INFORMATION SCIENCE 101

Anthony Debons

The Scarecrow Press, Inc.
Lanham, Maryland · Toronto · Plymouth, UK
2008

SCARECROW PRESS, INC.

Published in the United States of America
by Scarecrow Press, Inc.
A wholly owned subsidiary of
The Rowman & Littlefield Publishing Group, Inc.
4501 Forbes Boulevard, Suite 200, Lanham, Maryland 20706
www.scarecrowpress.com

Estover Road
Plymouth PL6 7PY
United Kingdom

British Library Cataloguing in Publication Information Available

Library of Congress Cataloging-in-Publication Data

Debons, Anthony.
  Information science 101 / Anthony Debons.
    p. cm.
  Includes bibliographical references and index.
  ISBN-13: 978-0-8108-5289-1 (pbk. : alk. paper)
  ISBN-10: 0-8108-5289-6 (pbk. : alk. paper)
  eISBN-13: 978-0-8108-6232-6
  eISBN-10: 0-8108-6232-8
  1. Information science. I. Title. II. Title: Information science one hundred one.
III. Title: Information science one hundred and one.
  Z665.D425 2008
  020—dc22   2008014769

∞™ The paper used in this publication meets the minimum requirements of
American National Standard for Information Sciences—Permanence of
Paper for Printed Library Materials, ANSI/NISO Z39.48–1992.
Manufactured in the United States of America.

To all present and future grandchildren.

Contents

Preface   xv

Acknowledgments   xix

UNIT I: NATURE AND ORIGINS OF INFORMATION SCIENCE

1   Introduction to Information   3
    Learning Objectives   3
    Overview   3
    Data, Information, and Knowledge   4
    Introduction to Information Concepts   5
        Signs   7
        Characteristics of Information   9
        Information and Communication   9
        Visible Information   11
        Variations on Decoding the Letter K   11
        The Philosophical Perspective   12
            Aristotle (384–322 BC)   13
            Karl Popper (1902–1992)   13
        Social Perspective   14
            Heidi and Alvin Toffler   14
        Technological Perspective   17
            Vannevar Bush—Memex   17
            Shannon and Weaver: Early Information Theory   17
                Claude Shannon and Technical Communications   17

Checking the Accuracy of the Received Message	19
Shannon and Bits of Information	21
Systems Theory and Cybernetics	23
Summary	25
Exercises	25
2 Professional Identities and Opportunities	**27**
Learning Objectives	27
Overview	27
Information Science–Related Professions	28
Documentation	29
Bibliographer	30
Indexer	30
Cataloger	30
Reference Librarian	30
Special Librarian	31
Archivist	31
Technology	32
Computer Scientist	32
Communications	33
Telecommunications	34
Information Scientists	34
Database Administrator	35
Information Specialist	36
Information Broker	36
Information (Knowledge) Counselor	36
Information (Knowledge) Consultant	36
Chief Information Officer (CIO) and Chief Knowledge Officer (CKO)	36
Information System Analyst	37
Information System Designer	37
Information System Programmer / Software Engineer	37
Decision Support Specialist	38
Interface Designer	38
Network Administrator	38
Webmaster	38
Information Architect	38
Competencies	39
Information Scientists' Interests	39
Information Scientists and Professional Organizations	43
Education of Information Professionals	43
Employment of Information Professionals	44

Summary 44
Exercises 45
3 Information Science: Nature and Function 46
Learning Objectives 46
Overview 46
Origins of Information Science 47
The Document 47
Alphabet and Language 48
Writing 48
Printing 48
The Book 49
Sharing the Document 53
The Library 53
Origins of Libraries 53
Librarianship 54
Technical Services 54
Acquisition 54
Cataloging 54
Access Services 54
Collection Management 54
Circulation 54
Reference and Information Services 55
Resource Management 55
Library Science 55
Computation 55
Origins of Counting 55
Computer Science 56
Communication Science 56
Some Shared Views of Information Science 56
Summary 59
Exercises 59

UNIT II: THE SCIENCE AND STRUCTURE OF AN ADIK SYSTEM

4 The Augmented Data, Information, and Knowledge
(ADIK) System 63
Learning Objectives 63
Overview 63
Introduction 64
Terms 64
Events and Situations 64

Conditions and Event Analysis 66
User Needs and Requirements 67
The Augmented Data, Information, and Knowledge System 69
Background 69
Composition of ADIK Systems 70
How about a Data System? 70
How about Information Systems? 72
How about Knowledge Systems? 72
ADIK Systems: How Do They Come About? 72
The System Development Cycle 72
Request for Proposal 73
Feasibility Study 73
System Analysis Process 75
System Design Process 76
System Management 76
GANTT/PERT 77
Testing an ADIK System 77
Simulation 77
System Maintenance 78
Summary 79
Exercises 79

5 How Do We Acquire Data, Information, and Knowledge?
The Sensing Subsystem 81
Learning Objectives 81
Overview 81
Background 81
The Nature of Data 82
Data Acquisition 82
Data Reliability 86
Data Validation 86
Data Discrimination 86
Data Reproducibility 87
Data Vulnerability 87
The Nature of Information Acquisition 88
General 88
Definition of Information Acquisition 88
Task Analysis 89
Information Retrieval 90
Organization of Information 91
Aids to Information Organization 92
Classification 92

　　　　Categorization　　　　　　　　　93
　　　　Indexing　　　　　　　　　　　93
　　The Nature of Knowledge　　　　　　94
　　　　General　　　　　　　　　　　94
　　　　Kinds of Knowledge　　　　　　94
　　　　Knowledge Acquisition　　　　　94
　　　　Knowledge Retrieval　　　　　　95
　　　　　　Aids to Knowledge Retrieval　　95
　　　　　　The Abstract　　　　　　　95
　　　　　　Citation Index　　　　　　95
　　　　Knowledge Management　　　　　95
　　　　　　Aids to Knowledge Management　96
　　Summary　　　　　　　　　　　97
　　Exercises　　　　　　　　　　　97

6　Movement of Data, Information, and Knowledge:
　　The Transmission Subsystem　　　　　99
　　Learning Objectives　　　　　　　99
　　Overview　　　　　　　　　　　99
　　Terms　　　　　　　　　　　　100
　　　　Transmission　　　　　　　　100
　　　　The Transmission Process　　　　102
　　　　The Role of Words and Symbols as Transmitters　103
　　　　Electronic Component Failure　　　103
　　　　Transmission of Knowledge　　　104
　　The Network　　　　　　　　　104
　　　　The Broad View of Networks　　　104
　　　　What Is Meant by Network and Networking?　104
　　Transmitters and Receivers　　　　　105
　　　　The Server　　　　　　　　106
　　　　The Medium　　　　　　　　107
　　　　　　Twisted Pair　　　　　　107
　　　　　　Coaxial Cable　　　　　　107
　　　　　　Fiber-Optic Cable　　　　107
　　　　Topology　　　　　　　　　108
　　　　Transmission Processing Protocols　110
　　　　Network Architecture: Combining It All Together　112
　　Advances in Teletransmission　　　　113
　　Summary　　　　　　　　　　　114
　　Exercises　　　　　　　　　　　115

7　The Computer　　　　　　　　117
　　Learning Objectives　　　　　　　117

Overview   117
Computer Science   117
The Computer and the Processing Subsystem: Hardware as
   Information System   120
   The Motherboard and Central Processing Unit   121
   Memory   122
   Input and Output Devices   124
The Most Important Technological Innovations   124
   Robots and the Computer   125
   Space Technologies: GIS, GPS Satellites   125
   Transportation   126
   Security   126
   Biometries   127
   Bibliometrics   127
   Medical Informatics   127
Challenges to Computer Science   129
Summary   129
Exercises   130

UNIT III: THE KNOWLEDGE SUBSYSTEM

8   The Utilization Subsystem: Decision Making—Problem Solving   133
Learning Objectives   133
Overview   134
The Study of Decision Making and Problem Solving   134
Definitions   135
   The Problem   135
      Problem Solving   136
      Problem Space   136
   Decision Making   136
      Decision-Making Analysis   136
Software Tools and Decision Analysis   138
Computer Tools That Aid the Problem-Solving and
   Decision Process   140
   Artificial Intelligence / Expert Systems   140
Summary   142
Exercises   142
9   The Transfer Subsystem: Communications   144
Learning Objectives   144
Overview   144
Background   145
Definitions   146

Communications 146
Information Science and Communications 146
Language 147
Mass Communications 147
Display: What is It? 148
Kinds of Displays 149
Displays and Communications 150
Display Factors 150
Application: The Third Dimension 152
Visualization 152
Wireless Communications 152
Summary 154
Exercises 155

10 **Human Factors (Ergonomics) and Information Science** 156
Learning Objectives 156
Overview 156
Definitions 156
Background 157
Origins of Ergonomics 158
General Area of Interest of Ergonomists 158
Theory 158
System Components and Ergonomics 159
Example: The Public Announcement
Communication System 159
Example: Audiovisual Presentation 159
Cognitive/Perceptual Functions 159
Cognitive: Information System Processing Models 160
Information Processing Model: Perceptual Representation 160
The Computer: Enhancing Human Activities 162
User-Centered Design 164
The Human-Computer User Interface (HCI) 164
Software Applications 164
Information Science and Ergonomic Challenges 165
Summary 166
Exercises 166

UNIT IV: SOCIAL ISSUES

11 **Value and Quality of Data, Information, and Knowledge** 171
Learning Objectives 171
Overview 171
Views on the Value of Information and Knowledge 172

Robert M. Mason   172
Robert Taylor   172
P. K. McPherson   173
Tefko Saracevic and Paul Kantor   174
Other Information Scientists   174
The Value of Information   175
  Benefit   175
  Cost   175
The Quality of Information   180
  Accuracy as Quality   182
  Timeliness as Quality   183
  Obsolescence   183
  Completeness and Format Check as Quality   183
  Age as Quality   183
  Source Availability as Quality   184
  Level of Summarization   184
  Format Check   184
  Security and Quality   185
  Other Dimensions of Quality   185
The Value of Knowledge   187
  Value as Process   187
  Value as Product   188
Administration of ADIK   189
Summary   189
Exercises   189

12   Security, Privacy, and Ethics   **191**
Learning Objectives   191
Overview   191
Security   192
Privacy   193
Ethics   193
Ethics and the Augmented Data, Information, and
  Knowledge System   194
  Event   195
  Acquisition Subsystem   195
  Transmission Subsystem   195
  Processing Subsystem   196
  Utilization Subsystem   196
  Transfer (Communication) Subsystem   196
Summary   196
Exercises   197

13	The Future of Information Science: The Knowledge Sciences	**198**
	Learning Objectives	199
	Overview	199
	Introduction	199
	The World Future Society	200
	Computing Research Association	201
	Professionalism and the Future	201
	Specific Areas of Implementation and Future Developments	202
	Distance Learning	202
	Computer Sensory Recognition	202
	Parallel Processing	202
	Intelligent Agents	203
	Embedded ADIK	203
	Expert Systems	203
	Computer Translation	203
	A Projection of Possibilities	203
	The Knowledge Sciences	207
	Library Science	209
	Computer Science	210
	Communication Science	210
	Information Science	210
	Summary	212
	Exercises	212
Appendix		213
Glossary		215
References		221
Index		235
About the Author		241

Preface

THE PRESENT GENERATION has seen a growing attention to information. Much of this attention has been the result of an explosion in data-processing technology, primarily in computers. Other national events such as hurricanes, floods, crime, and terror are clearly tied to the importance of information in our daily lives. These electronic machines are considered commonplace in almost all homes, at least in the world's industrial countries. Meanwhile, other developments have given us movies, the radio, then the television, and more recently the cellular phone. These engineering advances over the last three or four decades have been dramatic. Best estimates tell us such developments will continue.

For the last several decades, educational systems have responded to these technological advances through the introduction of (early in the studies of those entering college), the nature of, and the important role that data-processing technology presents and will continue to do so. Many schools now include courses in computer science as part of their curriculum. However, the fact that the computer represents an important technological facet of a broader social and cultural frame of reference remains to be developed. This text is intended to serve this purpose.

People have always tried to provide others with signs of their presence and intentions. A study of history gives us direct evidence of humans' ability to record human experience, thus extending their thought and purpose to others. People have long scrolled figures on physical substances as long as they had minds and hands to do so. The ancient abacus, the slide rule, and calculators have existed for many years. We all know of instances where someone placed a message in a bottle and tossed it to the sea, hoping someone would get the message when the bottle reached the shore. Paul Revere and the Pony Express delivered mail and packages over distances in pioneering days. Libraries have long maintained the record of human thought and experience. From birth and throughout life, humans possess an explicit interest in and dedication to explore the here and now.

Data, information, and knowledge-processing technology provide a medium for its realization and extension beyond that which was previously possible. In the process, however, there is a need and requirement that data, information, and knowledge-processing technology be understood in a broad context. Data-information-knowledge technology is just the beginning of a quest for a greater sense of awareness and understanding. This is one way that we can begin to understand how the science of information came about and what its role will be in the future life of the present-day student considering college.

Although some would be inclined to consider information science to be a new field, actually information science has been around for a long time. Information science, in its purpose and function, brings together a number of sciences. As long as the human has the need and requirement to record his or her experiences, the science of information exists. *The essential point in the science of information centers on one important idea. Humans are limited genetically in the capacity to deal with the world of matter and energy.* Fingers, feet, and brain are limited in capacity. Thus, we invent balls of strings and wire (abacus) to help us count. We invent wheels to help us move, paper to record our thoughts. Our eyes and ears can only see and hear certain things. We invent microscopes that enable us to observe the world of other organisms that is beyond our capabilities to observe. We have other senses such as touch and smell to provide us with an awareness of the world around us. We invent ways of moving energy from one place to another, giving us the telephone. We invent tubes and then transistors to move and conserve energy. We can go on and on presenting the many, many different ways humans have found to use tools (technology) to help them do things that they could not do without those tools.

In this context, *the information scientist is the trained professional who tries to understand how technology and services can complement and extend human capacities for a productive and meaningful life.* This requires an understanding not only of the technology but also the human physical, social, and psychological capacities and the institutions that have served as custodians of the record of human experience—both in thought and action. Specifically, the library has, for many centuries, been a strong institution directly concerned with acquiring and preserving the record of awareness (information) and understanding (knowledge). The immediate grounding of information science, like all sciences, lies in philosophy.

Unit I deals with the nature of information and knowledge as part of human interaction with the world about us. Chapter 1 ties the idea of a science of information together with the philosopher's perception. There are many views of philosophers that can be studied and applied to the study of information and knowledge. As a point of departure in this text, we have applied Karl Popper's Three Worlds of human experience. The first world is the physical world, with which we are familiar—the floor we walk on, the air we breathe, the bike we pedal that helps us move. The second world is that which we sense. In everyday experience, we interact with all sorts of things. It's this interaction that provides us with a sense of what we are doing, whether we enjoy it or not, and what we would wish in the best of possible worlds. The third world is the understanding that we get from our experiences. Chapter 2 identifies the information professionals who are serving the science, and chapter 3 describes the origins of the information science to the present.

The chapters in unit II, aimed at identifying information science, are anchored in the understanding of an augmented data, information, and knowledge (ADIK) system. Throughout the text, the living organism is used as a metaphor from which the major concepts of information science can be applied. To this end, chapters 4, 5, and 6 study three major components of the system—namely, the acquisition, transmission, and processing of data, enabling the human to be informed, the product of which is the essence of information science as developed in this text.

The focus in unit III is to extend the concept of information, both as process and product, to knowledge—that is, meaning and understanding. It is at this point that the human (cognitive/affective) aspect is central. The key point centers around an appreciation of technology, its design, and its influence on the individual's state of awareness and knowledge in meeting environmental (physical and social) demands. That issue centers on how technology learned earlier can influence human competence to solve problems and make decisions. This objective is extended in chapter 9 to the matters of human communications that are directed at serving individual and shared goals. An understanding of information is not complete without a sense of its social dimensions, including the impact of technology on social values, practices, and individual and collective integrity.

Unit IV sketches the major issues that are part of the science and its potential to those who are considering its challenges. Chapter 11 addresses the value and quality of information and knowledge, while chapter 12 covers security, privacy, and ethics, with respect to date, information, and knowledge acquisition and processing. The text concludes in chapter 13 with attention to the future of information science.

Acknowledgments

M ANY HAVE HELPED in the development of the text:

Edward Quigley and Christina Frank, whose work applied to the original draft of the text. Drs. Toni Carbo, Esther Horne, Glynn Harmon, Stephen Hirtle, Janet M. Waddel, and Michael Lewis reviewed and proposed suggestions on the technical content of the text; Sara Masters and Cyla Alcantara worked with the publisher in ensuring that the text met publication requirements. Mr. Thomas Dubis reviewed the initial draft, and both he and Dr. Ashli Molinero applied their professional wisdom to the technical content and expression. Thanks go to Mrs. Lynn Purvis-Yund for her work on the graphics, Mr. Terry Bennett and Ms. Susie Gratsky for their review of the original versions of the text, and to Ms. Rebecca S. Altes and Dr. Judith A. Jablonski for their assistance in generating an index for the text. The author is indebted to many students, both in high school and college, who were asked to review the text for relevance and clarity. Mr. Jonathan M. Spring, Mr. Mark Kurs-Lasky, Mr. Adam Hughes, and Mr. Jason Bryan Stewart are particularly cited for their attention and suggestions. Appreciation is extended to Elizabeth Mahoney and the extensive reference support rendered by the staff of the library of the School of Information Sciences, as well as William Senn, Lorna Kearns, and Yuri Sterostine. Appreciation is extended to many others in ensuring the quality of the graphics included in the text. Last but not least, thanks to Dr. Martin Dillon and the staff of Scarecrow Press for their patience and assistance in the development of the text.

I

NATURE AND ORIGINS OF
INFORMATION SCIENCE

1

Introduction to Information

What is information science?
The study of how best to use technology
Together with the knowledge of other sciences
In extending human awareness of the world;
Finding meaning and understanding
Applied to life's demands.

—*Anthony Debons*

LEARNING OBJECTIVES

- Define and differentiate among data, information, and knowledge.
- Explain how and why data, information, and knowledge are essential in our daily lives.
- Show how different founders of information science shaped the way that information is thought and studied.
- Explain the relationship between systems theory and information.

OVERVIEW

An overall view is presented of current ideas on data, information, and knowledge, both as process and product. This is related to the thinking of philosophers, the information revolution representing the advances made in theory and practice in information and communications.

Data, Information, Knowledge

- **The Symbol Data System**
- **Information**
  Who? What? When? Where?

- **Knowledge**
  How? Why?

**Figure 1.1.   Data, Information, Knowledge.
By A. Debons, drawn by S. Masters.**

Data, Information, and Knowledge

Information is also that which is in our heads (cognitive/affective), part of our state of consciousness. A primary source of information is our senses: sight, sound, smell, touch, taste, balance, etc. If you were listening to a Walkman or a radio while reading this text, you would be receiving audio messages as well as visual messages. It would be two channels of information coming at you at once. Here's another example: If you were reading this book in your home and noticed the smell of food cooking in the kitchen, you would be receiving two channels of information—one from the reading and another from the smell of the food cooking in the kitchen. We are surrounded by a constant barrage of messages containing information, both from our mind and from the physical world around us (see figure 1.1).

In the common view, data are the collection of numbers, measurements, and simple signals that surround us every day. Consider a child's science experiment involving a balloon, clock, thermometer, and ruler. The time is 9:30 a.m., the temperature is 70°, and the balloon is 6 inches in diameter (see figure 1.2).

The layman's view is that when we reflect on data and organize them into a structure, the result can become *information*, which is built out of patterns of data. For instance, if we took a series of measurements using the clock, thermometer, and balloon, we might end up with the above (see table 1.1).

So now that we have organized this data into a structure, the common view would say that we now have information. But let's look at our information.

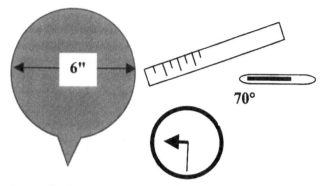

Figure 1.2. Data Collection. By A. Debons, drawn by S. Masters.

Looking at the chart, can you spot any patterns? Can you find an explanation for the changing size of the balloon? You might discover a pattern: the size of the balloon varies with the temperature; when the temperature goes up, the balloon grows; when the temperature falls, the balloon shrinks. So we think we have recognized a pattern: balloon size varies with temperature. The common view would say that this pattern, which we have found by looking at our information, would qualify as *knowledge*. So to restate: the common view holds that data are composed of the simple measurements around us, information is built out of an organization of data, and knowledge is built out of patterns in the information (see figure 1.3).

Introduction to Information Concepts

How can we describe information? Since information is all around us, the question is like asking a fish to describe water or asking a bird to describe air. We can start understanding information if we consider information as both a process and a product. Information exists through the processes engaged by our brains in responding to the conditions of matter and energy around us. Information can also be the product in physical form that we generate as part

Table 1.1.
Organized Data Becomes Information.

Time	Temperature	Size
9:30	70	6"
9:45	74	6.5"
10:00	78	7"
10:15	74	6.5"

Data—Information—Knowledge

Information is

awareness

Data

Account$1000Deposit$75$100ATM

Symbol: $

Ah! I have deposited $100 and taken out $75, leaving me with a balance of $25!

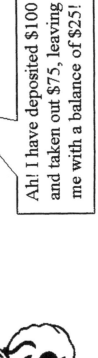

With Knowledge, make a decision

Question: Can I buy a skateboard?

Answer: No, the skateboard costs $75, which is more than my balance.

Figure 1.3. Data—Information—Knowledge. Data is composed of the simple measurements around us, information is built out of an organization of data, and knowledge is built out of patterns in the information. By A. Debons, drawn by S. Masters.

of this interaction (i.e., books, films, letters, etc.). We can understand this idea if we look at the many signs around us.

Signs

The way one can begin to understand information is through sensory experiences, the way information is presented in an environment. Signs provide examples of this concept (see figure 1.4).

What are the sources of information in this picture? Try to count as many as possible on a separate sheet of paper. Now try to see if there is some grouping of the information into categories that make sense. Are all of these messages equally valuable? Are all of the messages true? Are all of the messages equally reliable? Is it possible for a lot of unimportant messages to crowd out the important information? Say that you were going to the Driver License Center; would it be important to you to know where Ambridge is? Clearly not. A lot of information is targeted at us in messages, which actively seek our attention, but some of it is passive and we must seek it out. Is there any natural, rather than man-made, information in the first picture? Can you tell the time of day, time of year, the weather, and the latitude? Now study figure 1.5.

Since these signs are written in an unfamiliar language, how much information is there for you in this picture? This means that information is relative to the eye of the beholder. When we see a sign that says that the distance to a town is "20," then how much time will it take to reach a town that is "20" away? What will that mean to somebody in Berlin as opposed to someone in New York? The person in Berlin will think twenty kilometers, and the person in New York will

Figure 1.4. Signs Are the Products of Our Brains.
They help us to deal with the world around us. With
permission of Ed Quigley, photographer.

Figure 1.5.   The Influence of Language on the Ability of Displays to Communicate. With permission of Ed Quigley, photographer.

think twenty miles. Information is culturally based. This means that each group of people, wherever they are, use different words to label things around them or even use different languages to describe things around them. Our understanding of information is based on shared assumptions that vary from place to place.

Characteristics of Information

What are some characteristics of information? Some information is time sensitive. The food we buy at the grocery store often comes with a date stamped on it so we know when it will spoil. Most of the information in today's paper is outdated tomorrow. A billboard for a concert on July 10 contains little information on July 11. After a long while, however, bits of information will come back into the realm of importance. Historians and researchers may find that copy of the July 10 newspaper and find it useful for studying our time period, making the information in that newspaper valuable again.

The order in which you get information is also important. Imagine that you are trying to solve a problem, and an expert gives you some information that makes no sense to you. Later on, after becoming more familiar with the problem, you find one piece of information that sends you back to the earlier information that made no sense, and you can now understand it. This means that the order in which you receive information is important to your understanding of information.

Information is a relative thing; its value is relative to the person who uses or requires it. For example, a user manual for a French camera that is written in French may contain all the information that a photographer needs, but if the photographer cannot read French, the information is useless. But if the photographer could read French, the information is very useful because that person can now use his or her camera to its fullest potential.

Information can be explicit or tacit—that is, it can be clearly stated for anybody to use, or it can exist within the minds of a few people who share the information while not written down or available to outsiders. For example, you might obtain a guidebook that tells you how to behave at a Japanese restaurant; this is explicit information. On the other hand, if you went to a friend's house for Christmas, you may find yourself facing long-standing traditions, such as opening presents on Christmas Eve rather than Christmas Day. Information about these traditions is not readily available, so it is tacit information.

Information and Communication

Information and communication are two distinctly different things but are intertwined. Both are processes. When we communicate, we exchange information; information, in some physical form, moves from the sender to the recipient. When we see, hear, smell, touch, and feel, we are receiving information about the world around us. There are invisible streams of information everywhere, many in the form of different wavelengths. The air is filled with AM, FM, and shortwave radio signals that we cannot recognize until an antenna catches them, and a device (such as a radio) decodes them for us. There are signals that contain information running in and out of the world's many cell phone towers.

Information depends on communication for mobility and storage. The medium refers to the way the message or signal is moved from one place to another. When we send information through a medium, we are able to send it across distance and time. For example, say that you send e-mail to a friend in Florida; the information travels through the medium (computers and the e-mail system) and travels across time and space to reach your friend in Florida.

When the spaceship Pioneer 10 was launched on a journey into deep space, the spaceship bore the plaque shown in figure 1.6. The designers of the plaque hoped that if any other life form in outer space found the spacecraft, they would be able to read the communication, in picture form, and gain information about humans.

Communication is how we move information, and information is what is moved when we send a message. Without communication, information cannot move, and without information, communication has nothing to say.

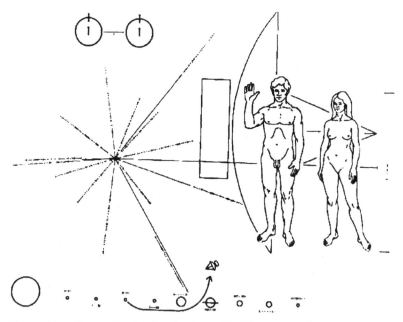

Figure 1.6. Plaque Carried by the Spaceship Pioneer 10. Source: www.aero spaceweb.org/question/spacecraft/q0225.shtml.

Visible Information

The information within our minds is invisible. Yes, there are devices that can scan our brains and develop information to make it visible for medical or research purposes. Still, no device yet invented can scan your brain to measure the quality or quantity of information that you have in it. But when you communicate a piece of information—either by voice, written message, or gesture—the information becomes observable, measurable, and recordable. This information is called visible information.

Sometimes information can be visible to us, but we don't recognize it. In our failure to "see" or apprehend it, we remain uninformed. We are ignorant of the information before us. An example would be to place both a stereotypical city dweller and an expert at survival in the wilderness. The nature expert may see trees, rocks, and clouds, or may see animal tracks that the city dweller missed; he may see food that can be found and water that can be used. The nature expert may be able to anticipate weather. The expert and city dweller both "saw" the same world, but the expert was able to decode and interpret the signals in the environment, or "problem space." To be fair, if the situation were reversed and the city dweller and nature expert were set loose in Manhattan, the nature expert would be out of his field and would miss a lot of information picked up by the city dweller. Each of us sees the world in a way we wish to see it. Sometimes we miss the trees in the forest!

Here's another example of visible information. Please examine the photograph in figure 1.7.

The photo is of a statue honoring a long-dead general. Is there any other information that is available? Would your response be different if you knew that the sculptor who carved the statue used a widely accepted code to communicate the manner of the general's death? Well, that is exactly what happened. If the horse has one hoof in the air, the subject died of wounds received during battle. If the horse has two hooves in the air, the subject died in battle. And if the horse has all four hooves on the ground, the subject died a peaceful death. Now that you know the code of communication for the statue, more information is visible. A prerequisite to "seeing" a new situation is learning about what information is encoded in the situation—that is, learning the context of the situation.

Variations on Decoding the Letter K

The signals used to communicate meaning are not unique; in fact, the same signal can have very different meanings depending on the context of the sender and recipient. It can be visible to two people but have two very different meanings to each person. Consider a very simple signal that could be sent in a message: the letter K. Depending on who is sending the message, the letter K could

Figure 1.7. Statue of Maj. Gen. John F. Reynolds. Source: www.virtual gettysburg.com/exhibit/monuments/pages/eq005.html.

have a wide variety of meanings. The same symbol is differently meaningful in each different context it is used. There are many examples:

- A chemist recognizes K as the symbol for potassium in the periodic table.
- A mapmaker using the metric system recognizes K as 10*10*10, or 1000.
- A computer designer recognizes K as 1024.
- A person scoring a boxing match recognizes K as a knockout.
- A pilot reading an aviation weather message recognizes K as smoke.
- A baseball fan recognizes K as a strikeout.

You can see that a message sent by the chemist to the sports writer could easily be misunderstood. These examples suggest that the symbol K itself has no meaning other than that which the sender and recipient mutually attach to it.

The Philosophical Perspective

Philosophy is the basic study of how we know things, matters of right and wrong, logic, and ideas and rules that come from studying it. Science has its basis in philosophical thought. Many philosophers from ancient times to the present have provided a way to look at information and knowledge. Aristotle's broad ideas of existence and the world have remained in the attention of thinkers for centuries. For our purpose, we will study Aristotle's interrogatives. His questions provide us with a sense of the relationship between information and knowledge. We will also examine Karl Popper's Three Worlds. His views help us put together our idea of data, information, and knowledge in our study of information science.

Aristotle (384–322 BC)

Aristotle (http://en.wikipedia.org/wiki/Aristotle), a student of Plato (http://en.wikipedia.org/wiki/Plato), was a Greek philosopher who contributed considerable amounts to our system of thinking, physics, biology, psychology, metaphysics, politics, rhetoric, and poetry. Aristotle divided the sciences into the rhetorical (the use of words) along with the practical and the productive. Aristotle also directed his attention to the role of questions in the development of categories of knowledge—a matter of some importance to our understanding of information and knowledge and, thus, to information science.

Karl Popper (1902–1992)

Like Aristotle, Karl Popper was a philosopher of science and a student of the scientific process. Popper (1965) describes a system of Three Worlds, which are very valuable as we try to discuss and understand information. Popper's worlds are shown in figure 1.8.

Popper's World-1 is the physical world, the world in which we live, which contains matter and energy, space, and time. World-2 is the realm of subjective reality, representing how we see the world from our own point of view,

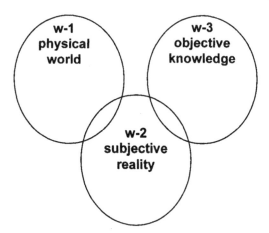

Figure 1.8.   Popper's Three Worlds.

our personal reality. World-3 contains scientific knowledge, which is all of the accumulated knowledge we have gained through various interactions with recorded information. Popper's Three Worlds interact with each other. These Three Worlds are linked to each other through their interaction. This can be easy to understand and important to our study of information and information science.

A World-2 observer, looking unto World-1, observes particular phenomena. Popper maintained that the activity of understanding consists of operating with World-3 objects. He described World-3 as an arena where ideas, expressed in language, can be critically discussed.

Popper describes science as a process that takes place in his Three Worlds. Events happen in World-1. A person tries to make sense of them in World-2. When the person comes up with a theory that seems to explain the events, he introduces the theory to others in World-3. The community can accept or dispel the theory, and that evolutionary process is at the heart of science.

How do we apply Popper's view and understanding of the world to our view of information and information science? Our minds bring the Three Worlds together by enabling us to respond to the physical states of matter and energy (World-1). This response we refer to as a state of awareness synonymous with information as a process (World-2). In the search for meaning, we conceive, create, design, and produce tools (technology) that add to our mental capacities. This technology helps us search, probe, and understand our inventiveness and creations (World-3). The business of information science is to find the connections between these Three Worlds. The approach is to identify the laws and principles that govern the environments of people, technology, and procedures we create that enable us to develop things, make decisions, and solve problems.

Social Perspective

Heidi and Alvin Toffler

Historians Heidi and Alvin Toffler (1984) have described human development as a series of revolutions they call the Three Waves. The First Wave was the agricultural revolution, when humans were farming. The Second Wave was the industrial revolution, when we began producing and working in factories. The Third Wave is the information revolution, when information became a mainstay of our economy. An easy way to remember the Three Waves is "farms, factories, and floppies."

In the Tofflers' description, humans began as nomadic hunter-gatherers. People wandered in small bands in pursuit of food supplies. When the agricultural revolution began, people planted crops, tended the land, reaped the harvest, and stored the bounty throughout the year. When people started relying on farming for their existence, new problems started to arise and these problems needed new solutions. For instance, it became essential that clean water supplies be protected. Storehouses were built and notions of ownership were developed. Laws were generated and penalties were established for violations.

The change from a hunter-gatherer society into a society of farmers was not painless. Roving bands of hunter-gatherers attacked early agricultural settlements. The farmers paid warlords to protect them, and local armies were developed. Farmers often did not own their own lands but worked as serfs for the warlords, paying a large share of their crops as tribute in a manner similar to paying taxes today. But the new life introduced by agriculture was an improvement and eventually became the way people lived in the First Wave.

The tools used during the First Wave symbolized human strength: the knife, the blade for plowing, the lever, the inclined plane, and the wheel and axle. People in this era lived on the family farm. They rarely traveled and often spent their entire lives within the same few miles. People were generalists, able to do many things: tend crops, butcher animals, and make clothing and candles. For instance, once an animal had been slaughtered, the family would make use of almost every bit of the animal. Everyone in the family, regardless of age, performed the work that needed to be done. When a specialized product was built, it was built by hand. Today, these products are generated by small individualized manufacturing units as a cottage industry.

In the 1500s, several forces brought about major changes to human culture. The Renaissance began an era of creativity and questioning of the status quo. The scientific revolution moved the questions of the Renaissance into the realm of the physical world. The Industrial Revolution brought the fruits of the scientific revolution into the workplace.

The Second Wave was the Industrial Revolution. Man developed new materials such as iron and steel. We learned to exploit new sources of energy such as natural energy (wind and water) and chemical energy (coal and oil). The combination of the energy sources and the new metals allowed us to build machines that far exceeded the brute strength of animals. Examples include windmills, watermills, locomotives, and textile mills, which augmented our strengths to remarkable degrees.

Work was done in factories, where specialized equipment was available. The factories required a large number of workers, so people left their farms and lived in homes outside the factories. The extended family broke down, and the nuclear family became dominant. In that nuclear family, the father often worked to make money, while the mother worked in the home. New social groups arose. Capitalists had the resources to invest in equipment and enjoyed the benefits of their investment. Laborers worked for an hourly wage paid in cash. Supervisors and managers oversaw the work of the laborers. None of these categories existed in the First Wave.

In the First Wave, barter (trading goods such as crops for other goods or services) was the economic medium. Money replaced barter in the Second Wave. Investments were made in money. People were paid in cash wages. When the economy shifted into a money-focused system, the methods of taxation also shifted, and taxes on profits and wages were introduced. Real estate taxes are a First Wave phenomenon, and income taxes are a Second Wave phenomenon.

In the Second Wave, work was done in factories, places with specialized machinery, specialized people, and specialized work. The change was not limited to the world of manufacturing. Schools were factories for learning. In the First Wave, learning and care were provided in the home, but with the Industrial Revolution, hospitals were created and they were factories for medical care. In the Second Wave, workers were no longer generalists; they became specialists, each trained only in one narrow technical skill. People left their farms to come to work in factories, and towns grew up around factories.

The Industrial Revolution introduced a life of material wealth to the people living in Second Wave countries. The entire world did not simultaneously move into the Industrial Revolution; some parts of the world remained agricultural while others became industrial. For example, the American Civil War was about slavery and succession, but it was also a conflict between a Second Wave economy in the industrial North and a First Wave economy in the agricultural South.

The transition from agriculture into industry saw its share of conflict. New technologies put many people out of work; one factory could produce more cloth than fifty cottage spindles. In France, workers threw their wooden shoes (*sabot* in French) into the machinery in protest, an act that gives us the word "sabotage." In England, people who opposed industrialization burned factories and equipment and honored an imaginary character named Ned Ludd as their leader. Today a person who resists technology is called a Luddite.

As the Industrial Revolution progressed, companies and organizations became more complex. Huge businesses employed large numbers of people, on a scale previously seen only by large armies. The companies developed information systems to keep track of their business, their people, and their money. This was the birth of bureaucracy. Because work was concentrated in factories, people focused on the efficiency of work. This required greater capacity to be "on top" of information needed and required for the management of resources, whether they be people or machines. The foundation of scientific management was born.

The notion of the factory—a central repository of people, equipment, and activity—is not as crucial in the Third Wave. Information work does not have to be done in any particular location. For example, reports from New York, Los Angeles, and Singapore can be e-mailed to the headquarters in Chicago, posted on the Web for distribution, and can be read the same day in offices around the world. Location is not a crucial factor in the Third Wave. Neither is the office. In the Second Wave, the office represented the apex of the organization and the "middle manager" worked there. Large staffs of secretaries and typists prepared reports that were sent to the office where middle managers compiled and compared the reports, building summaries and forwarding the information to upper management. The function of middle management has been largely replaced by small personal computers (PCs) that do the work of these people. The Third Wave workers need the skills to handle, manage, and troubleshoot information systems. They need to be able to work with people of other disciplines. They need to manage their own careers. When technology changes (which it quite often does), they need to adapt to the new systems. Education is a lifelong process for Third Wave workers.

Technological Perspective

Vannevar Bush—Memex

In the 1930s, Vannevar Bush had a vision that resembled modern computer systems. He called it Memex, which he noted as "a device in which an individual stores all his books, records, and communications, and which is mechanized so that it may be consulted with exceeding speed and flexibility" (Bush 1945). Bush envisioned a machine that made it easy to store and retrieve information. He wanted the information stored in a way that is uniform—that is, the same for each machine so that people will not have to relearn how to use the machine.

Shannon and Weaver: Early Information Theory

Warren Weaver described communications as "all of the procedures by which one mind can affect another" (1949, 1) and saw three different levels of communications problems: level A, the technical problem of communication; level B, the semantic problem of meaning; and level C, the effectiveness problem of changing conduct. The sections that follow explore Weaver's three levels of communication.

Claude Shannon and Technical Communications Claude Shannon was an AT&T (telephone company) mathematician. He was primarily interested in using phone lines to transfer signals and wondered what the cost of transferring information would be (Sveiby 1997). His first historic contribution was his recognition that transistors could be combined to perform as logical "gates," moving Boolean algebra from the theoretical into the physical and permitting the construction of digital computers. Shannon is a fascinating figure; his mentor was Vannevar Bush, Franklin Roosevelt's World War II science czar.

Shannon's second historic publication in 1948 (and republished with Weaver in 1949) was "A Mathematical Theory of Communication." Shannon provided a communications model that dealt exclusively with Weaver's Level A, the technical problem of communication. Shannon was dealing with the wartime problem of radar signals and how a signal could be transmitted effectively in the presence of noise like static or interference. Please study figure 1.9 below.

Shannon's communication model (involving an information source, transmitter, signal, noise, receiver, and destination) remains the accepted standard. In the picture that follows, an information source generates a message and gives it to a transmitter. The transmitter sends a signal, which is joined by noise known as static or interference. The received signal (the original signal plus the noise) goes to the receiver, which decodes the message, and gives it to the destination. Please note that the information source and the destination can be people, devices, or systems. Figure 1.10 gives us an everyday example of this communications model.

Consider Shannon's communications model in the process of sending a telegram. The sender generates a message to be sent and gives it to the telegraph operator, who generates a signal, which contains the message. The signal is sent over a network of wires that contains some static. At the other end, the receiving telegraph operator gets the signal, writes out the message, and gives it to the destination (the person to whom the telegram is addressed).

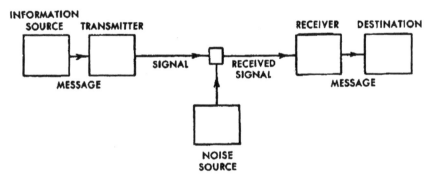

Figure 1.9. Communications Model: Transmitting a Signal in the Presence of Noise. "When I talk to you, my brain is the information source, yours the destination, my vocal system is the transmitter, and your ear . . . the receiver." Source: Shannon (1948, 2).

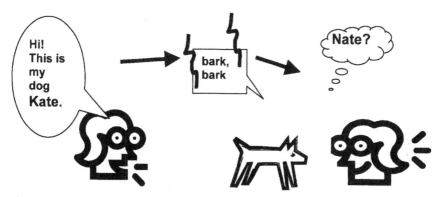

Figure 1.10. Shannon's Communications Model. Drawn by S. Masters.

Shannon's theory deals with transmission over a channel, minimizing noise and effective coding.

Although many have labeled it an information theory, it is more accurately a communication theory, focused on Weaver's Level B, the semantic problem of meaning. For instance, for Shannon, the messages "CONSTANTINOPLE" and "JFUEJSHUHESEF" were identical from a communications perspective: they were each fourteen-character messages to be transmitted accurately. Another coded example is in figure 1.11 below.

Weaver explicitly limited Shannon's use of the word "information" to a communications engineering perspective: "In particular, information must not be confused with meaning. In fact, two messages, one of which is heavily loaded with meaning and the other of which is pure nonsense, can be exactly equivalent, from the present viewpoint, as regards information" (Weaver 1949, 5).

Checking the Accuracy of the Received Message Let's say that you are the pilot of a bomber, and you've received a message to drop a bomb at a particular map coordinate. These numbers represent the latitude and longitude of the target, and could be transmitted as two seven-character words: 0395248 0750111, which would translate into north 039 degrees 52 minutes 48 seconds, west 075 degrees 01 minutes 11 seconds.

Message	*S E N D S U P P L I E S* $\cdots$
Key	*C O M E T S E N D S U P* $\cdots$
Cryptogram	*U S Z H L M T C O A Y H*

Figure 1.11. Codes According to Shannon's Information Theory.

Shannon's model describes a way for a message to be transmitted but really doesn't provide a way for the recipient to confirm the accuracy of the received message. It's important to be able to confirm the accuracy of a received message, especially when you're dropping bombs. Sometimes the transmission code employs a technique known as a checksum to confirm the accuracy of a received message. The way the checksum works is that the recipient adds up the first six digits of the message; the seventh digit should be equal to the rightmost digit of the summation. For instance, the original message is 0395248. The sum of all these characters $(0 + 3 + 9 + 5 + 2 + 4 + 8)$ is 31. The rightmost character of 31 is 1. So we add a 1 to the right of the original seven-digit number as the checksum, and the transmitted number is 03952481. If the target coordinates were transmitted with a checksum, the transmitted message would be two eight-digit character words: 03952481 07501115. The pilot who understood the checksum operation could then confirm the accuracy of the received message. See if you can use this process to validate the second coordinate, 07501115. Is this a valid message?

Activity

There are several bombing coordinates below that transmit six-digit coordinates in a seven-digit message, using a checksum. One of the coordinates has been incorrectly transmitted; identify which one. Two of the target messages are correct; identify the cities involved. This process permits the recipient to confirm the accuracy of a received message. Figure 1.12 illustrates the feedback that can now be achieved. It is an addition to Shannon's communications model, shown earlier.

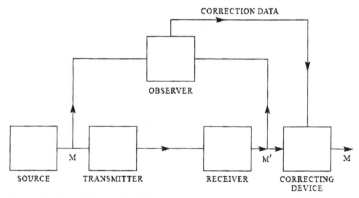

Figure 1.12.   Using a Checksum.

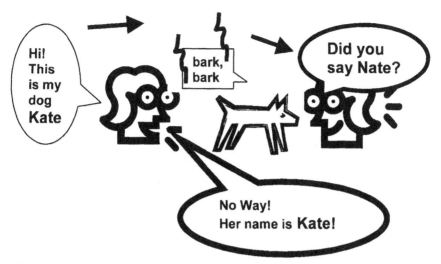

Figure 1.13. Errors Corrected by Feedback. Drawn by S. Masters.

In this example, when the destination receives the message, it sends another message back to the information source, saying either "Okay, I got that message, send me the next one" or "I didn't get that message correctly, please send it again." This addition to Shannon's basic model provides for a much more robust system that is more tolerant of interruptions, interference, and errors. This is illustrated in everyday life in figure 1.13, where the error created by noise from the dog is corrected with feedback.

Shannon and Bits of Information Shannon also gave us one of the first quantifications of information: the bit, or binary digit. A bit is defined as a single digit in a binary number, either one or zero ("on" or "off"). For example, when we buy a floppy disk that holds 1.44 megabits, or a hard drive that stores 300 gigabits, we are using the new word that Shannon invented.

Consider a person who lives on a houseboat and wants to be able to signal whether or not company is welcome to drop in for a visit. He rigs a light at the end of the dock. When the light is turned on, company is welcome; when it is off, company is not welcome. The signal device, the lightbulb, is capable of sending two different messages to people who know how to decode the message: welcome (on) and not welcome (off). If we were to write a list of all the possible messages and then number the possible messages, it would look like figure 1.14. If more light bulbs were added, the numbers would look like figure 1.15.

Shannon went one step further: he converted the numbers in the list to binary numbers and then counted the maximum numbers of binary digits necessary to carry all of the messages, as in the third column of figure 1.15.

Message To Visitors	Light Bulb	Code
Welcome!	ON 🔆	1
Not Welcome	OFF ●	0

Figure 1.14. Possible Messages.

Message To Host	Light Bulbs Sets of 2	Units	Binary Code
Expect 3 Visitors	ON 🔆	ON 🔆	11
Expect 2 Visitors	ON 🔆	OFF ●	10
Expect 1 Visitor	OFF ●	ON 🔆	01
Expect No Visitors	OFF ●	OFF ●	00

Figure 1.15.   Shannon's conversion of the messages from numerical expression of expected visitors to binary digits (code).

The largest number of digits required to count the messages in binary numbers is one binary digit, so Shannon would say that the message contains 1 bit of information. Here's another example: in Boston during the Revolutionary War, the colonists knew that the British were approaching in force but didn't know how they were coming (by land or by sea). This was crucial information that needed to be disseminated quickly and accurately. Henry Wadsworth Longfellow's poem "Paul Revere's Ride" immortalized this signal: "One if by land, and two if by sea." When the information was available, one or two lights were displayed in the church tower, as shown in figure 1.16.

Since the binary number for the last message contains two digits, Shannon's measure would say that this message contains 2 bits of information. Shannon said that information is the reduction of uncertainty and that the significant aspect of information is that it is one message selected from a set of possible messages. He explained that the number of bits of information in a message (H) could be calculated by H = log2(x), where x equals the number of equal probable messages from which it could be selected.

Systems Theory and Cybernetics

Let's say that your favorite baseball team just won the World Series and are the champions. Some claim that the reason for their win lies in the players' skills, but the other team has expert players as well. What could the difference be? A systems theorist would say that the team's organization (how the team was put together) led to the successful season. They would say that the overall organization of these expert players was the difference that gave them the edge against the other team. A system can be anything from a computer system to a baseball team to a coding scheme for libraries (such as the Dewey decimal system).

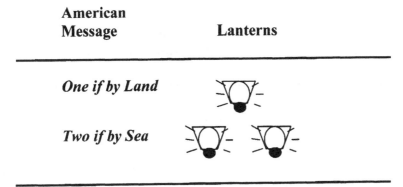

American Message	Lanterns
One if by Land	
Two if by Sea	

Figure 1.16.   Paul Revere's signals conceptualized. Drawn by S. Masters.

A system is anything that has organization of parts that are put together to achieve a certain purpose. Systems theory attempts to determine the principles that bring objects and processes together in achieving their objectives.

Many of the ideas associated with systems theory came from cybernetics, a word first used by Norbert Wiener (1894–1964). Cybernetics means "the science of systems of control and communications in animals and machines" (Wiener, 1948). Wiener used many ideas from Shannon's information theory, which we discussed previously. The idea of feedback was of specific importance to cybernetic system thinking. Many organisms and parts thereof live in the world of feedback. We eat and our hunger subsides. A student passes an examination and a grade is given that rewards the student's effort. Feedback is the key to Shannon's information theory. The idea of feedback is not as simple as it sounds. Much has been and continues to be studied about feedback. For our current understanding, it is sufficient to be alert to the role that cybernetics plays in our study of information science. To the extent that one of the major functions of the information scientist is to analyze, design, and evaluate data, information, and knowledge systems, cybernetics serves as an important foundation to the science. A distinction between the two theories is this: systems theory has focused on the structure of a system, how it is laid out and organized. Cybernetics, however, focuses more on the function of the system, how actions are controlled and how the system communicates with other systems as well as its own parts.

The ideas of systems and feedback were used heavily in World War II. The machines of the Industrial Age became more complex and specialized. Military operations have always required information systems to command and control the resources for battle. Thus, the first modern information system came out of the military. The early computers were built to compute ballistic tables for gunnery. We built radar systems that let an operator "see" ships and planes sooner.

We have always had information, but in World War II we started using information in new ways, even if written down. We built machines and systems that moved information just like factories moved physical goods. As the Cold War developed, we built command-and-control systems such as NORAD and the DEW line. These helped manage complexities that no one person could hold in his or her brains. These systems and the feedback they produced were vital in helping the United States engage in military operations.

These facilities replaced human lookouts at the fringe of a position with radar and other sensors, augmenting our capacity to observe threats. They also augmented the awareness of local military commanders, permitting one facility to deal with a strategic picture that no one individual could understand.

SUMMARY

Information is a fundamental property of life. No one on earth can live without it. Information is all around us, in all the physical things that meet our eyes, ears, and other sensors within the body. Information is also in our heads, the way the brain accepts and uses (processes) all that happens around us. Philosophers help our understanding of information—both as process and product, past and present, which combine information together with knowledge. Aristotle enables us to view the nature of questions (interrogatives), how we ask them, and their importance to our understanding of information and knowledge. Karl Popper provides us with a broad view of information as related to the physical world around us, that which we all bring to this world and the physical tools we create (engineer and produce) to bring these two worlds together in our lives. Our understanding and attention to information are also based on the great strides that science and engineering have made to enable us to receive, process, and communicate information. We see this in the rapid development and engineering of computers and other technologies (electronic displays, cable, fiber optics) that enable us to send and receive messages among ourselves and others (the Third Wave). Among these advances is our ability to measure information (Shannon's bits) and develop systems that can help us solve problems and make decisions. It's within all this that we can begin to understand information science as the integrator of each of these aspects of information.

EXERCISES

1. Is it possible to say that something is not information? Explain.
2. What is meant by the statement that information is in one's head or brain?
3. In the text, it is stated that information is a process. What can this idea mean? Provide an example.
4. State a problem that you have faced and discuss the role that information played in the problem and how it helped you understand the importance of information.
5. Claude Shannon and Warren Weaver were two important scientists that influenced how we transmit information. How did Shannon's thinking differ from Weaver's? Discuss their similarities and differences.
6. Let us suppose that you wanted to convey a message to one of your friends that you would not want others to receive. How would you develop a code to achieve such an objective?

7. What is the difference between transmitting and communicating information? What is the importance of this difference?

8. What is meant by visible information? Provide an example.

9. Discuss the idea of feedback. What importance does the idea of feedback serve in our understanding of information?

10. What is meant by reduction of uncertainty? Discuss the relationship between data, information, and knowledge.

2

Professional Identities and Opportunities

Vision

Establish a new information professionalism in a world where information is of central importance to personal, social, political, and economic progress by: Advancing knowledge about information, its creation, properties, and use; Providing analysis of ideas, practices, and technologies; Valuing theory, research, applications, and service; Nurturing new perspectives, interests, and ideas; Increasing public awareness of the information sciences and technologies and their benefits to society.

—From ASIS&T, an information science professional organization, www.asist.org/missionvision.html (accessed August 10, 2006).

LEARNING OBJECTIVES

- Compare the interests, study, and work of information scientists.
- State some common properties of jobs that information scientists hold and share.
- Describe the work of information scientists.

OVERVIEW

Although information science has deep roots in human culture, present-day information science differs in many exciting ways and offers new opportunities and challenges to the student. There are many avenues open in information science that those entering colleges and universities can consider. With the emergence of information-related technologies (computers, Internet/World Wide Web, and telecommunication systems), attention to information professionals has increased significantly. Information-related technologies offer real and challenging opportunities. This chapter describes a number of positions to which an education in information science can enable the individual to compete for exciting work in research and field application. It identifies those positions and the professional associations that provide an understanding of the current state of the field and the challenges of that field.

Information Science–Related Professions

There is increasing attention to information professionals and their importance to society, while an understanding as to who they are and what they do can be uncertain. They may be differently titled, depending on who hires them. The information professional can be a librarian, a computer specialist, a (tele)communicator, or all three at once. These three domains are incorporated in the information systems analyst, designer, and evaluator. The information professional joins other professionals, such as journalists, teachers, or almost anyone who serves the purpose of using various sorts of tools (technology) that enable humans to be aware of the world around them and in the process, understand it.

At the outset one should understand that information professionals have many titles and they perform different functions. These titles may differ in job descriptions. The titles and the functions related to them can also vary from one country to another. In 1981, the National Science Foundation awarded a grant to the School of Information Sciences to identify the various functions of information science professionals in the United States (Debons et al. 1981). These are presented in table 2.1.

Table 2.1.
Functions of Information Professionals.

Abstracting/indexing	Information analysis
Administrative services	Library/archives
Audiovisual media	Management information system
Command and control	Medical records
Communications	Public information/PR
Computer operations	Research analysis/planning
Databank/database	School/academic/department
Extension/outreach	System analysis/planning
Financial analysis	Technical information
In-company training	Technical reports preparation

Source: Debons, King, Mansfield, and Shirey (1981, 58).

Information sciences (discussed in detail in chapter 3) basically include three domains—namely documentation, technology, and communication. For each, there are categories (titles) of occupations and the educational programs that relate to them. It should be stressed at the outset that the professional trait that characterizes these vocations is the capacity to exercise interdisciplinarity, both in the way one perceives his or her vocation and his or her practice of it.

Documentation

The American Library Association defines the librarian as:

> a person responsible for the administration of the library; the chief administrator of a library; a class of library personnel with professional responsibilities, including those of management, which require independent judgment, interpretation of rules of procedure, analysis of library problems, and formulation of original and creative solutions, normally utilizing knowledge of library and information science represented by a Master's Degree. (*ALA Glossary* 1983, 130)

The trained librarian can be considered one of the oldest information professionals on record. Librarians existed as early as the tools were available to record human experience. These records can be called documents, so we can say they are engaged in documentation, which Vickery and Vickery define below:

> The field of documentation is most helpfully characterized if we take its scope to be all forms of document (i.e., any physical carrier of symbolic messages) and all aspects of their handling, from production to delivery. The document system then includes publication and printing, distribution, some forms of telecommunication, analysis, storage, retrieval, and delivery to the user. (2004, 7)

It is customary to account for the history of librarianship from the time of the monks in Alexandria and those who kept government records and archives. Educating librarians is a recent matter. Melvil Dewey founded the first library school in 1887. Basically, the education of librarianship has always amounted to serving an apprenticeship. A librarian was the person in charge of the library and nothing more. From 1920 to 1930, educating the librarian was defined for the first time. The education was American and originated at the University of Chicago (School of Social Sciences). The core courses taught included subjects such as reference work (aid in information, knowledge search, and retrieval), cataloging (listing the books in a collection), and classification (grouping things according to a particular system). Courses in library administration and management were also included.

Present-day education in librarianship and library science in the United States is extensive, including more than a hundred colleges and universities offering courses in library science. Of course, there are many library schools throughout the world, each having a distinct history and character of its own. During the 1960s, as part of the advances in information technology, some library schools included information science or information services as part of their title. Within the library profession, there are distinct specialties, with their own educational requirements and professional associations that represent their education and interests.

Bibliographer

A bibliographer is a librarian who is a subject specialist. "Bibliographer(s) . . . write about books, especially in regards to their authorship, date, typography, editions, etc. The Bibliographers are . . . familiar with systematic methods of describing the physical characteristics of books who prepare bibliographies, catalogs, or lists, subject areas" (*ALA Glossary* 1983, 21).

Indexer

An indexer is a librarian who provides "a systematic guide to the contents of a file, document, or group of documents, consisting of an ordered arrangement of terms or other symbols representing the contents and references, code numbers, page numbers, etc., for accessing the contents" (*ALA Glossary* 1983, 116).

Cataloger

A cataloger is "a librarian who performs descriptive and/or subject cataloging and may also perform such related tasks as classifying, shelflisting, etc." (*ALA Glossary* 1983, 37). Of course, today this includes the many and various electronic sources such as CDs, DVDs, microfilms, and movies, among others.

Reference Librarian

In addition to indexers and catalogers, who work mostly with materials and are not in contact with the library patrons, there are reference librarians who serve those who use the library to meet individual needs and requirements. These are the librarians with whom we are most generally familiar. They help us find answers to our information questions. "A Reference Librarian is a librarian employed in a reference department responsible for providing information service in a library that has a general collection limited to a special field, organized for consultation and general non-circulating information" (*ALA Glossary* 1983, 212).

Special Librarian

"A Special Librarian . . . serves the clients of a library supported and administered by a business firm, private corporation, association, government agency, or other special-interest group or agency to meet the information needs of its members or staff in meeting the goals of the organization" (*ALA Glossary* 1983, 212).

Archivist

Archivists are trained professionals whose function is to conserve, organize, and oversee

> the records of any institution, public or private, preserved because of their potential value . . . Archives administration shares a common purpose with library and information science: to acquire, preserve, and make available information, in the form of documentation as effectively and as economically possible . . . As an intellectual discipline, archives administration today embraces the study of records management, which may be defined as that field of general management that deals with the creation, maintenance, and disposition of records; records appraisal, accessioning, and disposal; archival buildings and storage facilities; records preservation and rehabilitation; archival arrangement, archival description, reference service, including photo duplication; exhibits and publication, including historical editing; and administration of personal papers. (*Ency LIS* 1968, 515–18)

Library schools vary in the offerings they provide students. All are at the graduate level as prescribed by the American Library Association. A typical academic program in library science can be found in table 2.2.

Table 2.2.
Sample Academic Program in Library Science.

Understanding Information
Organizing Information
Retrieving Information
Managing Change in Information Environments
Preservation Management
Records and Information Resources Management
Archives and Manuscripts Management

Sampling derived from available school catalogs for library science programs (2001–2004).

Technology

It should be understood that when reference is made to technology, as it concerns the information professional, technology can include many tools (hardware and software). In addition to computers, there are sensors (satellites), displays, printers, camera, film, and also tools including teletransmissions (such as telephony, cable, lasers, and remote sensors) and related telecommunication systems, such as voice, media, etc. Information systems often include all these technologies. The computer serves as the central technology and computer science as the main research and development source.

Computer Scientist

Computer science, like information science, is a marriage among several disciplines including electronics, mathematics, logic, linguistics, and other areas. The computer scientist is an information professional. The computer scientist studies the principles that govern the operation of a computer, with particular attention to the processing of data, information, and knowledge derived from and used by many sources. The computer scientist works with other information professionals to establish ways that the computer can help humans learn, make decisions, solve problems, and manage organizations.

The early computer science programs were either in departments of mathematics or electrical engineering. Computer science departments were slow in establishing their autonomy either in the college of arts and sciences or the school of engineering. Now, both undergraduate and graduate programs are offered by computer science departments in universities leading to either a major or minor as part of the undergraduate degree, or master's and doctoral degrees following the baccalaureate. Generally, these programs include the following areas of study, as shown in table 2.3.

Table 2.3.
Sample Academic Program in Computer Science.

Computer Programming
Computers and Networks
Discrete Structures for Computer Science
Information Structures
Computer Organization and Assembly Languages
Data Structures and Algorithms
Programming Languages

Sampling derived from available catalogs for cited computer science (2001–2004) programs.

Communications

Whenever we use language to share ideas or to interact with each other, we say we communicate; we share our awareness and knowledge with others (commonwealth). Often we use technology (telephone, wireless, displays, newspapers, TV, radio, etc.) to communicate with others. "Communication is the study of knowledge diffusion as used to reduce entropy by individuals, groups, and communities" (*Webster's New World* 1966, 423). Communications has been described by Beniger as part of the "control revolution," the "influence of one agent over another, meaning that the former causes changes in the behavior of the latter; and purpose, in the sense that the influence is directed toward some prior goal of the controlling agent" (Beniger 1986, 7). Beniger describes the basic technologies historically applied in communications: photography and telegraphy (1830s), rotary-power printing (1840s), the typewriter (1860s), transatlantic cable (1866), telephone (1876), motion pictures (1894), wireless telegraphy (1895), magnetic tape recording (1899), radio (1906), and television (1923). Colleges and universities offer programs in communication science stressing different applications. A student interested in communications is offered a wide variety of choices in selecting the institution in which to study areas of communications. A representative of some of the courses included in the communication science program offered in both undergraduate and graduate programs can be found in table 2.4.

It should be kept in mind that other functions and areas of specialization—education and journalism come to mind—can be subsumed as falling within the province of communication as a major domain of the knowledge sciences. These areas are not commonly included as part of the knowledge sciences, though they share objectives common to the other segments of the knowledge sciences presented. Telecommunications, however, has achieved acknowledgment in the thinking, practices, and education of information professionals.

Table 2.4.
Sample Academic Program in Communication Science.

Communication Process
Interpersonal Communication
Communication and Rhetoric
Theories of Persuasion
Freedom of Speech and Press
History of Mass Media
Small Group Communication
Political Communication

Sampling from available school catalogs (2001–2004) for communication science programs.

Telecommunications

In present day discourse, telecommunications includes the technologies that serve to move signals from one source to another and the properties of language and other human tools used to convey meaning and intention. Initially, telecommunications was primarily included in engineering schools, particularly electrical engineering. To some extent, this remains the case. But now, telecommunications goes far beyond the construction of telephone lines and cable (teletransmissions) between one place and another. There are satellites that do this. Our automobiles now offer TV screens. The breadth of telecommunications can be understood in the detail of a representative university program: "to prepare students as telecommunications network designers; analysts and managers; and data, voice, or image specialists with emphasis on the integrated voice, data, and image telecommunications network environment" (*School of Information Sciences* 1991–1993, 53). Some of the courses included as part of a program in telecommunications in the United States can be found in table 2.5.

Information Scientists

For as many information scientists are in the world, there can be the same number of views as to what they consider as the work of an information scientist. It may be helpful to understand that different parts of the world hold different views of what they consider to be "information science" and the function and work of the information scientist. Here is a useful general defi-

Table 2.5.
Sample Academic Program in Telecommunications.

Communication Devices
Protocol/Interfacing
Network Performance
Local Area Networks
Telephone Systems
Switching Systems
Telecommunication
Applications
Video Applications
Random Signal and Noise

Sampling from available school catalogs (2001–2004) offering telecommunication programs.

nition: "One who is highly competent or knowledgeable in the creation, use, and management of information, usually with an emphasis on the processes of acquiring, organizing, storing, and retrieving information rather than on its content. Sometimes called documentalist" (*ALA Glossary* 1983, 118).

As presented in this text, an information scientist is an information professional whose main function is the determination of those principles and laws that govern the analysis, design, and evaluation of augmented data, information, and knowledge (ADIK) systems. This function includes the integration and synthesis of the theories, laws, and principles that govern each of the domains of the knowledge sciences.

More and more, given the growing advances in information technology, there is an increasing shortage of trained information professionals to do the many jobs that are required. According to a recent study, many teens consider a career in information systems and the technology associated with them. Yet it is predicted (*Global Trends* 2000) that 900,000 workers will be required, with only 525,000 qualified candidates to fill them. Convincing young people, especially minorities and women, to incorporate technical skills and training in their education is a concern for all societies and the most prestigious of companies. The Bureau of Labor Statistics has found that the total college-level job openings between 1998 and 2008 will be nearly equal the number of college graduate entrants to the labor force (Fleetwood and Shelley 2000). More so, information technology positions such as computer engineers, computer system specialists, systems analysts, database administrators, and desktop publishing specialists are among the top ten fastest-growing occupations.

Along with the growing requirement for computer-competent employees, there is a growing requirement for specialists in specific areas. The responsibility for handling data and information is moving from the hands of clerical staff to personnel hired as part of the management information system (MIS) staff of a business. Subsequently, there has been an emergence of "new" positions. These specialist positions may have different titles within different companies and organizations. The background needed in these positions includes both business and an understanding of computers or information systems.

Database Administrator

A database administrator (DBA) designs, maintains, and integrates bunches of data. It is important that the DBA maintain the organization, integrity, and security of the data received and minimize the redundancies among the data. Examples of maintained data would be employee information such as hourly pay, projects worked on, or customer information such as orders taken, processed, and sent.

Information Specialist

An information specialist (IS) provides reference/literature-search service on a variety of business and technical topics utilizing online databases, print materials, and other resources to support research, engineering, management, and other corporate functions. They monitor, organize, and analyze relevant information needs of individuals and departments and implement services supporting a broad range of corporate functional areas and corporate goals. They also evaluate, acquire, and implement strategic information access and supporting technology, including but not limited to licensing for online and Internet databases, electronic journal subscriptions, books, journals, government, and education publications (Warren 2001; also see ASIS&T JobOnline at www.jobtarget.com/home/index.cfm?site_id=180 [accessed Jan. 16, 2006]).

Information Broker

An information broker (IB) is an individual or organization that, on demand and for a fee, provides information directly to individual and organizational consumers, using all sources available (*ALA Glossary* 1983, 117).

Information (Knowledge) Counselor

An information (knowledge) counselor is a trained information professional who aids clients in individual and/or organizational settings to meet tasks that require knowledge resources. He or she engages in the determination (diagnosis) of individual needs and requirements, formulates the necessary courses of action in the identification, retrieves and uses the knowledge resources (both human and technical), and evaluates the outcome of the process.

Information (Knowledge) Consultant

An information (knowledge) consultant is a trained information professional considered as an expert resource in applying assessment, diagnostic, and evaluative techniques acquired in the operation of data, information, and knowledge systems, usually in institutional, organizational settings.

Chief Information Officer (CIO) and Chief Knowledge Officer (CKO)

In business, there is a growing requirement to complement the work of the chief executive officer (CEO) with a CIO or a CKO. The responsibilities include development, maintenance, and corporate technology within the company. The use of tools (such as an executive information system [EIS] to analyze a company's progress or determine future goals of the business) is an everyday occurrence. As information technology has come to be used as a strategic tool, the CIO is expected to have more background than just in information technology. Typically, companies are looking for people with career success in a business and experience with a wide variety of technology and advances pertaining to them. The reasoning for this is that not only does a CIO have to understand the technology used by a company but also has to have the ability to negotiate, communicate, and delegate. Companies fear that if the CIO does not understand the underlying business requirements, he or she may hastily make purchases that will not address business problems. In other words, he or she might have an understanding about how the software operates but not have the first clue about how the user is going to apply it. The CIO must be able to view information technology as a way to accomplish business goals; therefore, he or she must be able to describe how a particular software package can add value to a business. A master's degree in business administration (MBA) can be an asset to the person who is looking to become a CIO of a company. The CIO of a company also works closely with the system analyst.

Information System Analyst

An information system analyst (ISA) works with the system users to develop a more user-friendly information environment (system) based on company needs and requirements. They are considered to be the "problem solvers" in a company's management information system department.

Information System Designer

An information system designer (ISD) works directly with the analysts in translating their work into software/hardware specifications that represent the data, information, and knowledge environment (people, technology, and procedures). The ISD has the additional task of undertaking simulation and other tests to establish the operational efficiency that is expected of the (design) system that is proposed.

Information System Programmer / Software Engineer

The information system programmer (ISP) is the information professional who ensures that the system software continues to operate the available computers efficiently. This is an evolutionary job because the systems must continually be updated to be faster and provide data on a wider range of machines. Both the ISP and the software engineer write code, the instructions that tell the computer what to do in order to perform a task to solve a problem.

There are several characteristics that a person must have to become a programmer. A career in software development is a very pressurized position. Employees must meet deadlines and the demand by users for bigger, better, faster application packages. Therefore, the person applying for a position in the field must be able to work effectively under pressure. Analytical reasoning and creativity are a must for programming to solve problems. And last, but not least, is knowing the language used in developing the software. Whatever the programming language, the programmer must have an in-depth understanding of the language to program and debug coded programming. The task or problem defines the type of programmer a person becomes: application programmer, system programmer, or maintenance programmer.

Decision Support Specialist

The decision support specialist supports management in scientific and support planning, provides data analysis to decision makers, and aids in organizing briefings and other activities.

Interface Designer

An interface designer considers the end user's perspective in software design. The user interface is probably the most important aspect of software engineering, and great strides are made to develop software that is user-friendly. It considers how the user prefers to view the information provided. Research is one of the major aspects of this position and is often referred to as "usability testing." This job attempts to merge the human aspect into the design of computer software.

Network Administrator

Within a facility, there is the physical connection between terminals so that information may be distributed and shared among the users. The network administrator oversees the design and maintenance of the physical system itself. Choosing hardware such as routers, switches, and hubs or installing system software are two duties listed in the network administrator's job description.

Webmaster

The webmaster uses development tools (such as HTML or other scripting languages) to provide website information about the company, entity, or organization and to collect and process information from the customers and users via the Internet.

Information Architect

An information architect supports the analysis and design of a system that manages data, information, and knowledge content important to the objectives and function of an organization (Warren 2001).

In 1989, the University of Pittsburgh Graduate School of Library and Information Science conducted a manpower study for the National Science Foundation to determine the composition of information professionals related to information science. It identified nine functions that were related to information work (Debons, Horne, and Cronenweth 1988):

1. Managing information operations, programs, services, or databases;
2. Preparing data and information for use by others;
3. Analyzing data and information on behalf of others;
4. Searching for data and information on behalf of others;
5. Performing other operational information functions;
6. Carrying out operational functions, including running of a library or automated information systems;
7. Designing and analyzing information systems;
8. Developing and researching information;
9. Educating and training information workers.

Competencies

Information scientists Jose-Marie Griffiths and Donald W. King have extensively studied the matter of identifying and stating the work competencies to be expected of information professionals. "An individual's competence is judged by his or her performance. Regardless of the type of work performed, a competent individual is one who can meet or surpass performance standards, whether they are explicitly stated or implicit. This competence can only be identified through performance" (Griffiths and King 1986, 121). In specific areas, they have identified the competencies for entry, middle, and senior levels for knowledge, skills, and attitudes of their work. Figure 25 on page 193 of their report provides a picture of the competencies they have identified, which are also reflected in appendix 3.1 of their report (Griffiths and King 1986). This information is redrawn in table 2.6.

Information Scientists' Interests

Information scientists' interests vary, based on their education and general interests. There is extensive opportunity for information scientists to apply these interests to a number of employment objectives. Some of these interests can be found in table 2.7, taken from the list of special-interest groups in the professional organization ASIS&T.

Table 2.6.
Information Scientist Competencies.

WORK SETTINGS	FUNCTIONS	COMPETENCIES			ACTIVITIES
		KNOWLEDGE	SKILLS	ATTITUDES	
Academic Library	Acquisitions	Entry Level	Entry Level	Dispositional Attitudes	Entry Level
Public Library	Cataloging	Basic Knowledge	Basic Skills	Toward Institutions	
School Library	Circulation/User Services	Subject Knowledge	Skills Related to Each Specific Activity	Toward Other People	
Special Library	Collection Maintenance	Library and Information Science Knowledge	Other Skills	Users	
Database Producer	Interlibrary Loan Management	Knowledge of Information Work Environments		Others in Workplace	
Database Distributor/Service	Reference	Knowledge of What Work Is Done		Personal Qualities	
Information Center/Clearinghouse	Serials Control	Knowledge of How to Do Work		Attitudes Related to Job/Work/Organization	
Records and Information Manager	Thesaurus Development/Control	Knowledge of Organization Served and Its Library			
Archive/Museum/Collection	Indexing/Abstracting	Mid Level	Mid Level		Mid Level
Information Analysis Center	Publications and Product Mgmt.	. . .	. . .		. . .
Information Service Company	Exhibit Management	Senior Level	Senior Level		Senior Level
Library Systems Supplier	Organization/Mgmt. Support	. . .	. . .		. . .
	Information Analysis/Research				
	Project Management				
	Reference/Analysis of Secondary Data				
	Research, Analysis, and Design				
	Marketing				
	Customer Support				

Source: Griffiths and King (1986, 193).

Table 2.7.

Information Scientists' Interests. As indicated by the list of special interest groups at ASIS&T (www.asist.org).

Arts and Humanities (AH): Application of information science to scholarship and creative endeavors in the humanities and fine arts.

Automated Language Processing (ALP): Interaction between linguists, who have a theoretical interest in the machine simulation of human language processing, and information scientists, who have more practical goals.

Classification Research (CR): Classification of data, information, and knowledge schemes and procedures by humans and machines.

Computerized Retrieval Services (CRS): Production of machine-readable databases and their use through computer-based retrieval systems.

Digital Libraries (DL): Development and use of digital libraries in corporate and public contexts.

Education of Information Science (ED): Provide a forum for the study of the education of information scientists in relation to the other sciences (computer, communication, and library).

History and Foundations of Information Science (HFIS): Develop theories, fundamental concepts, and models of information science and cybernetics that lead to better information systems and services.

Human-Computer Interaction (HCI): Serves practical and theoretical interests in research, design, development, and evaluation of how human beings use and communicate with computers.

Information Analysis and Evaluation (AE): Critical study of certain items from available information, assigning relative values and detecting meanings of interest for an expected use of information systems.

Information Architecture (IA): Interest in the entire structure (parts and whole) of a computer system, whose function it is to process information and make it functional.

Information Generation and Publishing (PUB): Theory, application, and standards involved in the processing of text-based information.

(continued)

Table 2.7. (Continued)

Information Needs—Seeking and Use (USE): Concerned with activities, both behavioral and cognitive, of people who are interacting with information.

Information Policy (IFP): Interested in the acknowledgment of legislation and regulation affecting field of information and/or members of the information professions.

International Information Issues (III): Promote better awareness among ASIS&T members and information professionals of the the importance of international cooperation through educational programs and other initiatives.

Knowledge Management (KM): Many-faceted interest in the acquisition, processing, and use of knowledge through technology, particularly toward effective organizational management.

Library Automation and Networks (LAN): Analysis, planning, management, and use of innovative technology in library operations and networking.

Management (MGT): Focus on the effectiveness of one or more stages of information process (creation to dissemination).

Medical Informatics (MED): Evaluate the needs and problems of developing and managing medical information systems and ethical problems pertaining to them.

Metrics (MET): All matters pertaining to the measurement of information from a broad perspective, including digital libraries, bibliometrics, scientometrics, and informetrics.

Scientific and Technical Information Systems (STI): Application of information science to the production, organization, and dissemination of scientific and technical information.

Technology, Information, and Society (TIS): How information technology impacts the individual and society. This includes a number of issues, such as ethics, privacy, and censorship.

Visualization, Images, and Sound (VIS): Study of issues involving graphic and visual information, including document images, still and moving pictures with or without sound, and other aspects dealing with the representation of the visual world.

Table 2.8.
Information Science Professional Organizations.

American Society of Information Science and Technology
(ASIS&T)
Association of Computing Machinery (ACM)
Institute of Electrical and Electronic Engineers (IEEE)
Electrical and Electronic Engineers Society (EEES)
American Library Association (ALA)
Special Libraries Association (SLA)

Information Scientists and Professional Organizations

A professional association is a society of people who usually meet periodically because of common interests, educational background, or work experience (*ALA Glossary* 1983, 210).

Information professionals can be represented by a number of professional organizations. Table 2.8 is representative of the many information professional organizations.

Education of Information Professionals

More than one hundred schools in the United States and abroad offer undergraduate major and minors in information science, although they may be referred to by different titles (e.g., School of Information, School of Information Studies, etc.). Some programs in information science are attached to the titles of departments that combine "computers and communication."

There are similar numbers of programs at the graduate level offering master's and doctorate degrees in the respective areas. Preparation for admission to these programs requires scores on the Graduate Record Examination (GRE). Students from abroad seeking admission to programs in the United States may be required to take the Test of English as a Foreign Language (TOEFL) as part of their admission requirements. Individuals who are seeking a career in research and teaching in the field are recommended to pursue the doctorate. Peterson's guides and directory of college programs (www.petersons.com/books) are valuable reference sources to those who are pointing their career direction to a major or minor in information science and pursuing graduate programs as well.

Employment of Information Professionals

Information professionals are employed in many public and private institutions and organizations. Each position has its own qualifications and requirements. A number of factors are considered important in acquiring a position as an information professional. Often, many positions at the entry level require the completion of an educational program enabling the individual to engage employment in that position. Positions beyond the entry level require evidence of technical experience supported by educational credentials related to that experience. Individuals who have completed their academic programs can expect to be placed in positions that may not necessarily represent their ultimate career goals.

Professional associations listed in table 2.8 periodically distribute announcements of positions open to applicants. Interest in these positions starts with the submission of a brief resume that includes biographic data, academic achievement, and experience. A resume is a summary of who you are, what you have done, and what you wish to accomplish in life. The objective statement included in the resume should be carefully considered and written; it should include immediate and long-range career interests.

SUMMARY

Information professionals include a broad range of skilled individuals who apply science and technology to the creation and operation of data, information, and knowledge environments (systems). These systems serve to augment the human capacity for awareness and understanding fundamental to problem solving and decision making. Information professionals are identified by different titles, functions, and work environments. Each shares a capability for interdisciplinarity, both in how they see the world, the tasks, and the tools that are applied to them.

Our capacity to deal with circumstances that are part of human existence is largely dependent on records that account for the experiences as they are encountered (documentation). The librarian, as documentalist, is the custodian of such records and the institution that insures their preservation and use. The work of the librarian is supported by a number of related vocations (i.e., cataloger, indexer, archivist, etc.), each of which requires specialized training. The library and each of the contingent vocations have been significantly affected by technology. The computer, as the main element of this technology, has significantly changed the way humans acquire, process, provide, and share with others (commonwealth, communication) data, information, and knowledge. Electronic displays (TV, holography, virtual reality) have added to the increasing potential that such tools provide to augment information and knowledge.

These advances have expanded the role of information professionals and the requirement for educational programs to meet the need. Academic institutions worldwide have responded by creating academic programs (at both undergraduate and graduate levels) that prepare individuals with the necessary expertise, technical skills, and sense of interdisciplinarity required of them. The primary charge for integrating all resources to help achieve the objectives we have discussed rests with the information scientist. The integration is based on the laws, principles, and theories that govern the analysis, design, and evaluation of the augmented data, information, and knowledge (ADIK) system and for which the information professional is educated and trained. The core of such ADIK systems will now be our focus in the next chapters.

EXERCISES

1. To what extent does the education and training of a librarian (documentalist) qualify an individual to be identified as an information professional?
2. Describe the role of an information professional with a specialization in the communication domain.
3. Identify an information professional whose main and sole function is in the area of language.
4. What could be considered the best preparation for an active career as an information professional?
5. What specific characteristics or requirements would identify the information scientist from others in the three domains of the knowledge sciences?
6. Which one of the following traits or skills should be considered most important to be shared by each of the information professionals serving the three domains (documentation, computation, and communication)?
   a) management skill
   b) programming
   c) view sharing
   d) speaking

3

Information Science: Nature and Function

The blind man asked his partner: Tell me what you see.
Lots, said the partner sheepishly.
But I see a lot, too. What do you mean?
It's all in my head, the partner replied.
Then, the blind man asked: Please place it in my hands.

—Robert Stone, *A Hall of Mirrors*

LEARNING OBJECTIVES

- Identify and define the three main sources of information science.
- Explain why the document is an important area of interest to the information scientist.
- Identify the technologies involved in documentation and situate them within a historical context.
- Relate library science and computer science to information science.

OVERVIEW

This chapter presents a general view of information science, its origins, structure, interest, and work of the information professionals who define its function and purpose.

Origins of Information Science

As we learned in chapter 1, information is part of our lives from birth to death, and the history of information science began when humans were first asking questions in order to create and discover answers. These questions were about the world around them. Information science originates from the time we used our hands to signal or used pebbles on a beach, goes on to pencils, ink, paper, books, and the printing press, and continues on to present-day computers. Information science is as old as life itself. But information science—the study of information and its creation, discovery, and use, especially as augmented by computers—was born in the twentieth century (Hahn and Buckland 1998; McCrank 2002).

There are many ways that the history of information science can be approached. Present-day information science is formed from three main sources, each related to the other. These three sources are the record of human thought and accounting (documentation), counting/computing (computation), and in service to the human instinct for self-preservation, the sharing of information for the common good (communication). The combination of all these sources can be considered the knowledge sciences, because they use data and information to create knowledge. This aspect of information science will be discussed in chapter 13.

The Document

The document, as a physical object, is one of several important ways of moving facts and ideas from one place to another (transmission), making others aware of their existence, helping others to be aware, and then extending this awareness (information) to an understanding of those things that exist and are important to them. A document is a tool that augments our capacity to communicate.

In recent times, an understanding of the role and the position of documentation in the definition of information science has occurred. We send (transmit) data, information, and knowledge across distances and times. We can look at ancient scrolls and decipher information and knowledge from long ago. For example, a note that you may pass to a friend in class or e-mail you may send to somebody can be considered a document.

The computer scientist defines a document as text (structure of symbols, words, and data) that is part of instructions (program) that tell the machine what to do (applications). According to this way of thinking about a document, a computer program that enables you to do things on a computer is judged to be a document.

The document is a technical tool for the transmission and transfer (communication) of data, information, and knowledge. This includes a number of different technical entities—namely language, writing, printing, the book, and the institution of the library that serves as the procurer, safeguard (archives), and distributor of the physical presence of these entities.

Alphabet and Language

Language and writing in all forms are critical for moving ideas (transmission) from one place to another. Evidence of some form of language exists from antiquity (ca. 8000 BC). It is difficult to track down when language, in its many forms, was first used (linguistics). Certainly it predates writing by thousands of years (Gray and Atkinson 2003). Yet signs and symbols are also older than writing as we know it. We can suppose that human activity would not be possible without it. The study of language (linguistics) is a science in its own right and very much related to the science of information. If, as stated, information is considered as a state of awareness, then language is the physical representation of that state, which occurs in our brain. This will be discussed further in a subsequent chapter on communications.

Writing

Writing is a way of storing information and knowledge (Gaur 1992). Writing occurs through a variety of means, from the practice of moving pebbles on surfaces, to using liquids, smoke, and odors to convey states and events. Ink and paper are examples of the application of chemistry to the act of writing. Ink was invented by the Chinese (200 BC) and has been an important tool in record keeping (documentation). Figure 3.1 shows papermaking in the Middle Ages in Europe, but the development of paper dates from much earlier, circa 866 AD.

Figure 3.2 shows the development of paper, from ancient China to recent times. Paper, in its present form, came into use in the seventeenth century. Writing came about much later than spoken language. The oldest forms of writing used pictures or symbols for whole words (logos). The origins of writing began with the origin of the alphabet (in the city of Ugarit) in the modern country of Syria during the second millennium BC, which evolved into Phoenician, the ancestor of all modern alphabets (see figure 3.3).

Printing

Printing is "a reproduction (as on paper and cloth) of an image from a printing surface made typically by a contact impression that causes the transfer of

Figure 3.1.   Papermaking in the Middle Ages. Source:
Christopher Weigel, *Book of Trades,* 1698.

ink" (Thompson 1978, 294–512; *Webster's New International Dictionary* 1961, 1803). The art of printing, that is, applying ink to paper, goes back several centuries, possibly to the Chinese and to the fifteenth century in Germany (*Encyclopedia Britannica*, 15th edition, 1989, vol. 26, 68–108). "It is the practice of producing multiple copies by pressing on another carrier of the printed image, again on facsimile of the original" (Halsey 1983, 785). The invention of the printing press and the first printing of the Gutenberg Bible in German in 1440 were important in aiding communication (transfer) of human awareness and understanding the printing press. With movable type in 1450 AD the distribution of information and knowledge was increased.

The Book

As we all know, the book is a physical object—a form of technology. The book is a document. The book is "a long written or printed matter or record" (*Webster's New Explorer Dictionary and Thesaurus* 1999, 59). One form of the book

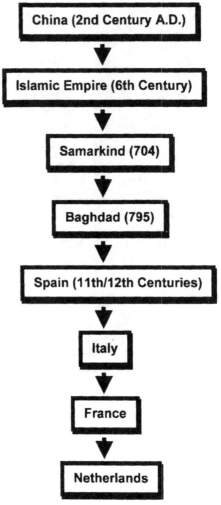

**Figure 3.2. The Development of Paper
(adapted from "Paper folding," *Encyclopedia
Britannica*, Vol. 17, 1966, 279–285).**

is the codex, which originated in the first century. The codex consisted of a
number of folded sheets sewn along one edge (www.leavesofgold.org/learn/
children/glossary.html). A codex allows for scrolling, the practice of moving
up or down a page's content. The book is a record of thought, spirit, and
work. The book has its origins in ancient Sumerian, Babylonian, and Assyrian
civilizations. The book is a technological innovation in printing that significantly influenced record keeping and communications in general. The history

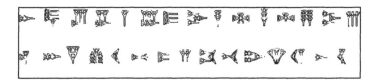

Ugarit Alphabet

Modern Roman	A B G D E F Z H	I K L M N	O P	Q R S T
Early Latin	A ꓐ < D Ɛ F Z H	ꙅ K L M N	O ᒥ	O P ꙅ T
Greek	Λ Δ ᒥ Δ Ⴈ ᐊ Z Β	Ⴆ Χ ꓘ ꓘ ꓘ	o Π	Φ Ρ Σ T
Phoenician	⟨ 9 ∧ Δ ∃ Ⴈ Y I Ⴇ ⊕ Ⴇ Ⴑ Ⴑ Ⴑ Ⴈ Ⴈ ꓘ ‡ o ꓘ Ⴑ Ϙ ۹ w †
Early Aramaic	Ⴈ Ⴈ Ⴈ Ⴈ Ⴈ Ⴈ Ⴈ Ⴈ 6 Ⴈ Ⴈ L Ⴈ Ⴈ Ⴈ o Ⴈ Γ Ρ Ⴈ Ⴈ Ⴈ
Nabatian	Ⴈ Ⴈ Ⴈ Ⴈ 9 I Ⴈ Ⴑ Ⴈ Ⴈ Ⴈ Ⴈ Ⴈ Ⴈ 9 Ρ Ρ Ⴈ Ⴈ Ⴈ
Arabic	L ل Ⴈ Ⴑ Ⴇ 9 ل Ⴈ Ⴇ Ⴑ Ⴑ Ⴑ ل ﻣ ﺟ ﺳ ﻋ 9 ﺻ 9 ﺟ ﺳ ﻟ

Phoenician Alphabet

Figure 3.3. The Evolution of the Alphabet.
Note: The Ugarit Alphabet slowly evolved into the Phoenician. The Phoenicians were great traders across the sea and their alphabet spread far and wide. With minor variations, this alphabet has evolved to all modern scripts in the world. To make them easier to remember, the symbols were taken from words beginning with the sound represented, such as *gimmel* (meaning camel) for "g." © 2002 Krysstal. Used by permission. Accessed June 22, 2006, from www.krysstal.com/writing.html.

of the book is important to our understanding of information science. The book developed, invented, created, and applied evidence of how humans, as a species, used technology—tools (e.g., books) to augment the capacity to communicate by providing others with the development and use of thought in physical form to meet the prevailing demands of the environment (see figure 3.4). This understanding includes the nature and history of language, writing, and the generation of print.

Figure 3.4. The level of detail and the artistry applied in the expression of information and knowledge desired to be presented. *Source: Encyclopedia Britannica, vol. 3, 923.*

Sharing the Document

The Library

All of us are familiar with the library. Basically, a library is both a physical place and an institution operated by people for social and educational purposes. The first libraries of record go back to the fourteenth century in monasteries and churches. There are almost countless libraries throughout the world—from the Library of Alexandria in Egypt, the Vatican Library in Rome, and the British Library in Great Britain to the Library of Congress in our nation's capital. It should be noted that before libraries existed, there were "storytellers": poets of old who carried "documents" in their heads alone! An overview of the structure of the present library is presented in figure 3.5.

Origins of Libraries

The establishment of the first library of consequence has been attributed to Ramses II. In Egypt (1309–1237), Ramses established a library of sacred literature in Thebes. The existence of libraries was prompted by the development of papers made from an Egyptian plant. One of the best known of the very early libraries flourished at Nurchev, the capital of ancient Assyria, about seven centuries before the birth of Christ. Assyrians wrote by making wedge-shaped impressions on clay tablets that, when dried and hardened, were

Figure 3.5. The Structure of the Modern Library. Source: *MLA*, Vol. 79, No. 3, July 1991, D. IV.

impervious to fire and dampness. Books existed in Athens in considerable quantity before the time of Aristotle (c. 384–322 BC). The Library of Alexandria in Egypt was established by the early Ptolemies (c. 300 BC) as a deliberate step in the hellenization of Egypt to preserve and extend the civilization of the old Greek world (adapted from Halsey and Friendman 1983, 558–60).

Librarianship

Librarians function actively in insuring that the products of data, information, and knowledge are available to those who seek the resources of the library to satisfy their needs and requirements.

Librarians work with information and other scientists to insure that the resources are managed and used effectively for this purpose.

The library incorporates and offers a number of technical services. These services are incorporated in support of public, school, and academic institutions. In addition, other functions such as archival and special libraries extend the scope of librarian function and interests.

Technical Services

Acquisition

In libraries, this is the practice of identifying and adding new volumes to their holdings (Wiegand and Davis 1994).

Cataloging

This practice identifies and describes material (books, recordings, magazines, etc.) within a library.

Access Services

Collection Management

This function provides for traditional collections, to control changes already occurring, to deal with new problems, and to develop opportunities into reality (Wedgeworth 1993, 215).

Circulation

This function includes all activities that are involved in making books, journals, and other materials directly available to the people who need them (Wedgeworth 1993, 201).

Reference and Information Services

This function helps library clientele use the internal and external resources efficiently to meet their information needs (Wedgeworth 1993, 703).

Resource Management

Resource management is defined as planning, operating, and controlling the human and material resources that are part of the library.

Library Science

Library science is defined as "the knowledge and skills by which recorded information is selected, acquired, organized, and utilized in meeting information demands and needs of a community of users" (*ALA Glossary* 1983, 132). Library science is one of the information sciences. In 1957, the late S. R. Raganathan, a prominent international librarian and scholar, proposed five laws of library science. These were to be considered as norms, guides to good practice.

- Books are for use;
- To every reader his or her book;
- To every book its reader;
- Save the time of the reader, and of the staff;
- A library is a growing organism (as quoted in Vickery and Vickery 2004).

More often than not, library and information science is considered as joined in both practice and science. This can be considered as similar to the practice of medicine and medical science, which incorporates the research of a number of related sciences. (http://en.wikipedia.org/wiki/Library_and_information_science).

Computation

Origins of Counting

Let us say that there was no way for our performance in class to be tested. You would probably like that! Great! But it would not be great if there were no ways to indicate your performance in baseball, soccer, or whatever activity in which you would like to engage. What if there were no ways to count money? We can go on and on to show the limits of our innate capacities and how important counting is to our ability to deal with the world around us. Information has one of its origins in counting. Counting is one way (act) to show ourselves and others how things are, can, or should be. We use our fingers, feet, and arms to count for whatever purpose. We use measures such inches, feet, yards, and miles to help us.

Computer Science

As information science, computer science can be defined in a number of ways: "The study of computers, including both hardware and software design. Computer science is composed of many broad disciplines, including artificial intelligence and software engineering" (www.webopedia.com/term/C/computer_science.html) and "the systematic study of computing systems. The body of knowledge resulting from this discipline contains theories for understanding computing systems and methods; design methodology, algorithms, and tools; methods for the testing of concepts; methods for the analysis and verification; and knowledge representation and implementation" (www.nitrd.gov/pubs/bluebooks/1995/section.5.html, in context).

Computers are an essential, important subsystem of the augmented data, information, and knowledge (ADIK) system. Computers process data captured from events, assist in the transmission of the characteristics (data) of the event occurring in time and space, expand our awareness of the world about us, and aid in our understanding of these events, enabling us to respond to them. The discipline of computer science will be studied in chapter 7 of this text.

Communication Science

Communication is difficult to define (Littlejohn 1978, 24). A science of communication can include research and study in a wide area of interests ranging from the use of symbols, language, understanding, interaction/relationship, binding communality, intention, the media, and the Web to many other areas of interest. Our attention will be directed to the linkage between how we acquire information, how we transmit to others, and how the computer aids the communicative/transfer function (chapter 9).

Some Shared Views of Information Science

We all think we know what science is about. We have heard about astronauts traveling to the moon, vaccines for disease prevention, cars traveling by electrical power, and much more. Science is an agreed method of asking questions about our existence and using established methods to find the answers. Science tries to discover and understand relationships that exist in nature, within and outside of us.

As we learned in chapter 1, there have been many ideas presented as to the nature of information. Also, many definitions of information science exist. Given our understanding of science, the problem rests on what most of us consider information. A view that most of us share is that information is something we have, use, and exchange with others. The newspaper, books we read, and any other media that may come to our attention, day in and day out, contain information. It is all around us physically; we buy it and we store it. We have discussed this aspect in chapter 1.

But where does the word "science" come into the picture? Science comes into the picture when, through study and research, we attempt to establish those laws and principles that enable us to understand our experiences with data, information, and knowledge. Then to analyze, design, and test systems (technologies and procedures) that extend our native capabilities of awareness, understanding, and sharing of these capabilities. The following views of information science have been presented by information scientists.

Harold Borko (1962), a pioneer information scientist, submitted his understanding of the science:

> Information science is the theoretical discipline concerned with the applications of mathematics, system design and other information processing concepts; it's an interdisciplinary science involving the efforts and skills of librarians, logicians, linguists, engineers, mathematicians and behavioral scientists. The application of information science results in an information system. The role of information science is to explicate the conceptual and methodological foundations on which existing systems are based. (quoted in Hahn and Buckland 1998, 8)

Other definitions of information science have been presented by Saracevic, Harmon, Flynn, Vickery, and Zins.

Tefko Saracevic (1970) stresses that Shannon's theory of communication is of fundamental interest when it is applied to information systems and their evaluation. Shannon viewed communications as the unifying theory.

Glynn Harmon (1971, 235–41), an information scientist at the University of Texas, Austin, states that

> Information Science may be viewed as one of a group of sister communication and behavioral science disciplines that emerged almost simultaneously around World War II. These sister disciplines included cybernetics, semantics, linguistics, decision theory, game theory, documentation, and information retrieval. The history of Information Science, then can be regarded as somewhat of an

amalgam of concepts rooted in these various sister disciplines. It might be tempting to view Information Science as having emerged from documentation and information retrieval-key concepts in Information Science.

Roger R. Flynn's 1997 text, "Introduction to Information Retrieval," relates the science to the question-answering process. In his concept, the creation, selection, coding, and manipulation of data and direct problem solving and decision making are points of interest to information scientists.

Vickery and Vickery (2004) defined information science as the study of communications and information in society. In their development of information science, they identify six major points of focus of the science (338):

1. The behavior of people as generators, sources, recipients, and users of information, and as channel agents
2. The quantitative study of the population of messages—its size, growth rate, distribution, patterns of production, and use
3. The semantic organization of messages and of channels that facilitate their identification by sources and recipients
4. Problems particularly associated with the function of information storage, analysis, and retrieval
5. The overall organization of information systems and their performance and transfer
6. The social context of information transfer, in particular, its economics and politics

Chaim Zins, an information scientist from Israel, conducted a five-year study in which he asked a cross-section sample of information scientists their views of information—its nature and interests of their science. Zins found that their interest centered around the application of technology (primarily computers) and how technology influenced all aspects of the management of data, information, and knowledge, the impact of these resources on society and culture and on "all types of biological organisms, human and non-human, and all types of physical objects" (2007, 335–50).

In the present text, information science refers to that activity directed to the search for laws and principles that are part of the analysis, design, and evaluation of information systems. These systems are environments of people, technology, and procedures that serve to augment/extend human capacities in dealing with the many states (decisions, problem solving) that are a part of day-to-day living. Our study of information science is focused on: the tools that humans have developed over time to account, preserve, and extend an understanding of their experiences for themselves and others; the methods and tools that have been invented/engineered/designed to aid humans to study, account for, estimate, and relate experiences; and how these experiences are shared with others.

SUMMARY

It is reasonable to suspect that humans, from the time of their origin, thought about themselves and the physical world around them. They developed tools to account for their experiences. They began to understand how some tools were better than others. They created new tools and found better ways to use old tools. These simple thoughts are the basis for understanding information science. Information science is concerned with how best to use tools (technology) to help deal with the common, individual, collective problems and questions that face humankind. Library science helps us understand how to order (organize) and retrieve the record (document) of times past and present. Computer science increases our ability to count and account and also discover, invent, and build (engineer) environments that help us make decisions and solve problems (hurricanes, tornadoes, floods, terror, economic mishaps, etc.). Communications is that vital function (both human and machine) that helps us spread the word, the thought, and the understanding that is achieved in the past, present, and future.

Information scientists express these properties of information science in different ways. One model considers libraries and information science to be interrelated (information sciences) through numerous contributions (human and technological) that have been made in the past and continue to be identified with the science. Another model stresses the impact of technology on the individual and the culture. The present text applies the functional and structural properties of the living organism as a metaphor in its attempt to develop laws and principles that govern the analysis, design, and evaluation of augmented data, information, and knowledge (ADIK) systems.

EXERCISES

1. Suppose no textbooks were around for the courses you are now taking in school. What sort of problems would you face, and how important would they be to your understanding (knowledge) of the subjects?
2. In what sense would things in a museum be considered documents?
3. How would one best explain the relationship between library, computer, communication, and information science?

4. Discuss how film can be a source of study by information scientists.
5. What is the relationship between information science and the information sciences?
6. What do the various definitions that have been presented with respect to the nature of information science hold in common? What are some of their weaknesses and strengths, if any?
7. In what sense is the distinction between information science and the information sciences justified?
8. In what way(s) do(es) transmission and communication relate to and influence each other, if indeed they do?
9. Discuss what you consider to be the problems information scientists face in defining their science, if indeed they do.

II

THE SCIENCE AND
STRUCTURE OF AN ADIK SYSTEM

Birth is the start of information; death the end.
From then to now, symbols command;
Symbols give essence to presence;
Through presence, meaning.

—*Anthony Debons*

"I thought these video games had more action."
By permission of Bunny Hoest, *Parade Magazine,* **2002.**

4

The Augmented Data, Information, and Knowledge (ADIK) System

Where is the wisdom we have lost in knowledge?
Where is the wisdom we have lost in information?

—T. S. Eliot, choruses from "The Rock"

LEARNING OBJECTIVES

- Explain how augmented data, information, and knowledge function together within an ADIK system.
- Compare and contrast examples of ADIK systems.
- Outline the evolutionary process of an ADIK system.
- Identify and describe the phases of the system development cycle.
- Give examples of how the word "system" as a title for something that exists (e.g., transportation system, medical system, etc.) is also a way of thinking.
- How would one determine if a system is achieving its purpose?

OVERVIEW

Our attention is focused on the meaning and importance of systems in our daily life. Systems are environments that respond to individual and collective needs and requirements. The nature of these needs and requirements is studied.

Specifically, attention is directed to the interest of the information scientist in the augmented data, information, and knowledge system that is directed to respond to these needs and requirements (see figure 4.1). This chapter will include discussion of how these systems are requested, analyzed, designed, and evaluated as well as how these systems are managed and maintained.

Introduction

This chapter is about human ingenuity and systems (people, technology, and processes) that define it. It is about the human ability to extend its native capacity through discovery and invention. It is about the human ability to go beyond the detail, to broaden the scope of immediate capacities to an understanding of their influences and impact. Information science is about systems past, current, and future, environments that apply and go beyond discovery and invention. In general, this is referred to as systems thinking, which is the guiding reference and application of the science. Systems (holistic) thinking starts with an accounting of the nature of the environment, the events and conditions that influence its state of being, the invention of tools, their use and management, and the establishment of institutions (discussed in chapter 2), which extend human capacities applied to events and situations that prevail (see figure 4.1).

Terms

We introduced the idea of an ADIK system. Terms that are used in relation to this idea can aid our understanding. At the outset, it is clear that information scientists may vary in their definition of the following terms and/or how they are used.

Events and Situations

All of us are familiar with the words "event" and "situation," but these are defined in a more careful way below. Combined together, the words become the term used in this book: "event world."

An "event" is defined as a "a happening; occurrence, especially an important occurrence (*Webster's New World* 1951, 503). A scholarly way to define "event" is given in current literature as "some occurrence that may cause a system to change" (Booch, Rumbaugh, and Jacobson 1999, 20). Every event must contain a time and, for most analysis, step-by-step procedure for calculations that are ordered in time (Ito and Sigg 2002). "Event analysis" is an umbrella

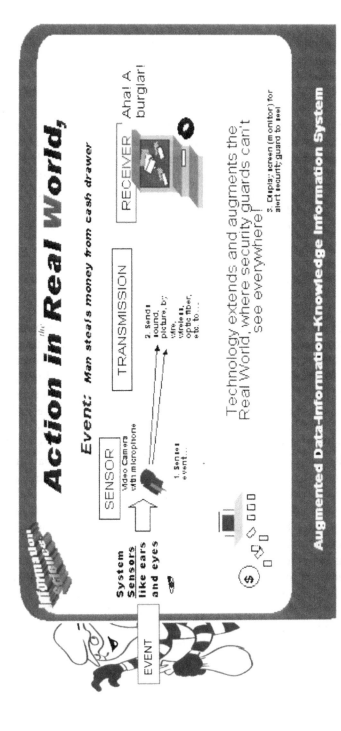

Figure 4.1. Action in the Real World—The ADIK System. An event (L) happens, such as a man stealing money from a cash drawer. A remote sensor (video camera) picks up the event, extending the senses of a human guard. The remote picture is transmitted to the security guard by way of a receiver (R), the display. The guard perceives an event he wouldn't have seen otherwise. Technology augmented his senses, and a thief is caught! Designed by A. Debons, drawn by S. Masters.

term for a set of procedures that identify events and situations to which each component of the ADIK system responds. Events such as 9/11, Hurricane Katrina, earthquakes, tsunamis, or the war in Iraq are significant events with corresponding situations. These occurrences serve to reflect the ability of ADIK systems to respond. The 1918 flu epidemic led to the deaths of many individuals worldwide. Unfortunately, we can expect the same—as well as contrasting—events in the future. The more unique an event, the more it is considered "noteworthy." For instance, a normal daily sunrise will not be put in the headlines of a newspaper. Events can include states at the micro-macro, individual, organizational, and cultural levels. Information scientists, working with scientists and technologists, serve to design ADIK systems that can effectively acknowledge and respond to such events and situations.

A "situation" is defined as the "place or position of things in relation to surroundings or to each other" (Murray, Little, and Onions 1964, 1904).

Conditions and Event Analysis

Events trigger some action (needs/requirements), such as the initiation—or stopping the execution—of a specific plan or an occurrence that may cause the state of the system to change. The attention of information scientists can focus on the ability to understand the event and the corresponding consummations at the molecular, molar, individual, organizational, and cultural levels. This quest extends to other physical, behavioral, and management sciences with their related technology. The course of events and situations related to them has had a profound impact on people, organizations, and commerce. Information scientists attempt to understand the principles that govern the analysis and design of ADIK systems that respond to events and situations.

Object-oriented analysis (OOA) is one approach to an understanding of events and situations (Coad and Yeardon 1990; Booch, Rumbaugh, and Jacobson 1999). OOA attempts to understand the principles that define the data flow within a system. These principles would then serve as models from which we may start object-oriented design. The products of object-oriented design can then be used as blueprints for completely implementing a system using object-oriented programming methods (Booch 1999, 40). There are other models that can be applied. These models rest on an understanding of how people see (perceive) and create new objects as part of the reality of an event and situation. This understanding then can serve in the reasoning and judgment of an event/situation that is applied in the analysis and design of ADIK systems (Heise 1979).

An understanding of events and situations is much broader than what may be implied above. For example, the analysis of events and situations can include methods that identify and define name and class of events, event condition, index, value, the application of histograms, and many mathematical tools (Ito and Sigg 2002). The important point is to understand the important role an understanding of events and situations plays in the analysis, design, and evaluation of ADIK systems.

User Needs and Requirements

The subject of user needs and requirements is of considerable importance to information scientists. Over the years, information scientists have studied various groups (scientists and others) to identify their needs for data, information, and knowledge. As could be expected, the findings from this research activity varied, depending on the group studied. The problem that exists rests on the double meaning of "need." A "need" is defined in dictionaries as "a requirement," and a "requirement" is defined as "a need." To the student, for example, a need is a textbook, which helps the student come closer to fulfilling the requirement—that is, the class. This understanding, however, omits *what* the student will do with the book (understand the material presented in the text). The book is a requirement that enables the student to understand (the need) the data, information, and knowledge presented in the class.

Michael Brittain, the late British information scientist, discussed the difference (1970) between information need and demand (requirement) below:

> The definition of "information demands" is relatively easy. It refers to the demands, which may be vocal or written, and made to a librarian or to some other information system. The definition of "information need" is more difficult. In some cases needs will be synonymous with demands: for example, where the user knows all the information that is relevant to his work, and makes a demand for an information source. At the other extreme, the user who makes very few demands but has many needs. He may have felt but unarticulated need (perhaps because of inertia or because he does not have sufficient specific details about the felt need to translate the need into a demand) or he may have an unfelt need (in which case he may not be aware that this is pointed out, which time he may readily agree that he has a need or he may not realize this until the need has actually been met). One of the problems in this aspect of user enquiry is terminological: there is no suitable word for "potential user" or "needier." (Brittain 1970, 1–2)

From the information professional's point of view, it is often difficult to obtain from the user a clear statement of what is needed from what is required. Over the years, information scientists have presented their views on information needs and requirements, often without coming to an agreement. In recent years, however, information scientists have come to consider information needs: the result of cognitive/affective processes (Case 2002; Nahl and Bilal 2007). Communication and information scientist Brenda Dervin, in her human need studies, proposes that an information need represents a "gap" between what the patron asks for and what is given the patron by the reference librarian (Dervin 1983). Other studies conducted by information scientist Nicholas Belkin suggest that the information need represents an anomaly, something given that is not consistent with what is asked and needed (Belkin 2005). Other concepts relate an understanding of the human need and requirement for information and knowledge to theories in pedagogy and motivation. Debons equates information and knowledge need to Bloom's taxonomy of cognitive and affective processes (see table 4.1). The taxonomy is used to identify the need and then to apply the determination as a tool to organize (prescribe) the physical requirements (i.e., books, reports, films, databases, specialists/experts, etc.) in response to the need that is represented by a task objective (see table 4.2).

There is much to learn about how and why people use the library and other resources in their daily lives. The information scientist, together with other scientists (library, computer, and communication), combines their collective wisdom to determine and find ways that extend the individual's ability in meeting the collective individual needs and requirements for data, information, and knowledge.

Table 4.1.
Needs and Requirements.

Needs	Requirements
Evaluation	Bring all the facts together in such a way that they make sense. Standards help; check for accuracy, effectiveness, economy, state of satisfying.
Synthesis	Organizing material for effective use. Determine the best way. Data, information are presented to promote meaning of material that is available or the possibility of making it available.
Analysis	Assemble resources in a way that brings out the positive/negative attributes of products (technology, subject matter, books, and visual-auditory material).
Application	Organize and present material following understanding so that it can meet the demands of the moment or in the future. Psychological principle of least effort is considered applicable.
Comprehension	Appropriate definitions of subject matter and area of focus.
Awareness*	Timeliness, completeness, ordering of data (what, where, when, who). Feedback to delivery of data for relevance and completeness.

Source: Bloom (1956b). *"Knowledge" in Bloom's taxonomy.

Table 4.2.
Bloom's Affective Domain.

Internalizing Value	behavior controlled by some value system
Organization	organizing values based on some priority
Valuing	value a person attaches to something
Responding to Phenomena	taking an active part in learning; participating
Receiving Phenomena	awareness; willingness to listen

Adapted from Clark, 1999.

The Augmented Data, Information, and Knowledge System

Background

Of course, the environment (physical and social) is forever a challenge to humankind. Human ingenuity in developing tools to deal with the challenge is the subject and study of history. The focus of information science is to understand the laws and principles that govern the generation and use of these tools (technology) that augment humankind's ability to deal with events that define and challenge its existence.

Synonyms of the word "augment" are "enhance," "amplify," "boost," and "build up." For our purposes, we will go to Douglas C. Engelbart, electrical engineer and computer scientist, who introduced the term in 1962 as part of his research work at Stanford University in California. Engelbart's research studied how computers aid human thinking, particularly intelligence. The expression "artificial intelligence" has reference to this work later adopted and extended by cognitive scientists (Newell and Simon 1972) of Carnegie-Mellon University in Pennsylvania. Engelbart wrote that

> By "augmenting human intellect," we mean increasing the capability of a man to approach a complex problem situation, to gain comprehension to suit his particular needs, and to derive solutions to problems. Increased capability in this respect is taken to mean a mixture of the following: more rapid comprehension, better comprehension, the possibility of gaining a useful degree of comprehension in a situation that was previously too complex, speedier solutions, better solutions, and the possibility of finding solutions to problems that before seemed insoluble. (Englebart 1962, 1)

As mentioned previously, systems are all around us. Human beings themselves are information systems. Information, as a state of consciousness or awareness, is fundamental to life. We use technology to help extend our awareness, solve problems, and make decisions. Joining these two ideas—awareness and technology—we have an augmented data and information system. By adding to awareness the technology to understand and search for meaning in what we do and in the world about us, we have an augmented data, information, and knowledge system.

There are many ADIK systems around us (see figure 4.2). For example, management information systems help institutions plan, operate, and control numerous functions within an organization. Information management systems ensure the right kind of data and information to run, operate, manage, and direct systems efficiently and effectively. Information retrieval systems help store and retrieve the data and information we may need and require from the many databases that are available. From an added perspective, command/control/communication (C3) systems are ADIK systems used by the military in engaging operations.

Composition of ADIK Systems

What makes up such augmented, enhanced systems? ADIK systems include people, technology, and the functions/procedures that bring these together to achieve a goal. Technology can refer to many physical things around us. For example, sensors that extend the limits of our ability to see things in space (radar, satellites) or under the sea (sonar) are ADIK systems. So are the nervous systems in our bodies that move impulses from many parts of our body to our brain, enabling us to be aware and act. Transmitters are a form of technology that move signals from sensors to computers. There are many examples of transmitters that we are familiar with, such as phones, flags, signs, and cable. These processors are like computers, only slower and with less carrying capacity. Transmitters augment our ability to speak and signal through motion and other forms of action. Where are such augmented, enhanced ADIK systems?

At the basic level, we can see elements of ADIK systems all around us. Pencils, pens, televisions, radios, fax machines, sensors, computers, satellites, and many other related technologies make up parts of ADIK systems. Although each of these technologies are systems in their own right and can be part of information systems, they are not what could be considered ADIK systems on their own. Yet when these various technologies are combined with people and procedures for the achievement of a specific objective or goal, then such technologies can be represented as part of ADIK systems. They add to the human sensory capabilities that we are born with and acquire.

How about a Data System?

Data systems consist of arrangements of symbols, the presence of which allow for the generation of rules as to their use for the representation of states

The Library: Systems within Systems

4. Producing more data
Librarians catalog books, count them and copy their IDs into a computer system

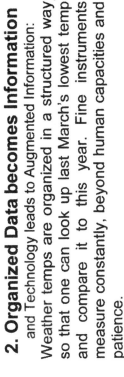

Farmer's Almanac

Knowledge is

. . . and Books

1. Knowledge begins as Data
such as weather

2. Organized Data becomes Information
and Technology leads to Augmented Information: Weather temps are organized in a structured way so that one can look up last March's lowest temp and compare it to this year. Fine instruments measure constantly, beyond human capacities and patience.

3. Recognized Patterns become Knowledge
Authors recognize patterns in the information and put this wisdom into Books, such as The Farmer's Almanac, which predicts weather.

Figure 4.2. Graphic showing Interrelation of Systems. Drawn by S. Masters.

or events in time and place. They can be represented graphically or linguistically, in both analog and digital form. They can be processed by humans and/or technology (adding machines, computers, etc.).

How about Information Systems?

An information system includes a sensing component that elicits the energy from an event through its sensor subsystem, transmission of this energy that is represented in some form (analog, digital) of a process (human or machine) enabling a response to a state or event. It responds to questions of what, where, when, and who.

How about Knowledge Systems?

The knowledge system is an extension of the information system. The knowledge element of the ADIK system relates directly to the various aids provided by the computer to enable problem solving and decision making. It includes the capacity to direct action by using all means of communication to transfer both information and knowledge to others.

ADIK Systems: How Do They Come About?

In answering this question, it is important to state that all of us (as noted previously) are data, information, and knowledge systems. We are part of the energy and matter system that surrounds us and to which we respond—sometimes willingly, other times unwillingly. Each impulse from this resource we symbolize and then order in the form of data that represent our state of awareness (information). Throughout our lifetime, we, as all scientists and artists, seek to find meaning in this interaction (knowledge). The focus of the information scientist is to determine the principles and laws that govern the use of technology (tools) that augment our native capacity to deal with this process. Based on theory and practice, information scientists work with information systems analysts, designers, and others to establish these principles and laws.

The System Development Cycle

ADIK systems come about after some person, institution, or organization recognizes a need and a requirement based on some task or problem to be solved, some decision to be made, or some activity to be initiated or managed. Technologies are applied to complement and extend human capacities that are deemed necessary to achieve goals and/or objectives. Goals are those ends for which the system is required (e.g., eliminate terrorism); objectives are the ways of achieving the goal (e.g., control bank accounts of terrorists) (see figure 4.3).

Request for Proposal

A request for proposal (RFP) is a document that is initiated by a user, generally by a government agency, institution, a public or private organization, or citizen in response to a need and requirement. It states the user's expectation about the work to be done, the amount of money available to complete the project, and when the system should be available. The RFP is communicated to the public using a number of different published news announcements and other means to solicit bidding. The RFP can be broad in scope. The need and requirement for which a proposal is submitted could also include any one of the following:

- Fix a current system available to the user. For example, the current computer system has broken down and requires immediate repair. Or, the current sensor system that acquires data from a source is capturing the data incorrectly. Or, a unit of the company is incurring losses that exceed the resources available to it.
- Upgrade a current system because parts of it may be getting old and/or obsolete. It can be replaced to achieve goals and objectives better or more cheaply. An example would be if a company or office has expanded its operations. The current computer system storage and processing capacity is not enough to deal with the increased amount of data that the company or office is required to deal with.
- Create an ADIK system from "scratch," because of a new need and requirement. This objective is less likely, but the possibility exists. Back in the early 1950s with the outset of Sputnik, new challenges to our understanding of the space environment (astronomy) have become evident. In our time, the aging population of the world requires new outlooks to deal with matters of housing and healthcare. Although ADIK systems presently exist that enable society to deal with such problems, the creation of new ADIK systems based on these issues could require new—as well as updated—ADIK systems.

Feasibility Study

In responding to the RFP, the interested agent initiates a feasibility study to determine if the project can be undertaken given what can be done (the state of the art), the people and the technological resources required to complete it

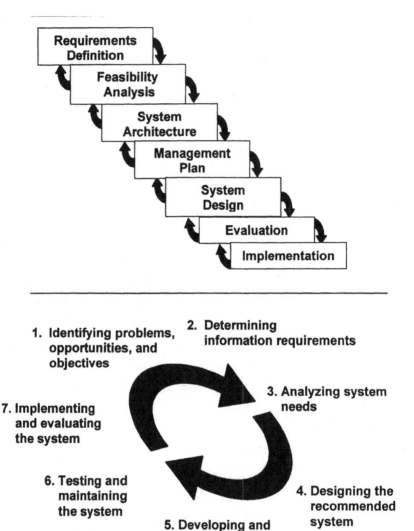

Figure 4.3. Two Illustrations of System Development Cycles. Adapted from Kendall and Kendall (2002).

within the time frame, and other constraints imposed by the user. This feasibility study will focus on the goal and function of the desired system. Once the contract is awarded to the successful bidder, the system analysis and design process will begin. Figure 4.3 provides two sketches of the various steps included in the cycle.

System Analysis Process

System analysis means exactly what the words imply. A system refers to an environment of people, tools, and procedures that are directed toward achieving or satisfying a stated objective. As discussed earlier, ADIK systems are assessed according to their ability to deal with events and situations that are confronted by the users of such systems. In the present case, analysis can refer to two related possibilities. One possibility (more often than not), as was suggested earlier, is that the system requires fixing or updating. The other possibility refers to the circumstances facing the user that would require an entirely new system. In each case, analysis refers to the careful breakdown of all the important factors in bringing together an environment (people, technology, and procedures) to enable the user to meet the needs that the event, situation, and/or condition demands. For example, take the case of the school superintendent faced with insuring the safety of all the students under his or her charge. This requires a study by the information system scientist of the current school environment (including teachers, students, maintenance people, and others as well) and the present ADIK system available to the superintendent or principal, as well as the likelihood of terrorist events and how to capture these events quickly to enable him or her to take action to respond to the event and avoid harm to people in the school.

In conducting a system analysis, it helps to have a picture—a system model. The model includes the details of the entire present environment: the people, the technology, and how these work together on a moment-to-moment basis, from one place to another during a normal day. The system model is similar to blueprints architects use in the design of physical structures.

Information system professionals may use different models to represent an ADIK system. The model may vary in how the basic working parts of the system are arranged in relation to each other (horizontally, laterally), but in general, the basic components of all these models are the same. The basic parts of the mode include input, that which enters into the system; throughput, the processing of the input; output, the result of the input; and feedback, the interaction between input, throughput, and output. In most models, the above are represented as arrows between the various components of the system.

System Design Process

Design refers to the general arrangement of people and technology related to each other to insure that the system given to the user(s) meets their needs and requirements. The system design process would include attention to the analysis completed by the system analysts, although it should be clear that, more often than not, the system analyst and system designer work together in the development of the system. In this process, the analyst's report is then translated and applied by the designer by detailing the use of all human and technological resources to be used in the system. The specifications are detailed in a document where each equipment and work process is fully described, including who will be using the equipment when, where, how, and why. The total cost of the ADIK system will also be provided by the designer at the time the design is presented, citing different design options with costs and risks pertaining to each, including any and all trade-offs. This is an estimate of the cost incorporating all these variables.

System Management

The system analysis and design project requires careful handling of available resources to ensure that the objectives of the system, as stated by the user(s), are met. Figures 4.4a and 4.4b include two charting schemes (PERT and GANTT) that information system specialists use to help them determine whether or not the development of the system (for which they are responsible) is on schedule and, if not, what must be done about it.

For example, suppose your "project" is to take a college course. There are several tasks your must complete: you must acquire the textbook, you must at-

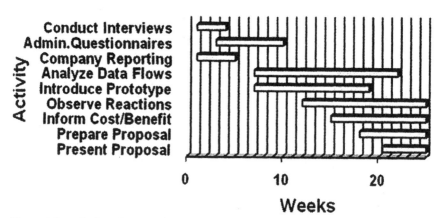

Figure 4.4a.   Project GANTT Chart. Drawn by S. Masters.

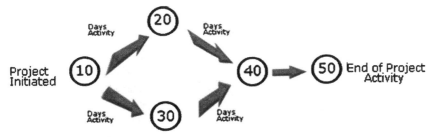

Figure 4.4b.   Project PERT Chart. Drawn by S. Masters.

tend the classes, you must read the assignments, you must do the exercises in the book, you must review, and you must take the exam. To track the path and progress of this project, you can use either a GANTT chart or a PERT chart.

GANTT/PERT

The left side of the GANTT chart in figure 4.4a lists the various tasks involved in the project. The right side of the GANTT chart is a bar graph, which shows how the tasks interrelate within the time schedule of the project.

The PERT chart in figure 4.4b takes a different approach, using arrows to represent tasks and "nodes" (small circles or ovals) to represent points in time at the start or end of activities.

Note that during the "project" described above, you cannot do the exercises in your book until you have finished the reading assignments. This is called a "constraint." Observe how this fact is represented in both the GANTT chart and the PERT chart. Both GANTT and PERT figures have been adapted from Kendall and Kendall (2002).

Testing an ADIK System

Simulation

Once the designer completes the design specifications, the proposed system is ready for a test prior to its submission to the user(s). One of the methods for testing the proposed system is to conduct a simulation. A simulation means submitting the system that the designer has proposed to a test to determine whether or not it will meet the user's needs and requirements.

There are two important parts of a simulation. First, the content of the simulation is based on the model of the system used for the analysis. This will guide the determination of the data to be collected from the simulation. Second, the simulation requires an understanding of the tasks in which the user(s) will be engaged in field situations. Task analysis tries to identify and bring together the various functions of the system and, for each, the level of proficiency to be achieved. The results of the simulation could lead to changes in the proposed design of the system.

The design of the system is now ready to be presented to the user(s). This will include software/hardware specifications, together with the specifications for a training program to prepare the individuals who will be using the new system. In this process, the intention is to increase the ability of the system to adjust to any number of changes that may occur. The user may be provided with more than one design for the system, varying in terms of costs and hardware/software trade-offs.

System Maintenance

Once the ADIK system is installed in the field, it will be subject to a maintenance program and schedule. These will be established to insure that the system meets its criteria of system performance under continuing changes that occur in the environment. This is particularly important to the information system specialist. Software/hardware design undergoes ever-rapid changes in function, design, and costs that occur in the field. In addition, there may be errors and bugs in the system, new demands on the various parts of the system, and new regulations from both inside and outside the organization. This may include government.

It is extremely important to realize that the maintenance of an ADIK system is most dependent on documentation. Documentation refers to the continuing physical record and accounting of all system activities on a time-to-time, component-to-component performance basis. This includes breakdown, loss of efficiency, and other elements of the overall ADIK system performance. In a world continually changing in purpose and function, individual discipline and skill by the information professional in detailing the state of any system at any particular point in time and space are critical. This system accounting could impact the function of both human and technological resources.

The maintenance of a system requires a training program at two levels: the work level and the development level. At the work level, the trainee is given the principles that make the system work. At the developmental level, the trainee is given specific instruction in the coding of specific tasks to insure they meet system objectives. With the application of new technology to a system, the information scientist is interested in understanding how the introduction of new technology in an ADIK system workplace can influence individual and group performance. Work skills must respond to different task procedures and functions. This requires careful attention by the information professionals in establishing training programs. In the case when a new ADIK system is introduced to the working environment, the information scientist is required to develop a training program for the work demanded by the new system.

SUMMARY

Throughout history, humans have developed tools to deal with circumstances (events and situations) faced. Each of these events and situations created demands for the use and extensions of native abilities in dealing with them. In the process, tools and procedures in their use were developed that met their mental (cognitive) needs and (physical) requirements. A major role of the information scientist is to determine the laws and principles that govern the application of these tools in meeting the needs and requirements of events and situations. These laws and principles serve the information system analyst and designer in analyzing, designing, and evaluating systems to meet the demands of events and situations. Thus, the augmented data, information, and knowledge (ADIK) system is an application of these tools. In the present text, the information system specialist is guided by a model (metaphor) that provides detailed mapping of the entire structure of the ADIK system and how each part (component) relates and contributes to the function of the entire system. The model also helps the information system specialist (engineer) in testing (using simulation and other methods) the output of the analysis and design before it is proposed to the user. The information system specialist is also engaged in the development of a maintenance and training program to ensure the efficiency and effectiveness of the system in the workplace or field over the extended life of the system.

EXERCISES

1. Describe something that you would consider to be a system.
2. Describe something you would not consider to be a system. Discuss why you think so.
3. Discuss the reason why documentation is important to any system operation. Why is it important to the information scientist?
4. You may wish an ADIK system to help you compete in a sport contest in which your skills would be important. Discuss how such a system could meet your ADIK needs.

5. Of what use is GANTT in the system analysis and design process?
6. Describe a situation where an information system analyst, and not a designer, would be called to help.
7. Event analysis is considered an important part of the system analysis process. Discuss a model that stresses this aspect of the process.
8. Of what importance is a feasibility study to a potential contractor in negotiating with a user a system analysis and design of an ADIK system?
9. What role can an ordinary camera play in meeting the user's needs (see figure 4.1)?
10. Discuss one of the many important needs that the present government faces in dealing with terrorism with respect to an ADIK system.
11. What is considered an important requirement in the system analysis and design process if it is to respond to new requirements?

5

How Do We Acquire Data, Information, and Knowledge? The Sensing Subsystem

It is difficult to realize that a shadow can move so fast
In the process it is telling us where we are, can, and should be

—*Anthony Debons*

LEARNING OBJECTIVES

- Define data acquisition.
- Recognize the important characteristics of data.
- Describe the major concepts involved in organizing and retrieving information.

OVERVIEW

The role of human and technological sensors that capture the events and situations facing an ADIK system are detailed. The account directs attention to the differences of data, information, and knowledge in the acquisition process.

Background

Just think of a world without data. Each of life's experiences would be just an experience, without any physical means for expressing it for us and to others. Fortunately, as humans, we have the ability to use symbols to record and give to others a record of our thoughts and experiences. A datum is actually a symbol created and used to account and represent that experience. All organisms acquire data, but many are limited genetically in their capacity to use data for extended purposes. All organisms acquire data through their senses at the time they are born and continue to do so until they die.

In the last chapter, we learned about systems, where they are, what they do, and what purpose they serve. We learned that we are all systems. We learned that technology adds to our capabilities to deal with the demands in our lives, to solve problems, and to make decisions. Various kinds of technologies augment our capabilities to deal with such matters. Information scientists are interested in how we can best obtain data, information, and knowledge.

Technology—such as satellites, cameras, and radars, to name a few applications—enables us to acquire data as never before. Information scientists study other ways also. For example, through the use of the computer, data mining extends our ability to be aware of patterns in data not available to our senses. There is the danger that technology and people can provide data on which we cannot depend or data that is not well founded. We depend on data for our awareness for the many things we do. At times, we are required to search and obtain information for the many things in which we are involved. Equally important, the information retrieved provides us with the knowledge required to make sense of the data. Information scientists are now interested in how we can best use our brains and institutions (schools, artificial intelligence, experts, documents, libraries, etc.) to plan, operate, and direct these rich resources, so that they can help us deal with the many problems we are asked to solve and the decisions to be made.

The Nature of Data

Data are part of our consciousness. Data are obtained as the normal process of living: through our various senses. Let's think of this in specific ways. When one awakes in the morning, one responds to light or darkness. The state of light or darkness tells most of us the time of day or night. These data guide us in our living day or at night. Just think of football. What would a football game be without a score? The score is a datum that provides us with information on how the teams are doing. Think of data, for example, relating to your health. You don't feel well. Your thermometer tells you that you have a fever and that something should be done about it.

Data Acquisition

Suppose, in one of your many experiences, you encounter a situation that you could not begin to understand. There were no words to express or explain it.

For example, you loved the vegetable garden that you carefully planted in early spring. You protected it from possible intruders in search of food. That morning, when you inspected your cherished garden, all the plants were wilted despite the fact that the garden was well watered and nourished the night before. The event puzzled you and you searched for an explanation. Could the plants have been overwatered or overnourished? You proceeded to check whether all the other plants from the neighbors suffered the same fate. You checked your plant encyclopedia. You approached the local nursery. You may have accessed the Internet for possible approaches to solving the problem. From the simple point of an awareness of the event—the state of the plants—you started to acquire data to extend that awareness (what, where, when, who) to understanding (how, why)—namely, knowledge. Acquiring data is a vital process of our existence.

This chapter, for example, is full of signs. The signs make up the language we use every day to tell ourselves and others who we are, where we are, and/or what we want and do. We use numbers, pictures, graphics, letters, symbols, sound, music, etc., to represent our experiences day in and day out. We do this by using all sorts of tools, technology, and the energy and matter that is available, from inside or outside of us. We refer to these ways that enable us to use these things as media. There are all sorts of media. Parchment paper, on which this was written, is a medium. Through this medium, we use carbon, ink, and paint to provide data to others about the state of ourselves and the things around us. We also use gases (smoke), electromagnetic energy (radio, TV), fluid pressure (water, blood), cloth (flags), body movements, wind, odors, etc. These are all kinds of media.

Data are symbols that we create that enable us to deal with the world (events/situations) around us. Let's now attend to how data is obtained. That should not be difficult. We have said that data is obtained with our first breath. We receive data through our various senses. We can miss getting data and that could be serious if life is dependent on it. We can receive a datum that is false, that is, it does not represent the real state of things and that leads us to do things that can even threaten our lives. If the technology we invent and use misses important data, the result could be important and serious. By using eyeglasses and hearing aids, we are hoping not to miss important data. Eyeglasses and hearing aids augment (extend) our capacity to acquire and respond to states of energy and matter around us.

If the data, as we stated, are a representation of some physical state or condition, then the question comes up regarding what happens when we don't receive them for one reason or another. You didn't see the car ahead crossing the middle of the road. You didn't receive the wedding invitation from your dear friend and you missed the wedding you wanted so much to attend. You attended a lecture that interested you, but the sound from the speaker was so low and noisy, you missed what was said. You didn't acquire data. Your chemistry teacher asked you to collect data on a particular experiment, but you didn't follow the test instructions. You collected data that were incorrect, which led to wrong conclusions from your experiment. You arrived at the airport to meet your friend, but you were not advised that the plane would be three hours late. You lost three hours. There are so many ways we can relate to acquiring data vital to our well-being.

It is possible for us to understand how little or how much we can respond to or are aware of in the world around us. What we receive from the world around us comes through our eyes, ears, and our touch. For example, what we smell and how we balance ourselves when we walk the tightrope or how we feel when we go on a roller coaster all are data that we acquire through our senses.

"Threshold" is the amount of energy required for one to respond to transmitted data. Threshold, an idea to measure human sensory behavior, was first thought of by physicist Gustav Fechner (1801–1887) and physiologist E. H. Weber (1795–1878). It's actually a very simple idea. The idea states that there is a certain level of energy that our senses must have to enable us to respond 50 percent of the time. If we want to be sure that we will respond to the energy (data), then what we are required to do is to increase the level in the amount of energy (light, sound, pressure, etc.) so we can respond more than 50 percent of the time. In case of a fire at your house, you want to be sure that the shrill sound from your smoke detector is loud and near enough to waken you in the middle of the night while in a deep sleep. So the first thing we learn about data acquisition is the matter of threshold.

Data, of course, can be a matter of technology as well. The optical camera, in its many varied forms, is a data acquisition device of considerable versatility. The car speedometer tells us how slow or fast we are moving. The compass tells us the direction that the craft is moving. The markers on a compass correspond to the relation of an object to true north. Waving flags tell us the direction and speed of the wind. The accuracy level of an instrument is a matter of calibration and is included as part of the instrument specifications. Generally, the data we receive from these sources result from applying what has already been learned to the current situation.

There are various ways that data can be acquired beyond those that have been mentioned. We discussed how data are acquired through our various senses. Quite often data are acquired through technologies that are included as part of the ADIK system discussed previously. Some of these technologies require a human interface to input critical data. For example, in an emergency, help can be acquired by dialing 911 and transmitting data that summon important personnel to an event. Also, some sensors like smoke detectors can alert humans to a fire or dangerous carbon monoxide or high level of radon that could threaten health without requiring human interface beyond that of installation. Medical sensing technologies such as magnetic resonance imaging (MRI), positron emission tomography (PET), and electrocardiography (EKG) create data from the recesses of our bodies, providing medical professionals with ways to see how our internal organs are working at the time and enabling us to establish our state of health and predict the onset of disease. Public safety agents and others, in order to control speed on our highways and locate aircraft in the skies, to use radio detecting and ranging (radar). Aircraft use sophisticated data-acquiring technologies to predict volatile weather and other conditions that could influence flight and the safety of passengers. Sound navigation ranging (sonar) provides the ability of submarines to navigate in deep waters and to identify objects and structures such as the long-lost ocean liner Titanic. Optical devices are used as data acquisition tools. Scanners, for example, give us the capability to take what we have written and digitize the script through the use of the binary numbers zero and one. This also enables us to present what we have written in picture form or by a computer that translates the numbers into text rather than an image. Light pens, by pointing, allow us to interact with the computer, enabling us to select objects and data of interest to be presented on an electronic screen. Yesteryear's phonograph discs, where music and other data were recorded, are now presented on compact discs, or CDs. CDs extend our capacity to record, store, and use manifold data that can be retrieved and used quickly for a number of purposes that include fast information retrieval. Today, we can digitize books and reports that contain a considerable amount of data, enabling their presentation on a computer screen.

An important data acquisition and processing resource is a database. A database is the arrangement of related data in a table, form, or report. These databases consist of anything from aircraft status to teacher/class schedules to hospital-patient status and train schedules. There are two kinds of databases. The flat-file database includes one table at a time (i.e., train schedule). Relational databases include two or more dimensions of an event. A database that includes grades for courses taken together with the number of previous courses taken would be a relational database. Databases show data in rows and columns known as records and fields. Databases are very useful because one can manipulate acquired data in different ways that provide subtle information important to problem solving and decision making.

Last, but certainly not least, the library, as an institution of people, technology, and procedures is foremost an instrument for data, information, and knowledge acquisition. The library has a long history in its role of recording human experience. The library is an important institution that supports all kinds of human needs and requirements for data that serve both individuals and organizations. We shall learn that the library and the professional librarian, who serves its patrons, are the critical elements of our culture, both as far as acquiring, retrieving, and distributing essential data, information, and knowledge. The library and information science are strongly related in purpose and function.

Data Reliability

Many of our actions and, of course, many of our decisions depend on reliable data. Data reliability is of considerable importance to the information scientist. Reliability means "capable of being trusted or depended on." Generally speaking, data reliability centers on three factors: the state of the event, the source of the data, and the capacity of the sensing mechanism to accurately represent the state of the event. For example, in matters of health, ability to capture blood pressure can be an important factor in maintaining personal health. Blood pressure (the event), we are told, is often unstable, fluctuating from moment to moment. The blood pressure instrument requires periodic calibration. In some instances, blood pressure data reliability is insufficient in its ability to provide a useful diagnosis of an ailment. But there are other instances when data reliability can be a matter of life and death. Consider the accurate reporting of the state of a tornado and the reliability and accuracy of the data reported in alerting people to the possible dangers to life and property!

Data Validation

We ask, "Another source for that fact, please!" "Validation" is defined as "proof; confirmation," while "valid" is defined as "sound; well-grounded on principles or evidence; able to withstand criticism or objection" (*Webster's New World* 1966, 1608) or "based on facts or good reasoning; true or sound (valid argument)" (*New World Children's Dictionary* 1997, 815).

The information professional is interested in ensuring that the data provided by the information system represents the actual state of the event to which the individual is to respond. Information professionals serve clients in different arenas, namely, instruction, research, and other scholarly pursuits. To this end, the importance of ensuring that these clients receive data representing actual states cannot be underestimated.

Data Discrimination

Discrimination refers to the ability to respond to similarities and differences in the data that correspond to the experiences we encounter. For example, not too long ago, the U.S. Department of the Treasury produced a metal dollar coin to replace the paper dollar, with which we are all familiar. It was not successful because the coin resembled a quarter. It had poor discriminability. The effort to create a dollar coin that the public will discriminate from other coins continues. This relates to the matter of acknowledging the human factor in technology, a subject that we will examine in a later chapter of this book.

There are many instances in our lives that data discrimination can be quite important. We should be able to judge correct from incorrect acts, given a standard to follow. It is a matter of judgment when we decide to pass a car on a two-lane road. This ability to judge how fast the other car is moving (data) can be a matter of life and death to you and others. It is important that our sensors and our technology provide us with data that correspond correctly to states of the world in which we live.

As we have learned previously, one of the reasons we have ADIK systems is to augment our capacities to deal with the world around us. The purpose of the ADIK system is to discriminate between various aspects of an event, or to help us make a decision and/or solve a problem. This understanding is an important function of an information scientist. Fortunately, engineers are now developing sensor systems that can be placed on the road and installed in a vehicle that will increase the driver's ability to estimate distances and conditions that are likely to be encountered during travel.

Data Reproducibility

Did you see that? Tell me what you saw. Can you transform a source medium into a different medium given the present technology (e.g., natural science onto film)? What was different between the two books on the same subject? Data reproducibility refers to the ability of an information system to provide the data obtained from a source at a different time and space. Generally, this is an important idea that governs the conduct of scientific research. It has applicability to the information professional's interest from several different points of view that we have discussed previously (i.e., reliability, validity, etc.).

Data Vulnerability

Social Security numbers, credit card identifications, and PINs represent data that can be compromised. The information professional's interest includes the protection of these valuable elements of human activity and interaction. Data vulnerability can be quite costly to individuals and organizations alike. The military has always been careful about the access to important data that could mean the winning and losing of battles and the life and death of military personnel as well as the loss of important battle equipment. In a community threatened by terror, for example, it will be necessary at times to safeguard important data for national security. National information systems (command, control, communications) are to be protected from those who threaten individual and collective security.

The Nature of Information Acquisition

General

All creatures on earth are born to acquire information. Some are better suited than others through the genes they inherit. The available energy and matter stimulate the sensors, eyes, ears, skin, and muscles. These sensors acquiring matter, energy, and time in space enable us to be aware. We can refer to this awareness as the state of being informed. Meanwhile, each sensor is limited in the amount and kind of energy and matter it can acquire. Further, there are limitations of another kind that can influence the ability to be aware, to acquire information. The energy that is captured by the sensor is given identity. This identity is represented as a symbol. For *Homo sapiens*, these symbols are organized by a set of rules that represent a system of symbols—letters and/or numbers that help us communicate with the world around us.

Our state of awareness can lead us to action. We are reminded, however, that inaction is a form of action. Whether action or inaction, the manner or physical product of its expression can be quite varied. It can be a spoken word, or the lack thereof, or the presence or absence of a letter, document, film, musical score, etc. These forms of expression provide information and are the products of our awareness.

Information is process and product. Information as a process is a function of the mind, the brain. Information is also the physical result of the process. Symbols are the means through which process and product occur. First, we should be clear that the absence of data could be information. If, for example, you were expecting your parents and they failed to arrive at home, then there is an awareness that something must have occurred to create that experience (event). You are aware of their absence, and that is information.

Definition of Information Acquisition

What is meant by information acquisition? Information is the content of awareness. The content of awareness is represented by data that define an experience—the what, where, when, and who. A red light from a traffic signal is not simply a red light. It makes us aware that there is possible danger and we should stop at a particular place to avoid a mishap. A green light tells us to go ahead. An "A" on a report card is not simply a letter. It makes us aware (information) of our performance in one of our subjects of study. The scoreboard in a sports game is not simply a data score represented by numbers or letters. It tells us something about who is winning or losing the game. These are all examples of data-to-information transformation, which is a matter of considerable importance to the information scientist. Information acquisition is the next step beyond data acquisition. It moves our awareness in certain directions.

Humans and organizations can acquire information in a number of ways, from parents, friends, teachers, computers, books, films, newspapers, radios, TV, satellites, and many other sources of observations. The critical information science issue and task is to establish how humans and organizations can store such data when needed and required so that the data can be retrieved as part of their needs. There are other issues of interest to the information scientist: security, confidentiality, privacy, censorship, etc. These will be discussed in a later chapter.

In information acquisition, there is a certain relationship that extends our awareness in certain directions. Generally, information scientists are interested in how best to obtain information demanded by someone or some organization faced with a specific need or material. It may require asking other questions in the process to obtain the best evaluation. The process requires a systematic and careful development of questions by the information professional.

How we obtain or ask for information (cognitive/physical) to do (search for) what we want or are asked to do depends on several factors: the task for which we seek information; the need and requirement for the information demanded of the task; the way we develop and ask the question; the way that information is organized, whether in someone's head, in the library, or at the information desk; or the relevance of the material retrieved for the task.

Information acquisition centers on tasks for which data are required to support the user's accomplishment. Individuals and organizations acquire information that is related to the tasks faced. Tasks demand the proper identification, recruitment, and use of data to ensure that the state of awareness meets the demands of the task.

Task Analysis

Almost anything we do depends on data and information. Whether we are asking for information on the best route to drive from New York to California, how to overcome dietary problems, or how to play the best defense in a football game, the key is to ask the questions in a manner and format that can get the best answer without asking many other questions in the process (e.g., drive to California with the least cost of fuel, lose weight and maintain good health). If an instructor's task is to obtain a good evaluation of a student's understanding of the subject matter, the skill is asking the right question that would give the instructor a measure of the student's understanding of the material.

In obtaining an understanding of the task for which information is sought, it may be necessary to obtain an understanding of other related tasks that could influence how a question is asked. Acknowledging the impact of other tasks on the main question being asked could lead to better retrieval of the information being sought. The task of selecting a college that will allow you to complete your degree in four years is one thing. Asking for information about the college program that would enable you to complete the program in four years (task 1) and allow you to work (task 2) is another. The retrieval of information that is sought to support both tasks can be influenced significantly. If the two related tasks are not part of the task analysis for which the questions are directed, information retrieval can malfunction. Information retrieval is work that requires, more often than not, the expertise of a trained information professional (e.g., reference/special librarian, information counselor).

Information Retrieval

Robert Korfhage, the late information scientist, defined information retrieval as "the location and presentation to a user of information relevant to an information need expressed as a query" (Korfhage 1997, 324). Among those who drafted the Constitution of the United States, who died first? Who, if any, among the terrorists reportedly responsible for the 9/11 disaster was born in the United States? A general definition of information retrieval can be proposed for our present purpose: the identification and collection of literary material and other graphic, human, and electronic resources required for human awareness demanded by a specific task.

Of some attention for the information professional is obtaining an understanding of the experience of establishing relevance of the subject material to the demands of the task confronting the user. Retrieval of relevant information remains one of the more important issues of interest to the information scientist. The following are examples of information retrieval.

Your instructor asks for a term paper to describe the last event of the French Revolution. You proceed to the library to retrieve the information on that subject. Or, you may ask a friend, the teacher of the French course you are taking.

In six months, you graduate. Where should you apply to college? What information can you obtain about a particular college?

You are interested in your great-grandparents, who are no longer living. And your parents are just as interested as you are to obtain the information about them. Where did they live? Where did they come from? How did they live throughout the years?

You can ask questions about the world. Who was Plato's mother? Where did Plato go to school, if indeed he ever did?

The president of the United States would like to obtain the material that President Kennedy used in his 1961 inaugural speech: "My fellow Americans, ask not what your country can do for you—ask what you can do for your country." What can the president do to obtain that information? (Hint: the text and audio for this speech are at www.hpol.org/jfk/inaugural.)

Considering the attention that information professionals have applied to information retrieval, it is often considered synonymous to information science. It is certainly directly related to the search process. It can cover the special reference services that librarians provide to individuals. It can also refer to the information desks found on interstate highways at rest areas when driving from one state to another; information booths at airports, railroad stations, and hospital entrances; and now the Internet and World Wide Web. Information retrieval is quite important when a crisis of any sort (medical, crime, weather, etc.) is faced. Korfhage defines information needs as "the requirement to store information (data) in anticipation of future use, or to find information (data) in response to a current problem" (Korfhage 1997, 323). We can adapt the following definition of "information retrieval" based on Korfhage's views: the identification and collection of literary and other sources (graphic, electronic, film, human) required for human awareness demanded by a specific task.

Organization of Information

The way we identify, compose, record our experiences, and arrange records is central to how we can best use the information we need, require, and how it is retrieved. Humans have always been inclined to identify objects of interest to them by placing like things in some order. Many of the ways that we use today in placing records in ways most easily accessible and usable derive from the time of Greek philosophers: Aristotle (http://en.wikipedia.org/wiki/Aristotle), Plato, and scholars before their time.

Melanie J. Norton, information scientist, provides an interesting metaphor that can be applied in our understanding of the organization of information:

Why are fruits and vegetables usually located together in a market? Why not have the apples on the shelf next to the applesauce, apple pie fillings and apple juice?

Why not have the market arranged by alphabet order; first aisles could all be all the "a" things? Why not just unload the trucks and put everything in the store in the order it comes off the truck that day? Why are standard phone books arranged in alphabetical order rather than numeric order? Simply, it makes it easier to find things if they are organized in some manner. Since fruits and vegetables require refrigeration and are valued for their freshness as well as appearance, it seems reasonable to keep them together, usually on the countertop displays to maximize refrigeration and presentation. They are usually sorted into fruit, with all the apples next to one another, all the pears next to one another, while the vegetables are also grouped together, such as red, yellow, and white onions, and different squashes together and so on. This is organization by association. (Norton 2000, 52)

Aids to Information Organization   Many human experiences are never physically recorded. Some are retained in memory. Psychologists tell us that we use a number of schemes to help us place things in memory so that they can be effectively retrieved. We organize things and experiences while we are aware of them. We also organize our understanding of these experiences. Thus, the aids that are available for the organization of information are directly applicable to the organization of knowledge that we will now consider.

Arlene G. Taylor, library and information scientist, considers the organization of information as a natural and necessary aspect of living. "Regardless of one's personal style . . . human learning is based upon the ability to analyze and organize data, information and knowledge . . . we organize because we need to retrieve . . . retrieval of information is dependent upon its having been organized . . . information is needed in all aspects of life . . . for health reasons, to understand each other, to learn about one's relationship, to fix things that are broken, or simply to expand our knowledge" (Taylor 1999, 2).

Taylor refers us to the organization of information that is manifested in libraries, archives, museums, art galleries, the Internet, data administration, and office environments. Of course, there are numerous schemes available for the organization of information. These include classification schemes, indexing, cataloging, citation indexes, clustering, associative terms, and other directly related aids to information retrieval.

Classification   Classification is placing thought, ideas, and documents into certain groups or categories based on some established standard. Knowledge, in physical form, can be presented in pictures, mathematics, and language. Knowledge can be presented physically, alphabetically, chronologically, in reports, essays, abstracts, encyclopedia, dictionaries, indexes, catalogs, and bibliographies using various standards and specifications.

There are different classification schemes. The Dewey decimal classification and colon classification are examples of such schemes. Each of these has received extensive study as to their functionality by library and information scientists. The Dewey decimal classification is based on specific areas of study with subjects for each and included as many times as required. Colon classification is based on the idea of facets, that is, the features of an object.

Categorization A category can be considered to be a class (common characteristics) of many different objects, including ideas. A catalog is a physical way that a person can use to help to identify and store ideas and experiences for others to find and use. How a separate thing (object, idea, process) can be identified so that it can be located and gotten back efficiently remains of major interest to librarians and information scientists. This includes how the object can be identified and found when needed and how best to describe the object (or idea) so as to provide the individual who is searching for the idea a means to locate it quickly and efficiently (Lubetzky and Hayes 1992, 436). "The ability to collect an item after it has been stored is based upon the organization and subsequent representation employed to describe its potential retrieval" (Norton 2000, 51).

An important factor in classification and categorization is the use of natural language. Of course, we use natural language each day of our lives. Natural language is a system of signals (labeling) that humans have established that enables the identification of things and the feelings that we experience.

Indexing An index is an indicator of content; it helps to identify the location of an item among a number of items to be retrieved. An index is part of a lexical device intended to aid the search process. It is related to the abstracting process, a process that reduces the substance of a document to basic essentials.

There are many kinds of indexes ranging from alphabetical, author, permuted, string, word, etc. One type of index that has received research attention by information scientists is the citation index. A citation index lists documents citing a given document (Korfhage 1997). The citation index has achieved considerable research attention and application (Garfield 1979).

Although it was developed primarily for bibliographic purposes, and in spite of its recognized utility as a search tool, the most important application of citation indexing may prove to be nonbibliographic. If the literature of a science reflects the activities of that science, a comprehensive multidisciplinary citation index can provide an interesting view of these activities. The view can shed some useful light on both the structure of science and the process of scientific development (Cleveland and Cleveland 2000, 50).

The Nature of Knowledge

General

Philosophers have struggled with understanding the nature of knowledge for centuries and continue to do so. For our present purpose, knowledge can be considered an extension of our cognitive state of awareness (information). In our present study, knowledge represents the "how" and "why" of our experiences. The state of understanding enables us to produce, in some physical form, the physical representation of the experience that enables us to process, store, and provide others with the nature, content, and significance of this experience.

Kinds of Knowledge

There are different kinds of knowledge: explicit knowledge, tacit knowledge, and declarative knowledge. Each has its own properties of how they are acquired and used. These properties command the attention of the information scientist.

Explicit knowledge is that which we are all accustomed to, such as is presented in commercial publications, the World Wide Web, e-mail, databases, etc. Your grade in the course is explicit knowledge, for example.

Tacit knowledge is that gained from face-to-face conversations, all the experiences in our heads, unspoken, inferred, and unconscious. For example, a good score on the SAT could mean one will be allowed to enter the college or university of his or her choice.

Declarative knowledge is that which we determine by study and other means as fact, like DNA and the nature of individual differences.

Knowledge Acquisition

Humans acquire knowledge informally through day-to-day contact with the world about them, basically information. All of us are aware that we go to school to acquire knowledge. Education, or schooling experience, is often considered to be synonymous with acquiring knowledge. We can apply this understanding to a definition of knowledge acquisition. Knowledge acquisition is the receiving, extending, and ordering of human consciousness (awareness) directed at meaning, understanding, wisdom from individuals, or from the records of individuals (the how and why of experience).

Information scientists are interested in establishing how technology can help us acquire and use knowledge. They are also interested in how technology can be used to teach students remotely or how surgeons can direct critical operations by personnel located in distant places.

Knowledge Retrieval

When information retrieval was considered earlier, different aspects of how information could be organized for retrieval were presented. We studied classification and categorization, cataloging, question-asking, etc. In that context, the task was to establish the place that related a literary identity to a physical product in a specific location. Information professionals were organizing records of human experience for retrieval in a physical space (location, manner of identification and assemblage, etc.). This served a logistical function, that is, how to arrange things that are alike in content or appearance. In knowledge retrieval, the recovery concerns the presence of ideas, concepts, declarations, matters that we relate to understanding and wisdom. It is important to stress that aids to information retrieval also serve knowledge retrieval. Knowledge retrieval cannot be independent of information retrieval. As a matter of fact, having the ability to retrieve information may not serve the purpose for which knowledge is retrieved. For example, a common habit of students, reported in their study of mathematics, is to search for the answer to a specific problem in the back of the book. Having retrieved the answer, however, does not guarantee the student an understanding of the problem. Also, possessing all the facts that underlie the signs of a disease, though necessary, does not ensure the knowledge required for its cure.

Aids to Knowledge Retrieval

The Abstract An abstract is an abbreviated statement that often accompanies a literary document identifying the basic ideas and conclusions that can be found in the document. This tool is an aid in identifying basic information by minimizing the time to search for critical ideas that are considered important to a task. It also helps in identifying ideas in documents in another language.

Citation Index With respect to books, articles, films, etc., an index is an alphabetical listing of subjects or authors by name pertaining to the subject. Another related aid to knowledge is called the citation index. If you want to find out what John Doe or Sally Blake wrote, then you would look for John Doe or Sally Blake in the index by name. This will tell you how many works John or Sally has written and how many of his or her publications are referenced by other authors. In addition, there is a subject index with which one can ascertain who has been writing in a particular field.

Knowledge Management

Humans have been involved in the process of knowledge management (KM) for centuries through writing, speaking, and other means (music, art, etc.).

Education and librarianship, for example, like other professions (law, medicine), have been involved in managing knowledge for some time. KM goes back to when teaching (education) first started and that could be from the earliest recorded time in antiquity. The book, discussed in an earlier chapter, is one of many forms used by humans to represent the meaning and understanding of the human state, action, and thought.

Knowledge management, from the present-day point of view, refers to the use of a number of human and technological resources, particularly computers, to capture the "how" and/or "why" of an experience and to apply this to the planning, operating, and control of organizations. The following is one of the definitions of "knowledge management": "A discipline that promotes an integrated approach to identifying, capturing, evaluating, retrieving, and sharing all of an enterprise's information assets. These assets include databases, documents, policies, procedures, and previously captured expertise and experience in an individual worker" (The Gartner Group's definition, quoted in Duhon 1998, 10).

Knowledge management in its present form refers to the acquisition (retrieval) of knowledge resources (human and products) to support planning, operating, controlling, and evaluating how a company, a school, or the government acquires and uses knowledge to deal with the world it confronts each day. The information scientist is directly interested in understanding the principles that govern the extension of a data and information system to a knowledge system.

As expressed in the current literature and texts, knowledge management centers on how the knowledge resource can use these technologies in planning, operating, and controlling functions of organizations and institutions. Knowledge management, so considered, directs attention, for example, to the efficient and effective use of the World Wide Web and the Internet, increasing creativity and personal competency, crisis response and control, ethics, and other vital issues that influence the achievement of institutional goals and objectives (Srikantaiah and Koenig 2000).

Aids to Knowledge Management

One of the interesting aspects of information science has been its continuing attention to how the computer can help solve problems and make decisions. In the late 1960s and early 1970s, Douglas Engelbart studied how the computer could enhance our mental (cognitive) ability. This research was the forerunner of artificial intelligence, a term first used by cognitive psychologists who became intensely involved in research that applied the computer to an understanding of human learning and intelligence (chapter 7). It culminated in the famous chess match between Russian chess champion Gary Kasparov and the formidable IBM machine, Big Blue.

SUMMARY

Data can be acquired by our senses, but our senses are limited as to what they can capture. Technology—especially computers, electronic displays, and telecommunications—can help us deal with large amounts of data, information, and knowledge. There are numerous other technologies in the marketplace (from eyeglasses and hearing aids to cameras and microphones) that help us to see, hear, touch, smell, and feel, using devices we can associate with Radio Shack down the street. Technology enables us, as individuals and organizations, to do what has to be done to meet the demands of daily living. But having data is not enough. Data have to be linked to what we do, whether pursuing a subject in school, figuring out what's best to do after graduation, going out on a date, buying and driving a car, getting more involved with sports or a band, etc. Answers to the basic questions of the what, where, when, and who of our lives, we have learned, represent information. We search and retrieve the what, where, when, and who (information) for tasks (problems, decisions) that we face and pursue. The computer is a helpful tool because it enables individuals and organizations to gather and order the data acquired from our human or technological sensors, to retrieve data and information now in libraries, museums, etc., worldwide, and to see and understand different information (data) in different ways. Our lives are not limited to awareness (information). Humans and organizations seek to understand, that is, extract the meaning from our experiences. Knowledge is an extremely important resource that defines and supports the human quest for meaning and understanding. Classification, cataloging, indexing, and abstracting are organizing tools that aid the use of both information and knowledge. Knowledge management covers a broad area in determining how the intellectual and physical resources of an organization can be identified, retrieved, and used. Knowledge management, although an old activity, is receiving increased attention through the computer, which redefines it in specific ways, that is, as artificial intelligence and expert systems.

EXERCISES

1. The postman has little difficulty delivering your mail in your mailbox. What makes this so easy to do considering all the different streets, different people living at various streets, moving in and out of houses?

2. You are asked to start a Little League baseball team for your neighborhood. There are close to fifty kids who could qualify as members of the team. How might you use the computer to help you identify the potential members of the team and their position on the team?

3. You are faced with the task of selecting a college that you could go to and that would correspond to your interests. How would you use the computer to help you select the school you would want to go to?

4. What is the difference between searching for something you want from the school library and searching for something you want from Blockbuster (other than the fact that the library has books while Blockbuster has DVDs, tapes, and films)?

5. What is a data dictionary? Why is this of interest to an information scientist rather than a computer scientist?

6. What is the main difference between a keyboard and a typewriter other than the fact that one is electronic and the other mechanical?

7. Your neighbor has asked everyone in the neighborhood to help find a pet cat that was reported lost. Posters were attached to lampposts throughout the neighborhood providing pictures of the cat. What aspect of this situation would be of interest to an information professional?

8. The end of the class term is a week away. You gathered many notes throughout the semester. What aspect of this problem would interest an information professional?

9. How would acquiring data be different from acquiring information?

10. What is the difference, if any, between acquiring information and acquiring knowledge?

6

Movement of Data, Information, and Knowledge: The Transmission Subsystem

It (telecommunications) is powerful and it empowers, with far reaching consequences. It has demonstrated the potential to transform society and business, and the revolution has just begun. With the invention of the telephone, human communications and commerce were forever changed. Time and distance began to melt away as a barrier to doing business, keeping in touch with loved ones, and being able to immediately respond to major world events. Through the uses of computers and telecommunication networks, humans have been able to extend their powers of thinking, influence and productivity, just as those in the Industrial Age were able to extend the power of their muscles, or physical self, through the use of heavy machinery. (Goleniewski 2002, xv)

LEARNING OBJECTIVES

- Compare and contrast transmission and communications.
- Categorize the various ways of sending (transmitting) signals from one place to another.
- Recognize the features of effective transmission.
- Identify and describe the role of the components of network architecture.

OVERVIEW

Movement (transmission) of a signal from one to another, in time and place, is a subsystem of an augmented data, information, and knowledge (ADIK) system. If we could move our bodies through space at the speed of light, we could do things that are shown to us in movies. Of course, we can't. Yet, wheels help us move faster. Wings enable us to fly. Before the telephone, we were limited to pebbles, smoke, flags, horseback, and written messages as a means to transmit our intentions and action to others. Now we can talk across oceans and through space, bringing together cell phones, TVs, radio, and other electronic devices to help us deal with many things before, while, and after they happen. The information scientist works with the electrical engineer, the computer scientist, and the psychologist to determine what kind of ADIK system meets human needs and requirements. This chapter will examine the transmission of data, information, and knowledge as a subsystem of an ADIK system. It will discuss the importance of transmission in the day-to-day experiences of both individuals and organizations. This chapter will also introduce networking and the technologies that make it possible. Throughout the study of transmission its relationship to communications, what is transmitted for human meaning and understanding, is of central importance.

Terms

Transmission

"Transmission" is defined as the movement of signals from one point in space and time to another. Teletransmission refers to the electrical movement of signals. Signals represent states of events captured by sensors coded and moved (transmitted) to human/machine processors (satellites, telephone system, computers, e-mail).

It should be clear at the outset that the transmission of data may obey different principles than the transmission of information, and the transmission of information may differ from the principles involved in the transmission of knowledge, although the three are interrelated in important ways. Communication, as applied to transmission, refers to the electronic and other devices that move signals from one place (medium) to another. Exchange between senders and receivers can be at different points of time and place. This aspect of transmission of these resources is discussed as part of a communication or transfer subsystem (chapters 9 and 10 of this book).

Wireless transmission, simply stated, is without wires; the cell phone is the most common example. Wireless transmission has been a human activity for a long time, from the time when smoke signals were the means for asserting battle intentions to the present-day radio at home or in the car. Currently it is most predominant in the cell phone, where much of individual and collective activity and commerce occur. Study of wireless transmission is a subject of some technical complexity. Only a brief view can be provided at this point in our study of information science. The key issues rest on the effective use of bandwidth, the capacity that a connection has for carrying data. The technical problems rest on the retention of signal strength, the influence of signal echo, fading interference, and noise. The design and position orientation of antennae enter into the assessment as well. Problems center around standards for use and design, political regulation, and spectrum allocation.

More often than not, communication and transmission of messages and signals are considered as synonymous experiences. Communication, in this text, refers to the human ideas, meanings, understanding, and intentions (transmitted by a carrier between a human sender and receiver: e.g., language, mail, etc.). In the literature the terms "teletransmission" and "telecommunications" are cojoined both in theory and practice (Thompson et al. 2006). Telecommunication refers to the process of electronic communication (e.g., radio, TV, media, etc.). Communication is not possible without transmission. The absence of transmission, however, can also be a source of communication (i.e., the fact that you did not receive the letter from the college you applied to can be a signal suggesting the possibility of an event or a number of events regarding your admission). See figure 6.1 for some of the differences between transmission and communication.

Communication vs. Transmission

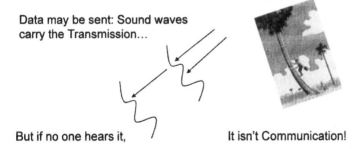

Data may be sent: Sound waves carry the Transmission...

But if no one hears it,

It isn't Communication!

> **If a tree falls in the Forest and no one hears it...it is Transmission→ the Sound Waves are moving across air. However, to be Communication, someone has to hear it!**

Figure 6.1. Communication vs. Transmission. Drawn by S. Masters.

Why is the difference between transmission and communication important? An increasing number of countries and regions have become reachable, and in turn, the world is a more accessible place. It has become a necessity for doctors in large cities to reach doctors located in remote parts of the country. Surgeons in California have concluded successful operations on patients living in Alaska. It is important for businesspeople to be able to get together and move their ideas from one place to another.

As ADIK systems, we write and place letters in the mailbox, dial a phone number in our home, chat with our friends. In all of these experiences, we are engaged in the process of transmission that facilitates communication. When our sensors (organic/mechanical) pick up energy from the external world, this energy is expressed in the form of a signal (chemical, electrical), which moves either to our brains, our hands, or to the computer. When we pick up a newspaper, book, or letter, these documents (products) serve as transmitters of states that are occurring or not occurring, represented in physical form. The important point for our understanding of information science rests on the fact that without transmission, ADIK systems would not exist, let alone operate. When transmission fails, ADIK systems fail. When they do, the information scientist attempts to understand the cause of such failures and integrates this understanding in the analysis, design, and evaluation of ADIK systems.

The Transmission Process

Signals from events captured by ADIK systems are coded, and when so represented, they constitute data. These data in turn provide the means to generate messages over distance and time from one source to another. Transmitters and receivers are two hardware devices with a physical connection between them. For simplicity's sake, let's say that one of the devices is a computer and the other is a printer directly wired to a network. Inside the computer, there are two essential parts needed to establish data transmission: software and a network interface card. The software includes a director and a network driver. The role of the director is to tell the information where to go. In other words, the director determines whether the request made by the user can be handled by the computer itself (a local service) or if the request has a need for a network service (remote service). For example, you finished an English paper that is due tomorrow and want to print it. The printer is not directly connected to the computer, yet it is connected through the network, and the printer sits across the room. Remember, the characters that were typed into the computer through the keyboard have been translated into binary code (ones and zeroes) and transmitted. Since the printer is a network service, the director guides this binary information to the network driver with notification of destination. At this point, the network driver engages and acts as a conveyer between the director and the network interface card. It takes the information to be delivered and packs it up according to the rules established by the network, called network protocol (more on this later in the chapter). In our example, the binary word-processing document has descriptive information attached to the beginning of it, which includes where the message originated and its destination.

The Role of Words and Symbols as Transmitters

Language is a system of words and symbols used to transmit our intentions, feelings, and other states of our lives. Language plays an essential role in communications. For example, you received a letter from a friend whom you met on a recent visit to China. The letter was written in Chinese. Although you received the message, you would not be able to read and understand the message because it was in a different language. You were not able to translate the symbols, thus no message was received. It provided no meaning to you. Information scientists working with computer scientists, linguists, and others are now making advances in computer language transmission and translation that would bridge this language gap. But in addition to lack of transmission, we need to consider that there are errors in transmission that need to be accounted for.

Electronic Component Failure

Whenever any electronic or mechanical device is used for whatever purpose, the possibility of equipment malfunction or failure in transmission can occur. There are also other errors that can occur. Whenever we send a message from one source to another, human or technological, there can be an error in understanding (knowledge) of that which is intended. The error can occur as part of noise (random energy) that impairs the reception of the message. Humans have the capacity to return the message to the sender for clarification, thus reducing the impact of the error in the application of what is intended. Yet noise (random energy), the result of technical interference, can directly influence the transmission of the message in many ways.

Errors in the transmission subsystem can occur at many parts of an ADIK system. For example, failure to replace the batteries in the fire detection device in your home renders that sensor unable to transmit to—and thus inform— the inhabitants about the fire, leading to serious consequences. The delay in transmitting the message from the human lookout to the ship's captain on the ocean liner Titanic cost the lives of many passengers.

Transmission of Knowledge

One view (among many) that could distinguish between information and knowledge centers on the question that individuals ask about themselves and the world around them. Knowledge centers on the questions of "how" and "why." Answers leading to an understanding of these questions may rest with philosophers, psychologists, educators, and many other professionals. Meanwhile, the transmission of knowledge is well within the bounds of many institutions, from the press to education. The work and focus of information scientists will center on how technology, primarily computers, can aid human access and application of knowledge. It should be mentioned that in the post-9/11 era, the access and management of knowledge (intelligence) would offer increased challenges to the information scientist.

The Network

The Broad View of Networks

The sharing of data, information, and knowledge across distances is a necessary tool in everyday life in today's society. The demand has fueled research and development of better ways to connect nodes of computers through networking. In the construction of a network, several specifications must be considered before putting it all together. What types of data will be shared? How many bytes is a typical quantity of data? How fast does it need to be shared? Who will be the users of the database? What are the limits to their capabilities? How many users will want to share this information? How much reliability is needed in the network? All these questions—and more—should be considered when analyzing, designing, and evaluating ADIK systems (in this case, networks). The answer to these questions will help determine what network devices are needed, what medium should be used, what network architecture software should run the system, and if any other hardware devices are needed to advance the sharing of data, information, and knowledge among users. There are advantages, disadvantages, data size, and rate limits to be considered. Most of all, the cost of building such networks usually determines the materials involved. All these matters are of direct interest to the information scientist in the analysis, design, and evaluation of these systems.

What Is Meant by Network and Networking?

A network is a series of computers that work together to serve users at the same or different locations. Networking is data, information, and knowledge transfer (from one point in space to another) made possible by teletransmission technologies. These technologies function in a medium—the physical surroundings (air, water, etc.) in which the signals are carried. Networks augment the human capacity to communicate. It's the same as having a conversation. It takes at least two communicators (transmitter and receiver device), a medium between them, and some service to be provided. For example, in a face-to-face conversation, two parties communicate. Air is used as a medium (voice) to carry sound (acoustic signals) between the two, and the service that is provided is the language that is used by each person involved, each having an understanding of the rules of its use. By definition in a technological sense, networking is the connection between two or more computers (or other devices) through some type of medium, with the ability to transmit according to set rules and protocols that form a local area network (LAN), metropolitan area network (MAN), or even a wide area network (WAN). So now let's examine the three basic parts of any network: the transmitters and receivers, the media, and the services.

Transmitters and Receivers

There are other hardware devices used in constructing a network that become useful depending on the needs of the network configuration. These hardware devices are hubs, switches, bridges, and routers. Each sends data along a network, but varies in capabilities. For example, the hub (figure 6.2), which is located at the center of the network, takes the data from one node of a star topology and broadcasts the data to all other nodes (computers) on its network. It does not concern itself with the address of the receiver when forwarding the data. It only repeats data to all the nodes connected to this single network.

When two or more networks connect together, a slightly more complex device must be used. For example, a bridge is used to connect two networks that use the same protocols or rules in sending data (protocol is discussed later). The software capability must contain addressing and switching intelligence. This means that the bridge is aware of the location of all the nodes connected and the unique identifying addresses. However, if I wanted to connect two or more networks or different protocols, a router must be used. Since this hardware device connects two or more networks of different protocols or rules, the data might have to be adjusted to be sent across another network. Let us consider that data are prepared by sending from a node in network 1, where the protocol requires the same size of ten megabytes (Mb). The data are being sent to a receiving node in network 2 that requires a data

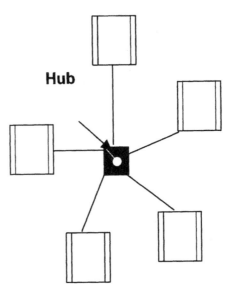

Hub

Figure 6.2. Multiple Computers Connected through a Hub. Drawn by S. Masters.

size of only 1Mb. It is the router's job to make adjustments between the two networks. Therefore, the original signal of 10Mb data packets have to be broken down into 1Mb data packets before they are sent across network 2 to the receiving node. These concepts will be discussed in greater detail later in the chapter.

The Server

Most computers that are part of a network are connected through cabling to a bigger, faster computer with more storage capacity, known as the server. The server is just that—it serves the other computers connected to the network. There are several services provided by this technology such as printing, file storage, messenger services, and others. A request is made from one computer to print the word-processing file to the print server computer. That server controls the print queue, the order of the files to be printed. It is there that the file is formatted and printed back into the characters that were visible on the user's monitor. There are other services such as messenger services that send and receive electronic messages (like e-mail or bulletin boards) or file services where the served files are stored and retrieved from the file server instead of one's own computer.

The Medium

The medium is the surrounding material in which signals exist and move around (air, water, etc.). In the present sense, the medium refers to the device that enables signals to be transported from one point to another. We can understand the kind of medium technology and the function that such technology serves. There are several types of mediums. They are twisted pair wiring, coaxial cable, and fiber-optic cabling and wireless.

Twisted Pair

Otherwise known as "phone wire," unshielded twisted pair (UTP) cabling is a pair of copper wires twisted around each other to prevent interference of signals. The fundamental physics concept of electricity and magnetism behind this technology is that when electricity runs through a wire, a magnetic field is created and surrounds the wire. Wires that are close together will have their magnetic field interfere with one another, thereby corrupting the electrical signal in the wire. By twisting the wires together, the fields are cancelled out, and the wire is then insulated, or the signal is protected from corruption. There are several types of unshielded twisted pair cabling.

Coaxial Cable

Coaxial cable, or "coax," is the wiring used for cable television. It consists of a solid copper wire surrounded by insulation and a shield made of copper braiding. It is then further coated with a protective covering to prevent further external interference. There are two types of coax: thicknet and thinnet. Just as the name implies, thicknet is the thicker of the two, able to cover longer distances when networking: 500 meters as opposed to 185 meters by thinnet. A British naval connector (BNC) is used to connect cable to its hardware.

Fiber-Optic Cable

Fiber is the premium choice of cabling. It uses light signals traveling along glass or plastic, instead of electrical signals along copper wire. The glass is then surrounded by more glass to act as an insulating layer to prevent leakage or allowing the trapping of light inside. It is then coated with permanent virtual circuit (PVC) or Teflon as a protective covering. The advantages and disadvantages in the use of fiber optics in communications are listed in table 6.1.

Table 6.2 compares how long it would take to transmit a book, using several different methods including telephone (twisted pair), LAN (coaxial cable), and fiber-optic cable.

Table 6.1.
Advantages and Disadvantages of Fiber Optic Usage.

Advantages That Fiber Offers:

1. More bandwidth;
2. Allows one to add additional equipment that provides for increased transmission capacity;
3. Not subject to interference (electromagnetic);
4. Low in weight and mass.

Disadvantages:

1. Special test equipment is needed;
2. Shortage of components and manufacturing sites;
3. Subject to physical damage;
4. High installation costs;
5. Vulnerability to damage by wildlife.

Source: Goleniewski (2002, 91–92).

Topology

Now that we are aware of all the hardware possibilities and wiring types, we must put all these together so that data, information, and knowledge can be shared. How these devices are connected is called the physical view of local area network (LAN). By definition, the physical view is the physical location of all the hardware and the physical connection between them. The topology used, also known as the "wiring orientations," is a very important consideration when designing a network. Which topology to use depends upon which network architecture is implemented. These are critical aspects for an ADIK systems analyst and designer.

Table 6.2.
How Fast?

- One page of single-spaced, word-processed text is equal to about 2,000 bytes of information, or 16,000 bits (8 bits per byte). The text of Cohen's book is approximately 200,000 bytes long.
- Old-fashioned (1970s) teletype was transmitted at 110 bits per second (bps). At that rate, it would take *four hours* to transmit this book via teletype.
- If we transmitted this book over a typical telephone (dial-up, twisted pair cable) computer link (2400 bps), it would take approximately *eleven minutes*.
- If we transmitted this book over a typical LAN (2.6 million bits per second [Mbps] on coaxial cable), it would take *less than one-half of a second*.
- If we transmitted this book over a special fiber-optic cable-based network (100 Mbps), it would take less than one-fiftieth of one second. *Looking at it another way, we could send fifty copies of this book in a single second.*

Source: Cohen (1991, 7).

Four LAN network topologies are presented: star, bus, ring, and tree. These are displayed in figure 6.3.

The star topology is probably the most popular. All hardware devices of this segment of the network (otherwise known as "nodes") are connected to a hub or some other multiaccess hardware unit. Any data sent by the computer must pass through the central device before continuing on to another node of the network. If a node were to have problems, it would not interfere with the operation of the rest of the network. Also, the failed node could be easily detected. On the other hand, the physical wiring of this orientation could get ugly and expensive! The bus topology is a "linear" orientation that has two distinct endpoints or terminators; each node branches off a common line having its own address. The advantage of the bus topology is the minimal wiring needed; it is more cost-effective. The main disadvantage of the bus topology is that if a node were to fail on this topology, the rest of the network beyond this point would be unable to transmit across the network. The nodes of a ring topology are connected in a circle. While it is similar to a bus topology, it has no terminators. All the data sent by a node travels around a ring until it reaches the address of its destination. The physical connection can get expensive, and if one node fails, the whole network goes down until the problem is fixed. In the tree topology, the root is the head end where all the transmissions must pass. The root of the tree contains the trunk cable where user devices are connected. The head end translates the frequencies of

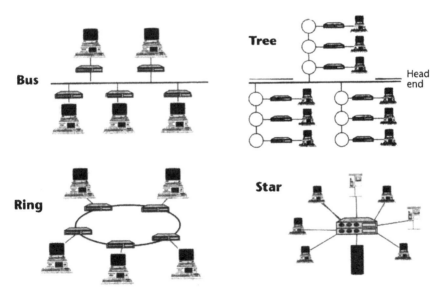

Figure 6.3. LAN Topologies. Source: Goleniewski (2002, 225).

one device to the frequency of another (remodulation). Many network administrators have designed LANs using combinations of all these topologies.

Transmission Processing Protocols

As stated previously, the method used in the transmission of data is of direct interest to the information scientist in the analysis, design, and evaluation of these ADIK systems (networks). Sending data across the wiring of a network is very similar to sending a letter via U.S. mail using a standard addressing method. This standard addressing method, called Internet protocol (IP) addressing, is a system that applies a unique identifier to a node or a host connection to a network. IP addressing assigns a logical address to every device and gives an address for internetworking.

By definition, a protocol is a set of rules that describe a method of transmission between systems. There are several protocols working today, but for our purposes, we will focus on the most widely used, which is transmission control protocol / Internet protocol (TCP/IP). They all have similar functions but differ in the handling of translation, encryption (code to restore original data), security, and comprehension techniques. Each basically achieves the same goal, namely, sending data to its destination across a network. So how does it work? Let's look at the open systems interconnection (OSI) model to understand protocols (see figure 6.4).

But what guarantees are there to ensure delivery of the data? In 1984, the International Organization for Standardization (IOS) presented the OSI model for sending data over a network (figure 6.4). The goal of this model was to help eliminate network incompatibility and transmission problems between different types of networks. It was not designed to be an absolute standard, but it is used in developing network protocols or rules for sending data over a network. It is a great reference model to use in understanding how networks function and computers communicate.

A protocol takes data to be delivered and breaks it down into understandable parts, in terms of machine language. The OSI model can be compared to an onion; it has several layers. So, like an onion, the data sent can be "peeled" apart and translated by another machine somewhere else along the network. The OSI has seven "layers," if you will. Working from the top down, figure 6.4 shows these layers. Starting with the application layer and continuing down to the physical layer, the data is broken into chunks, also called packets, with control data being added at each layer on the way down (transmitting device) and then stripped away on the way back up (receiving device). This process is referred to as encapsulation. For example, you have an English paper due tomorrow and you have been typing into the computer. Along with the typed document, the application

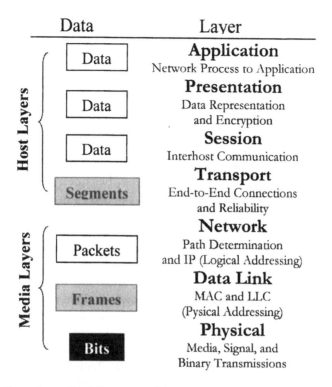

Figure 6.4. The OSI Layer Model (Open Systems Interconnection). This is a set of international network protocols (rules). See http://en.wikipedia.org/w/index.php?title=OSI_model&oldid=6521 7570 for interesting diagram showing parallel with business world and more. Redrawn by S. Masters.

software adds at the "head" of the document called "header information." Header data could include such specifics as the version and software package data used to create the document, how large the document is in terms of byte size, where the document begins and ends, and other data pertinent to the receiver.

Altogether, the software header and the document itself make up the application layer. This is the innermost layer of the set of data to be sent. Other examples of application layer data could be created in e-mail, Hypertext Transfer Protocol (HTTP) requests, or file transfer protocol (ftp).

The presentation layer refers to data that is translated, formatted, restructured, encrypted, and compressed. It is then encapsulated by identifiers of the types of software used to manipulate it in such a way. The presentation represents the combination of the adjustments made with the added software data. Now that the data is packaged and its destination determined, it is now prepared for delivery. All protocols have a limit to the number of bytes of data that can be sent across a line at one time. The transport layer takes care of this issue by dividing data into packets. Then, it ensures that the packets will get to the destination. If for any reason not all the data reaches the destination address, it is the transport layer that is responsible for retransmission of the packets. Before the data packets are transmitted, three layers of network protocol must process them. First, the network layer determines the best path to send the data across the network and adds this data to each packet. The data link layer adds error-checking information to the back of each packet. The receiver of the data packets then uses this data to determine if the data packet has been corrupted somewhere along its transmission path. Also, the media access control (MAC) address is added. This is the unique identifier given the network interface card (NIC) when it is manufactured. This number is a way to distinguish between computers on the same network and, thus, packets can be traced back to the source.

Lastly, the entire data packet is converted into binary digits. The physical layer then takes the ones and zeroes and converts them into voltage, light, or radio signal, depending on the network medium used. Isn't it amazing that all this occurs in a matter of fractions of a second? So much detail is monitored when designing the protocol software needed to handle the packaging of data that is sent across a network. Remember, the OSI model is only a reference for programmers that design protocol software. Not all protocols have these seven distinct layers but have taken care of the functions in the combination of layers. For example, the TCP/IP protocol application layer combines the duties of OSI's application, presentation, and session layers all at once. Regardless of the protocol used, the names of the layers may be different, but the concepts are virtually the same. All of this is of critical importance to the information scientist. The main concern is to ensure that the data as a total packet reaches its destination, has not been corrupted all along the way, and that the interpretation of the data is not corrupted.

Network Architecture: Combining It All Together

The medium, the physical layout of the transmitters, the access method, and the protocol (services) all combine to make what is known as the network architecture. Table 6.3 provides a chronology of network architectures.

Some current common network architectures are Ethernet, AppleTalk, ARCNet, Token Ring, and FDDI (fiber distributed data interface). The Ether-

Table 6.3.
Time Line (Chronology) of Network Architecture.

Time	Architecture
1970s	Stand-alone mainframes
Early 1980s	Networked mainframes
	Stand-alone workstations
Early to late 1980s	Local area networking (LAN)
Mid-1980s to mid-1990s	LANs work together (internetworking)
Mid-1990s	Internet commercialization
Mid- to late 1990s	Application-driven networks
Late 1990s	Remote-access workers
Early 2000s	Home area networking

Source: Goleniewski (2002, 154).

net is the most common network architecture. The access method is known as carrier sense multiple access / collision detection (CSMA/CD). This refers to a computer that is ready to send data across a medium that will "listen" to the wire to detect if it is carrying a signal, that is, another device sending data. If no signal is detected, the computer will send its data; otherwise, it will wait for a random time period before trying again.

Advances in Teletransmission

For the information scientist, teletransmission and telecommunications offer significant challenges. These challenges are defined in the vast, fast, and significant advances in technology represented to some extent by networking and wireless transmission of signals. These advances that aid in the processing of data, information, and knowledge provide significant opportunities for the planning, operating, and controlling (managing) of many individual organizational resources. The functions of teletransmission and telecommunication can be seen in the many advances in technology, which support and advance national and international commerce as well as geopolitical initiatives. Networking and wireless communications are examples of two such advances. Of particular interest and importance in the role of remote sensing is serving in extending the science of data, information, and knowledge transmission. "Remote sensing is the science of deriving information about the earth's land and water areas from images acquired at a distance" (http://fwie.fw.vt.edu/tws-gis/glossary.htm). See figure 6.5 for an application of remote sensing.

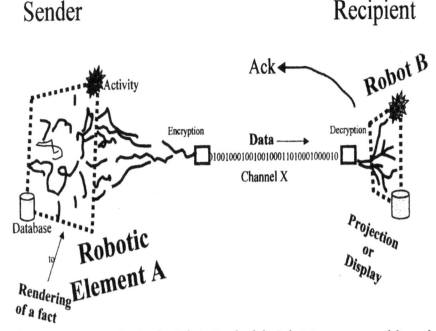

Figure 6.5. Remote Sensing by Robot. On the left, Robot A senses an activity and translates what it perceives into zeroes and ones. These are sent to Robot B, which decodes the message and reconstructs the activity on its display. Also, it sends an acknowledgment that it has received the message back to the first robot. Drawn by S. Masters.

SUMMARY

Our lives depend on our capacity to receive, note, and respond to the activities and ideas around us. The movement (transmission) of signals that transmit our ideas and intention is a normal human activity, yet also a complex affair. Transmission (movement) of signals from one component of an ADIK system to another is an essential function and requirement of such systems. Failure of transmission corresponds to the failure of the system. The content of the transmission is represented as the signal. The signal contains the data that is transported through the medium. The expression of data in a transmission is considered the language of the transmission. The matter of the language used to convey the message can vary based on cultural applications that require translation. This difficulty in transmission is increased when the equipment used or the human action involved in the transmission fails, or, when there is lack of precision in the use of the language in conveying the intended idea adequately. These considerations apply to the transmission of information and knowledge alike although the impacts and consequences may differ. Advances in transmission and communication media (twisted pair, coaxial cable, fiber optics) that continue to be made are important to our understanding of their role in information science, particularly in the analysis, design, and evaluation of ADIK systems. Networking of these technological advances, with the combined use of computers, serves to increase the human ability to use transmission and communication hardware and software more efficiently and effectively in the engagement of problems and making decisions. Wireless transmission is a case in point. As we can note, wireless (cellular) transmissions have influenced and continue to influence the way that individuals and organizations relate to each other and form a broad perspective of national and international commerce and geopolitics.

EXERCISES

1. You are interested in sharing your homework experiences with a fellow student who shares the same course and instructor with you. You are finding some of the ideas in the text difficult and would like to share this with your classmate. What are some of the problems that you would likely face if the exchange would be with your home PC or laptop? What is the information scientist's interest in your problem?
2. You are communicating with a friend a long distance from your home. Suddenly, you encounter static in the reception of the message you are receiving. Explain the interest of the information scientist in your experience.
3. Describe a situation, an occasion, or condition when and where the lack of transmission of a message led you to do the right or wrong thing. In each case discuss the transmission and communication factors involved.
4. In what way can a fire alarm system at your school be considered a network? How is the network part of an ADIK system?
5. A book that is important for the paper that you are writing for your history course is not located in your school or local home library. How can the idea of a network help you obtain the book you need in time for you to write the paper?
6. Almost everyone is using a car/cell phone these days to communicate with his or her friends or business partners. Differentiate the transmission from the communication problems that one is likely to encounter.

7. Data, information, and knowledge can be transmitted from one person to another in different ways. Discuss how the computer can help a person in ways in which other forms of transmission (sound, light, odor, touch) would not be as successful.

8. It is claimed that when transmission fails in the ADIK system, communication is not possible. Discuss.

7

The Computer

LEARNING OBJECTIVES

- Examine the essential components of a computer.
- Explain the role of computers within an ADIK system.

OVERVIEW

As human beings, we are constantly taking in data and information and trying to make sense of the world around us. In this respect, the computer extends our capabilities in the attempt to understand ourselves and the environment. This chapter examines the basic elements of the computer that are relevant to its role in data, information, and knowledge processing. See table 7.1 for an overview of the history of computers.

Computer Science

Computer science as a formal discipline was given expression by George Forsythe, a numerical analyst. The first computer science department was

Table 7.1.
Brief History of Computers.

500 BC	The abacus is invented.
1617	John Napier introduces a system of multiplying numbers and dividing automatically.
1822	Charles Babbage conceives of first computer.
1896	Herman Hollerith starts the first computer company.
1930	Vannevar Bush creates differential analyzer.
1936	Alan Turing conceives of the computer.
1937	Claude Shannon sets the stage for digital computers.
1942	High-speed vacuum tube devices are created for calculating.
1942	ENIAC, the first electronic numerical integrator, is developed.
1945	John Von Neumann invents the Electronic Discrete Variable Automatic Computer (EDVAC).
1948	Claude Shannon develops his information theory.
1951	The first business computer is sold commercially in the United States (UNIVAC).
1960	Common Business Oriented Language (COBOL) is invented.
1961	IBM develops a computer with 100 times the power of any other computer (STRETCH).
1962	Doug Englebart invents the computer mouse.
1965	Ted Nelson creates the term "hypertext."
1965	The first floppy disk is produced.
1971	The first microprocessor is developed.
1982	The first spreadsheet program is invented.
1990	Microsoft releases Windows 3.0.
1991	A menu-driven search-and-retrieval tool (Gopher) is created.
	INTERNET wireless is introduced.
1996	Online auction sales begin.

Source: *Computing Dictionary* (1999).

formed at Purdue University in 1962. The first person to receive a PhD from a computer science department was Robert Wexeblat at the University of Pennsylvania in December 1965 (www.cs.uwaterloo.ca/shallt/courses/134/history.html). Computer science enjoys an extensive heritage of human invention and creativity, as indicated in the aforementioned brief history of the science.

The computer is a powerful tool for the manipulation of data (information) from many sources (events/situations). Its power derives from its ability to receive, store, and process a large amount of data based on simple rules for dealing with the presence or absence of states (yes/no, true/false). A computer is a machine for carrying out simple instructions quickly and accurately. Computer science derives its identity from research that determines the machine's ability to mimic and extend human capacities in problem solving and decision making (to think and talk as human beings do). Thus, research attention of computer scientists focuses on several critical facets of machine-processing of data (information). The following are some of the areas of interest and research applications. Computer science has broader interests and applications beyond those that are cited.

- *Power of computer programs (subtraction and recursion)*: How the computer solves a problem. The most important attribute of a computer is that it is programmable; when it leaves the factory, no one knows how it will be used. The application of computing power to a particular type of problem is entirely dictated by software.
- *Machine language and its translation*: The means through which computers function internally. Humans know English (or some other language). Computers know one and zero, electricity on and electricity off. Some of the first software was written to translate ones and zeroes into a form that humans could more easily understand. These programs, called compilers and interpreters, have continuously evolved to make computer programming easier.
- *Increasing machine memory*: The place where data are held to be used. Computer memory, like human memory, is a hardware component that gives the computer's "brain" (CPU) ready access to data and instructions. Early computers had a few thousand memory addresses; current computers have *billions*!
- *Communication among computers*: With advances in telecommunications, one computer can access data stored on another, anywhere in the world, rapidly. Information stored in books is physically limited because there needs to be a copy of the book in every city or town or home where a person needs to access that information. Via computers and the Internet, anyone in the world can sit at home and access all the information on all the computers in the world.
- *Information organization and retrieval*: Ways that data are assembled and stored for use. Though originally conceived of as a mere computational tool, today's computer has evolved into a personal library, which we use just as our grandparents used the local library. Still, the enormous volume of data on the world's computers would be of little value if there were no way to find specific facts quickly. Computer scientists, such as those at Google and Yahoo, spend a large amount of effort devising efficient and scalable indexing schemes to cope with this ever-increasing volume and to enable us to search for and find things quickly.
- *Application of artificial intelligence*: The ability of the computer to think for itself. Science fiction has long predicted the arrival of the "self-aware" machine, as in the movie *The Terminator*. When the first computers were invented, scientists predicted that they would quickly outsmart the

human brain. Now sixty years later, computers are far more powerful than we ever imagined, and yet we cannot begin to match the complexity of the human brain. The cause of this paradox is that until we started building computers, we had no appreciation for the power of the brain. Computer scientists, psychologists, and other scientists continue to investigate the mysteries of the human mind, in the hope of developing smarter computers.

- *Data mining:* The vast amount of data obtained from sensors and processed by computers provide a rich resource with respect to applications in problem solving and decision making faced by individuals and organizations. Computer scientists study the many ways that the vast amount of data can be searched and processed to enable the discovery of knowledge applied to varied problems and decisions.

- *Virtual reality:* An artificial computer-generated environment in which users interact with the environment and objects in it through specialized input devices such as goggles, headphones, and gloves. This area is a physical manifestation of artificial intelligence, involving learning, perception, and other properties of human activity. The vast challenges presented to computer scientists in this field are being met through advanced object-oriented programming techniques and the development of specialized hardware such as Microsoft's Xbox and Sony's Playstation.

- *Robotics:* Use of computers to simulate and control physical activity. Since the Industrial Revolution, humans have had the ability to power machines and do useful work. Computer programming makes possible at least low-level decision making by machines. These two abilities combined enable us to build machines that can "think," both detecting physical events and enacting physical responses. Robotics applications are commonplace in manufacturing today, but are also important in specialized areas such as space exploration and homeland security.

The Computer and Processing Subsystem: Hardware as Information System

The computer stores, processes, and manages data at greater volume and efficiency than is humanly possible and is an essential part of an ADIK system. Truly, technology extends our activities of daily living. Computers come in many forms, shapes, sizes, and applications (ubiquitous). Some computers try to mimic what people do but without their presence. In virtual reality people interact with a simulated environment. Most familiar is the desktop PC commonly found in homes, schools, and offices. However, they are so engrained in our everyday lives that it is very easy to overlook the many types that we interact with daily. There are handheld computers—such as personal digital assistants—and there are mainframe computers that can take up entire rooms. There are tiny computers—"chips"—in many familiar household items.

Regardless of their size, all computers share fundamental characteristics. Computers are comprised of hardware and software. Hardware refers to the physical components like the disk drive, and software refers to the applications or programs that run on them, like Microsoft Office. All computers have a motherboard, central processing unit (CPU), input and output capabilities, and data storage. Depending on the computer's specifications, in one nanosecond (or one billionth of a second), these simple components are capable of processing more data than a human might in one month. Each of these components serves a unique function, which we discuss below.

The Motherboard and Central Processing Unit

One of the fundamental parts of a computer is found in the motherboard. This is where all the various components of a computer meet. It holds the CPU, the memory card, and the expansion slots and ports that connect the input and output devices such as the keyboard, monitor, and printer.

The central processing unit is where all of the data processing occurs (see figure 7.2). It is comprised of thousands of tiny interconnected transistors. The bits of data are shifted and organized here, either in the arithmetic logic unit (ALU) or the control logic unit (CLU). The ALU is responsible for the

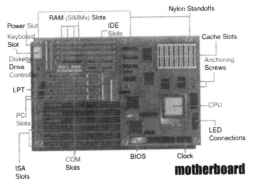

Figure 7.1. IBM System/360. A new concept in computers which creates a "family" of small to large computers. The concept of a compatible "family" of computers transforms the industry. By permission of IBM Corporate Archives, www.ibm .com/ibm/history/history/year_1964.html.

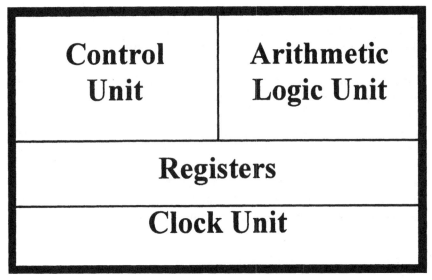

Figure 7.2. The Central Processing Unit (CPU).

mathematical calculations and logical decisions. The CLU keeps track of the steps that occur in the processing. Sometimes, this is referred to as the "brain" of the computer. While our brains enable us to perform many tasks, we also store thoughts in our brain. The computer also has "memory" and can store nearly infinite amounts of data.

Memory

Memory is essential to computers. This is where all of our data is stored in many different file types. It is essential because computers must be capable of holding vast quantities of data and information. There are two main types of computer memory: random access memory (RAM) and read-only memory (ROM).

RAM is the primary memory source, sometimes compared to the human short-term memory. It runs the operating system and software applications. The more RAM a computer has, the more applications it can run simultaneously. Types of RAM include SRAM (static RAM), DRAM (dynamic RAM), and SDRAM (synchronous dynamic RAM). DRAM is the cheapest of these, and the amount of memory per chip is very dense. SRAM is significantly more expensive than DRAM, but it is also more efficient and faster. SDRAM is the fastest and the standard for the RAM in most personal computers.

If RAM is the short-term memory, then ROM is sometimes compared to the human long-term memory. Here, data is permanently stored and cannot be erased. This memory holds programmed instructions for the computer that can only be read by the CPU. ROM comes in different types, including PROM (programmable ROM) and EPROM (erasable programmable memory).

The ability to access all of this memory and utilize the processing power in daily activities is provided to us by the input and output devices, which also come in several forms. The input and output devices are connected to ports on the computer, usually located in the back of the case. Through these ports, the monitor, keyboard, printer, or other so-called peripheral devices are connected to the computer (see figure 7.3).

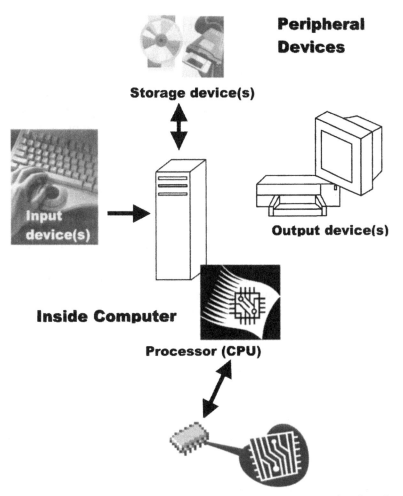

Figure 7.3. Peripheral Devices and Memory. In a computer, the CPU is connected to peripheral devices by external ports, but the memory chips are usually inside the computer (connected by bus). Drawn by S. Masters.

Input and Output Devices

Peripheral devices are the input and output devices that allow us to access and manipulate the data stored on our computer. Input refers to the data that we enter into the computer. There are multiple devices that allow us to enter data into a computer. Most familiar would be the keyboard or touchpad. However, there are many others, some of which include the digital scanner, digital pad and stylus, and speech input. Once the data is entered and stored, we can manipulate or move the data with the use of devices such as the trackball, mouse, head pointer, joystick, digital stylus, or voice recognition, to name the best-known sources.

Output refers to the information that the computer generates, or puts out. A screen or monitor attached to a computer allows the user to interact with the data via a graphical user interface (GUI). As with input devices, there are many output devices. These devices allow us to view or access the data, including the printer, sound speakers, and screen-reading technologies. People with a hearing impairment use a printer that generates paper documents, a screen reader. Another technology automatically announces or "reads" the information that is visible on the screen to give access to individuals with visual impairment.

When combined, all of this technology allows us to use, access, and store information more efficiently and for different purposes. To this point, we have discussed the fundamental components of computers in their most basic form. We described the "parts" of a computer. However, as we will discuss below, the computer augments much more than our ability to process, manipulate, and store data. With human ingenuity, computers are increasingly faster, smaller, and less expensive. This has enabled us to apply computers for broader and often quite significant uses in our daily lives. This is what makes them the most important technological innovation of our time.

The Most Important Technological Innovations

Computers and information technologies are an integral part of the ADIK system. Through graphical and statistical analysis, we can identify patterns or trends in the data that lead us to explanations for both best and worst practices in business, health, education, and government. These explanations give us the power to change and refine our existing systems and to improve them. As we know, optimized systems yield the highest rates of production. Higher productivity leads to increased profits and strong economic systems. Increased wealth leads to greater well-being for society's residents. Well-being for individuals leads to a healthier society.

When societies share their best practices, the entire global community can benefit. Computers and the Internet support world collaboration and exchanges of information. This is why it is imperative that we make the information on the Internet accessible to as many people as possible, available via as many technologies as possible. Because the computer supports our ability to share information, and this impact serves the global community, the computer is the most important technological invention of our time. To demonstrate this, we offer the following examples of practical applications in space, transportation, security, and medical informatics.

Robots and the Computer

Robotology, that is, the study, design, and engineering of robots that can simulate human actions driven by specific functional objectives, is a new area of interest to computer scientists. It allows the study of motion and other processes to serve a diverse set of objectives and interests. Robotology spans a wide area of scientific and technological interests (e.g., medicine, space), particularly for computer scientists (Desiano 2002).

Space Technologies: GIS, GPS Satellites

Computers are used in space to give us information that we cannot gather here on the ground. A growing application of computer technology is geographic information systems (GIS). GIS includes the computers, software, and other equipment mounted on satellites launched from earth. This equipment collects, analyzes, and maps information about the environment (Ganzorig 2002). These systems allow us to view our environment from space. They are used to monitor ground water levels, forests, soil erosion, mineral exploration, natural disaster management, wasteland mapping, coastal studies, forecasting agricultural output, irrigation, drought assessment, and flood mapping. This is accomplished through a satellite-based remote-sensing system that provides aerial photography and data collection through airborne sensors. When processed, the data provides ecological insights that can aid economic development and environmental protection in the most remote areas of our planet.

Global positioning systems (GPS) are another expanding application. This remote-sensing technology monitors the longitude and latitude coordinates of a device on the earth's surface. It sends that data to a satellite for retrieval and retransmission. The data reveal the exact location of the device. The automobile industry has begun to equip cars with these systems to aid drivers when they are in need of directions or emergency assistance, and for tracking stolen vehicles. In some states, these tracking devices are being used to monitor convicted criminals who are serving time under house arrest.

Transportation

While GPS is enhancing the automobile industry's abilities to ensure safe travels, its impact on safer air travel is also significant. Airports themselves are complex information systems monitoring the logistics of people, cargo, and aircraft. Computer technology is also used to monitor flight instruments of aircraft from the ground to ensure our safety.

Security

When used appropriately, computers and information technology have the ability to reduce hazards in our lives. An example is when they are used to deter terrorist acts against the public. Subways and other public areas have security systems. Cameras and closed-circuit television capture everything that happens remotely. Such data enable security personnel to monitor all activity. In 2005, London's Underground was subjected to a terrorist attack that consisted of multiple explosions. As part of the built-in security system, cameras that monitor the activity that occurs throughout the Underground were in place. Closed-circuit television cameras captured everything that happened on the platforms and in the cars, remotely. This data enabled authorities to see which passengers were in each of the cars involved in the blasts. This information—combined with real-time reporting facilitated by mobile telephones equipped with digital cameras, Web access by people who were also in the blasts, and live television feeds from news agencies—led to the quick capture of the surviving terrorists.

Another field related to security is called biometrics. It is based on the fact that all humans are physically different from each other, just as snowflakes are. According to the U.S. government's Biometric Consortium website (www.biometrics.org/intro.htm [accessed May 2006]), "biometrics are automated methods of recognizing a person based on a physiological or behavioral characteristic. Among the features measured are face, fingerprints, hand geometry, handwriting, iris, retinal, vein, and voice."

Because each of us has unique facial characteristics, facial recognition is one application of biometric technology that is increasingly being used in crowded public spaces to enhance our security (Norton 2000). A formula is created to find features. Also, a database of many people's features is found to compare the single set to. Optimally, it would follow the "three bears" rule (see below)—it is neither too difficult nor too easy to compare the features. If too many details are given—such as if there is only the fact they have noses and eyes—in such case, everyone would be a match (Norton 2000, 663–77). Biometrics is an important area of study to the information scientist, who is concerned with individual freedom and security in the use of data, information, and knowledge.

The "three bears" rule is named after the traditional English children's story in which Goldilocks enters the vacant cottage of the three bears. Inside, she samples everything she finds. The great huge bear's porridge/chair/bed is too hot/hard/high, the middle bear's things are too cold/soft/low, but the little small wee bear's things are "just right!" (Biometrics Working Group 2002, 2).

Biometrics

Biometrics refers to a number of processes such as finger printing, face structure, hand geometry, eye profiles (IRIS), hand writing, and voice that are used for a number of objectives (security, criminology, etc.). Biometricians attempt to utilize a number of these applications to understand events and the many human and organizational factors influenced by them. See www.biometric.org/introduction.php for more information.

Bibliometrics

Another area of information science interest that *sounds* similar to biometrics, but is really much different, is called bibliometrics. Bibliometrics is a study that attempts to trace relationships among various citations included in documents to determine their importance to a particular work: interrelationship among authors, their schools of thought, and academic affiliations (Norton 2000).

The game "The Six Degrees of Kevin Bacon" might be called an informal form of bibliometric mapping, representing the networks of relationships between people. It is:

> based on the theory that Kevin Bacon is the center of the entertainment universe, and that any actor or actress can be linked back to him, typically within six degrees (six connections) (variations on this game are based on the assumption that almost anyone in the world can be linked to anyone else in the world by six or seven degrees). (www.distance.syr.edu/bacon.html [accessed May 16, 2006])

Medical Informatics

While biometric technologies are helping to improve security, medical technologies (medical informatics) are also helping to improve our quality of life. Today, many new medical devices and procedures are possible because of computer technology. The fusion of technology and health care allows both patients and physicians to reap benefits. For the patient, the benefits include less pain, less invasive procedures, faster recovery, shorter hospital visits, and rehabilitation. For the physician, the benefits include safer procedures through enhanced digital imaging diagnostics, observation, and surgical tools.

Even medical education is enhanced through digital operating rooms. At the University of Pittsburgh, medical students are able to view surgical procedures in a digital operating room (Roach 2003). This operating room is equipped with voice-activated and digital surgical equipment, as well as teleconferencing capacity. While surgeons perform live operations, students observe via teleconferencing in the adjacent web lab. They simultaneously practice the same procedure on simulated anatomical models, which allows them to perfect their technique before attempting to work on live patients.

Students watching doctors perform surgery in the next room via teleconferencing equipment is certainly impressive. However, it is even more impressive when the doctors are performing the procedure and the patient is in another country! Not long ago, this may have seemed like science fiction, but it is a reality today thanks to fiber optics and surgical robots. The first telesurgery (a gall bladder removal) was performed in 2001 by two doctors in New York, while the patient was physically located in France (Osborne 2001). Remotely guided robotic arms equipped with tiny cameras and computers allowed the surgeon to be on the other side of the world, but they are just as helpful in performing medical procedures when the doctor and patient are in the same room.

For example, SPY is an intraoperative imaging system used in coronary bypass surgery that lets doctors see the blood pathways they have created while the chest is still open, confirming the success of the surgery (Gerhardus 2003). Before this technology, a doctor would have to close the patient's chest, test the pathways, and if they were not functioning properly, the patient would have to be reopened. Obviously, the information from the imaging technology shortens the procedure and reduces the physical stress on the patient.

Another way technology is making surgery safer is radio frequency identification (RFID) (*FDA Consumer* 2005). Surgichip Tag Surgical Marker System uses RFID to mark parts of the patient's body for surgery. This ensures the surgeon will perform the correct procedure on the correct side of the correct patient! With so many patients being seen in a hospital at a time, managing the patient data in an accurate and timely manner is a complex yet crucial task. While this technology increases the accuracy of information, the timeliness of medical transcription is another area benefiting from technology.

Consider this scenario, provided by Thomas Friedman in his book, *The World Is Flat* (2005): Late at night, a patient comes to an emergency room in the United States. The doctor on call determines that tests need to be performed. The tests are completed, but no one will be available to transcribe the results until the next shift of technicians arrives in the morning. This means the patient will have to wait until the afternoon of the next day for diagnosis. However, thanks to technology, physicians can send the test results to India for transcription overnight, and because of the time-zone difference, a patient can get much faster diagnosis in the early morning hours as opposed to the early afternoon! Again, just another example of enhanced patient care made possible by computer technology.

Challenges to Computer Science

There are many challenges to the present and future computer scientist and correspondingly to the information scientist. Only a few can be suggested. Important developments in hardware, software, and engineering aspects of computers offer several important challenges to the computer scientist. Like most advances in technology, the more that components are added to the computer system, the more the advances approach limits with respect to the upper limits of system application. Computer scientists will continue their research in advancing the ability of the computer to reach every quarter of life (ubiquitous computing). Computers will become invisible (virtual); they will come in different sizes, each suited to particular task. Research in the practical applications of virtual reality and artificial intelligence will present new challenges. The Internet and Web will continue to influence almost all quarters of civic interest and management. Meanwhile, understanding the upper limits of computer technology with respect to individual and organizational usage offers new opportunities for research and applications. This challenge rests in part on the ability of computers (hardware/software) to aid individuals and institutions in dealing with the many human aspects of living—namely, the individual and organizational management and operations of health, economy, privacy, or terror, to cite a few. The future will increase the ability of sensors and other sources, both human and technological, to elicit data from events. This will require close collaboration of the computer scientist with other disciplines in data, information, and knowledge organization and management. In turn, this challenge will include determining the objectives of the science and how these can be applied to the education of the future computer scientist (Weiser 1991).

SUMMARY

The present-day computer has a long history in its development. Each component of the computer, as a technology, evolved as electronic engineering and other advances made possible wider usage in the ability of the computer to process data, information, and knowledge. Research and development in memory storage capacity, input, and output broadened computer applications. In this chapter, the basic parts and functions of the computer are detailed. In addition, professional applications of the computer in extending our abilities to several areas of interest—space, medicine, bibliometrics—are briefly presented together with the challenges that face computer science.

EXERCISES

1. Modern automobiles are being equipped with global position systems. Of what interest are these technological advances to the information scientist?
2. Relate what was learned in this chapter with that of chapter 5: the sensing subsystem.
3. Discuss what you consider the most important challenge computer science faces, stating your reasons why.
4. Which component (part) of a computer would you consider to be more "virtual" than others?
5. Given your understanding of information system analysis and design, what do you consider most important to problems of terror generated by events?
6. Computers, as well as all technologies, may be limited in what they can do. Discuss.
7. You have been assigned to conduct research that requires the application of the computer in the library. Discuss the advantages that the computer could present in such an assignment. What are some of the problems that can be expected?
8. Of all the challenges to the computer scientist discussed in this chapter, which one would you consider the most difficult to confront?
9. Discuss the difference between *virtual* and *ubiquitous* computing.
10. Considerable research has been applied to space technology. What aspects of these advances are of importance to the information scientist?

III

THE KNOWLEDGE SUBSYSTEM

Awareness shapes our thought.
Thought defines our action.

—*Anthony Debons*

"Can you help me with my ethics homework, or
would that be missing the point?"
By permission of Bunny Hoest, *Parade
Magazine*, November 24, 2002, 26.

"We're deciding! We're deciding!"
By permission of Bunny Hoest, *Parade Magazine*, January 13, 2002, 6.

8

The Utilization Subsystem: Decision Making—Problem Solving

The three fishermen decided to fish for the day. At the camp, they arranged to rent a small motorboat for their outing. The agent at the camp, who arranged for the rental of the boat, alerted the three fishermen that they would have to return the boat no later than 5 p.m. that evening, just before sundown. He could not insure their welfare beyond that point in time. He also informed them that the main lake flowed into three adjoining lakes and that the second lake represented a better source for catching the big fish. The three fishermen boarded the motor craft, hoping for an enjoyable day fishing. The three explored the first lake without success. They explored the second lake with a similar outcome. While on the third lake, they were so successful that the time of day escaped them. At one point in time, one of the fishermen informed the others that it was late and that they should return so as to obey the time deadline presented by the agent earlier that morning. While returning, a major problem surfaced. There were so many outlets to the three lakes that it was impossible to establish which outlet they had left that morning. Without a map or another source of information, they were unable to decide which inlet would lead them to the camp safely. In addition and unfortunately, there were no other craft on any of the three lakes that could be summoned to provide them with the information they required to help them to return safely to the camp. Fortunately, the camp who had leased them the motorboat had an adequate information system to locate them and return them to camp safely [true story].

LEARNING OBJECTIVES

- Develop a typology of decision making.
- Assess the role of information in decision making.

- Summarize the contribution of artificial intelligence and expert systems to decision making.

OVERVIEW

Each day, individuals are faced with making decisions. Ways of thinking, as well as conduct, can influence the quality of our lives and the objectives and goals that we set to achieve. Human decision making has challenged many minds throughout our history. The arrival of the computer has stirred even greater interest for many scientists attempting to identify the properties of human decision making. In fact, an augmented data, information, and knowledge (ADIK) system's most important role is to aid the decision process. It extends our native cognitive capacities. This chapter describes those aspects of interest to the information scientist, whose challenges are extensive and sometimes difficult to face. First, the critical terms and ideas related to decision making are defined. The focus of attention is our current understanding of the decision process, including problemsolving and decision analysis and the computer tools that aid these processes. Included is a discussion of artificial intelligence and expert systems and how these relate to the human decision function.

The Study of Decision Making and Problem Solving

All of us are familiar with the words "problem" and "decision." A "problem" is something difficult to deal with and understand. More often than not, it involves decisions to be made, decisions that will affect the solution of the problem. We make decisions in almost all the things we do, from going to school, to the baseball team we watch, to the kind of work we want to do. Decisions require making choices.

Decisions often do not come alone. They are generally part of problems we face. A problem is related to some goal, such as the best place to go to college and support oneself in the process. Problems are obstacles; decisions involve finding ways of facing and overcoming these obstacles. There may be no single, best way to achieve the end goal. There are countless conditions and states we face each day. Each involves decisions to be made. Even postponing a decision could have important consequences. Each of these decisions demands data, information, and knowledge to support actions to be taken.

The possibility that terrorists would apply biochemical warfare to achieve their goals raises many problems and may require many decisions to be made.

The events of September 11 present a horrendous number of problems and with each, an important decision must be made.

No other area in information science merits more careful and direct attention than human problem solving and decision making. Each of the segments of the knowledge sciences—documentation, computerization, and communication—includes the human action of problem solving and decision making.

Humans have an enormous capacity to solve problems and make decisions. We can see this all around us. Particularly, think of the many advances that have been made in transportation, medicine, and other fields based on the advances in physics, chemistry, astronomy, and the other sciences.

Much of our capacity for solving problems and making decisions is based on the capacity of the human brain. However, the technology that humans have invented and created extends this capacity. Whether it is in private or public life, the human requirement to augment human capacity to make decisions and solve problems is paramount. Decision making and choice go hand in hand. Humans have a significant capacity for making choices, particularly in certain societies. The greater the choice base, the greater the requirement for aids that help or assist in making choices and resolving problems. One can say that a core issue in information science is understanding how technology aids individuals in meeting conditions that require actions, whether these actions are to resolve conflicts, take advantage of opportunity, or safeguard personal welfare.

Definitions

The Problem

A problem is when there is a difference in the actual state of a situation and the desired state. A person is confronted with a problem when he wants something and does not know immediately what series of actions he can perform to get at it. The desired object may be very tangible (an apple to eat) or abstract (an elegant proof of a theorem). It may be specific (that particular apple over there) or quite general (something to appease hunger). It may be a specific physical object (an apple) or a set of symbols (the proof of a theorem). The actions involved in obtaining desired objects include the physical actions (walking, reaching, writing), perceptual activities (looking, listening), and purely mental activities (judging the similarities of two symbols, remembering a scene, and so on) (Newell and Simon 1972, 72).

Problem Solving

What is problem solving? Problem solving is "cognitive processing directed at transforming a given situation into a goal situation when no obvious solution method is available to the problem-solver" (Mayer 2002, 37).

Problem Space

A problem space is a set of elements expressed in symbols representing a state of knowledge; operators that change an existing state of knowledge; an initial state of knowledge; a problem representing a desired state of knowledge and prevailing knowledge in the area of interest to the person faced with the problem (adapted from Newell and Simon 1972, 810).

The important point to information scientists, as we have learned, is that all humans are limited in our innate capacity to solve problems and make decisions. The challenge is to determine the best ways to use the tools that we have made possible to help us create, invent, or revise the ways to do things better, faster, or cheaper when the need and requirement arise. That is the function of an ADIK system.

Decision Making

John Dellen had to make a decision: go out for the basketball team or work for a 3.5 grade point average to get into his college of choice. In this case, being on the basketball team and obtaining good grades depend on each other. Both require equal amounts of effort. Having to work after school so that he could enjoy the few hours he had with his friends came into the picture as well. How to manage all these options was a problem for John. What could be done about all this? Perhaps a little thinking on his approach might help. Decision analysis is such an approach.

Decision-Making Analysis

The decision refers to making a choice among different alternatives, such as going to school or going to work to earn a salary to support a family. Analysis means finding out similarities and differences about states, conditions, aspects of problems, etc. In a word, decision analysis is understanding a situation. It includes estimating risks and minimizing losses. It refers to deconstructing or breaking down problems; understanding their structures; determining their inherent values; and developing a model of all of the various aspects of the problem and the decision required. The key to decision analysis is reducing a problem to its basic element. Some decisions are easy to make; others are more difficult. It depends on the problems one faces and the consequences of the outcomes.

We should realize, at the outset, that almost all of our actions involve decisions. Now and then we have problems to face, such as how to study for tomorrow's exam and still watch television tonight. Or how about what we should do after graduation: go to college or get a job? Your mom bought a new VCR to watch and record your favorite TV shows, but its manual is really unclear on how to set up the recording. The problem: how to operate the new device. The decision to be made: should you bother your mom about it or just not use it? Which decision would be wise?

Problem solving and decision making are part of everyday life. Decision making and problem solving have been studied by behavioral scientists, economists, management scientists, and others for many years and much has been learned about decisions and how we make them. The information scientist uses this knowledge when he or she analyzes and designs ADIK systems to deal with the many events and situations we are presently faced with and those that we are expected to face in the future.

One of the basic aspects of problem solving and decision making is that we can develop tools that help us solve problems and make decisions. There are so many tools that we might mention. It would be almost impossible to list them all. The ordinary pencil and pen, for example, are used each day to help us solve problems. We use symbols to create all sorts of things including numbers, letters, and pictures, which we put together on paper or in our heads in an attempt to come up with an answer or approach to a problem. We use the old-fashioned barometer outdoors to tell us whether we should wear a heavy coat or take an umbrella to school on a particular day. We use a car speedometer to help us make a decision as to when to speed up and pass a car within a certain speed limit zone; the pilot watches the altimeter to establish how high an aircraft is above the ocean or a mountain. We can go on and on giving examples of technologies that we have invented to help us make decisions and solve problems.

So where and how does our study of decision making and problem solving fit in our study of information science? If one was to ask what tool can be considered to be most important in helping us solve problems and make decisions, we most certainly would consider the computer as the obvious choice. The computer, however, is not the only choice. If we take into account the data, information, and knowledge systems that we study, we would include all the technologies we mentioned above plus, most importantly, such technologies as sensors, eyeglasses, binoculars, cameras, radar, sonar, telephones, satellites, and much more. There are other candidates such as artificial intelligence, expert systems that information scientists include, that we will look into later in this chapter.

Software Tools and Decision Analysis

We know that software enables humans to use computers for their own purposes (applications). There are many software programs that can be used for a variety of decision analysis applications. Information and computer scientists are continually developing new software to support human problem-solving and decision-making functions. There is a chain of logic that helps us structure a decision, that is, to see how various parts of the required action follow from each other in achieving an objective. There are software programs that help people make a decision while taking into account the value of the information that comes into play when a decision is to be made. There are software packages that provide us with the options that are available in dealing with a problem or decision situation, given the information at hand, and the best way to act (Clemen and Reilly 2001, 10). Although decision analysis provides a good way of looking at how we make our choices—while providing ways of looking at alternatives—it should not induce us to accept the alternatives that it provides. As a matter of fact, if good decision analysis is engaged, there should be no need for blind acceptance of decision alternatives. It should provide a better understanding of the problem rather than provide solutions. Decision analysis is an information source to clarify objectives, alternatives, and trade-offs. Decision analysis does not take over the decision maker's job. It helps do the job. Decision analysis helps us make inferences about what is happening or is likely to happen. It offers possible alternatives to action and a trade-off for each, thus helping us negotiate appropriate actions to be taken. Decision analysis allows for personal judgment to enter into the decision process. In fact, it requires it. Table 8.1 shows an example of decision analysis modeling.

There are certain aspects of a decision that relate to its difficulty. The decision may be hard because it involves numerous factors, some related and others not. Decision analysis can help group these factors together, examine each carefully, and evaluate similarities and differences before taking action. Another difficulty with decision making is the uncertainty of outcomes. There may be many objectives desired, all with different costs and values to each (see figure 8.1).

Passing an exam may get one into college, but on the other hand, one may not be able to gain a scholarship based on athletic competition. So there may be a question of the price for achieving one objective at the cost of another. It can come down to the matter of having to see a problem in different ways. For example, a mom and a dad could have different views of the achievements of their son. Again, the decision may be difficult if the father is factored into the decision process opposite the mother. So how can anyone establish the best

Table 8.1.
Decision Analysis: An Example of Modeling.

Objective: Establish the best standard of living (value) for me and my projected family.

Decision: • Should I find work, earn a salary, or
 • Should I go to college now, or
 • Do both?

Go to School	Get a Job Now	Do Both
No money	Money	Compromise quality of life
Delay family	Limited job range and opportunities	

Choose best alternative.
Apply sensitivity analysis: What if parents move?

Decide.

Source: Clemen and Reilly (2001, 10).

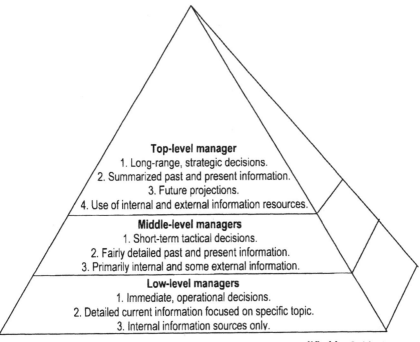

Top-level manager
1. Long-range, strategic decisions.
2. Summarized past and present information.
3. Future projections.
4. Use of internal and external information resources.

Middle-level managers
1. Short-term tactical decisions.
2. Fairly detailed past and present information.
3. Primarily internal and some external information.

Low-level managers
1. Immediate, operational decisions.
2. Detailed current information focused on specific topic.
3. Internal information sources only.

Figure 8.1. Decision Analysis. Source: Marakas (2003, 91); amplified by S. Masters.

decision for any particular situation? Figure 8.1 shows how different types of decisions are made by different managers.

Decision research tells us that a good decision is one that provides the "best" attainable outcome. We can say, "Of course." But then, where does luck come into the picture when decision analysis is applied? Decision researchers tell us that decision analysis cannot improve your luck. Yet it can improve your understanding of how to make better decisions. This understanding includes the structure of the problem and how to deal with the uncertainty related to it. Decision analysis helps those who are sufficiently intelligent and thoughtful to look at the problem and the decision carefully and then establish or prescribe the action that could lead to the best results. Although we are not perfect decision makers, we could do better by looking at a problem carefully and systematically. Information science is a major player applied to this end. Matching the human with the technology could do the trick.

With this background, we can now examine the various programs computer scientists have provided that can be applied directly to our study of decision analysis. In this process, we will also examine how artificial intelligence and expert systems complement decision-making and problem-solving functions, acknowledging that each could be a study in its own right.

Computer Tools That Aid the Problem-Solving and Decision Process

Computer programs have been designed to help the modeling and the solution phase of the decision process. All of these programs work together. One example is Microsoft Excel. Excel is a program that employs an ordinary spreadsheet, that is, a working sheet consisting of columns and rows that help in viewing and working with data. Such a tool is best used to model uncertainty. Uncertainty is a major human cognitive (mental) state related to information which enters in many decision-making activities. These may include managing the research and development of projects and programs; determining the best way to discover and use resources (human, oil, energy, etc.); bringing new products to market; or how best to deal with disaster (9/11, hurricanes, tornadoes, medical epidemics, etc.).

Artificial Intelligence/Expert Systems

Artificial intelligence started with the idea that computers can really help us think and learn. How can computers help us solve problems and make decisions? How can ADIK systems help us solve problems and make decisions? Let us first define terms and then show how information scientists and others are applying and conducting research to understand the best way to aid decision making and problem solving in specific applications. Artificial intelligence (AI) has been defined as "the ability of a computer to 'think' for itself. AI studies usually focus on understanding how humans think and how these capabilities might be instilled in the computer which includes speech recognition, deductive reasoning capabilities, creativity, and the ability to learn from experience (as opposed to memorizing data)" (*Computing Dictionary* 1998, 86).

Expert systems are considered to be a form of artificial intelligence, "an application that makes decisions by using facts, rules, and a reasoning ability called an inference engine. The facts are supplied by human experts in a particular field. Common categories include medicine, investments, automobile routing, insurance, equipment repair, and science" (*Computing Dictionary* 1999, 154).

Expert systems have, at times, been referred to as "knowledge systems" when applied to practical problems that information professionals face. "Knowledge systems in general do not necessarily mimic human experts, but do provide the electronic means to collect, store, distribute, reason about, and apply knowledge. Expert systems are a specialized case, incorporating know-how gathered from experts and designed to perform perishable human expertise; distribute otherwise scarce expertise; reduce costs of Medicare or poor human performance; provide help to humans trying to access information and use computers" (Smith 1987, 51).

At the outset, it is understood that almost all activities engaged in by information professionals include a large measure of problem solving and decision making. These functions include the access to and acquisition of data, information, and knowledge, the processing of these resources, and the actions (decisions) demanded by the task.

The following are some of the current interests of information scientists in applying artificial intelligence and expert systems to problem solving and decision making:

1. What are the means for updating data automatically to meet needs and requirements of users?
2. How can one organize knowledge in such a way as to aid us to think, learn, and use the literature efficiently and effectively (Heilprin 1989; Hjerppe 1992)?
3. How can one establish the best interface between the human and the computer in getting things done?
4. How can one identify ways that the computer can help human memory in processing and updating of information and knowledge?

5. How is it best to apply expert systems in reference work in libraries?
6. How does one codify and improve what we know when it is broken up, full of mistakes, and make what we understand more precise and reliable?
7. How does one determine the social impacts of AI and expert systems on decision makers and problem solvers in our present institutions and environment?

SUMMARY

Most of our lives involve problems that we have to confront and decisions that we must face before we act. Data, information, and knowledge systems are analyzed, designed, and evaluated to serve this purpose. On this basis, we can act prudently, knowing how the information systems we create truly augment, that is, extend our capabilities to perform these two important human functions. Decision making and problem solving consume much of the capacity of our brains. They provide the experiences we accumulate in the course of dealing with life's circumstances. Analysis of problems and decisions related to them is a matter of historical reference. The approaches to them, however, have changed over time as insight and technology have become more available to deal with them. One tool, among many, is decision analysis. This method of dealing with decision making includes procedures such as detailed identification of the variables (factors) of the problem faced, modeling of the problem space, the sequential tracing of steps in the problem, a solution phase, identifying alternative options for problem solution, and determination of the risks and costs related to them. Toward this end, information and computer scientists have provided a variety of software programs that aid these processes. Artificial intelligence and expert systems represent a class of such tools. They seek to have computers help us think, learn, and hopefully act. Information scientists are continuing to study how these resources can be applied to help us deal with the many complexities of life we face.

EXERCISES

1. You have been admitted to three colleges to which you have applied. Each has merits that can be easily identified. The selection of one, however, could be difficult due to the fact that they have equal advantages to you. Identify and discuss those factors that are included in this problem decision. How could an information professional help you make a decision?

2. What is the factor that is considered most important in analyzing a problem or making a decision?
3. Discuss why decision making and problem solving should not be solely centered on computer technology.
4. Select a problem of your preference and show how modeling can help in the solution of the problem.
5. Identify how information professionals apply an understanding of decision making and problem solving to library operations.
6. How does decision theory relate to information retrieval?
7. What is the relationship between a knowledge system and artificial intelligence?
8. How and when might an expert system fail to support decision making and problem solving?
9. Describe a current problem you face. Sketch a model of such a problem that could serve as the basis for decision analysis.
10. Most, if not all, problems relate directly to an objective. Discuss how the satisfaction of an objective can be evaluated.

9

The Transfer Subsystem: Communications

LEARNING OBJECTIVES

- Define, compare, and relate communication, displays, and transmission.
- Analyze technologies that support transfer and describe how they work.

OVERVIEW

Information transfer is concerned with all the processes involved in transferring information from sources to users. In many cases there is some form of document associated with some stage of the transfer, even though other stages may be by word of mouth. The volume and variety of documents are immense (Vickery and Vickery 2004, 7). If what one speaks is not understood, there is an absence of the transfer of ideas. Thus, there is a lack of communication. Communication is an indispensable function of an augmented data, information, and knowledge (ADIK) system. At the very least, action is not possible without the ability of conveying (moving) thought and action to others. Thus, communication is a kind of commonwealth created through the sharing of thoughts and experiences. The media and related (tools) technologies, such as displays and the Internet, are introduced as part of this experience.

Background

Consider the state of a tropical storm threatening life and property on the mainland. The data captured by the sensors tracking the storm indicate that the storm will hit the mainland at a particular time with an estimated state of intensity. The exact location where the eye of the storm will hit cannot be accurately determined at the time. The individual users who are responsible for insuring the safety of the citizens and for minimizing the possible damage to property are uncertain as to the actions to be taken. With the aid of an ADIK system, the decision makers are provided with varying options for alternative actions (with accompanying probability of risk) that could be taken. The staff develops a plan of action, given the different models of the storm. These are provided on an electronic display. The data on the display show the attributes—for example, strength and direction—of the storm. Based on the data, the decision is made to warn the inhabitants of a particular area to leave their houses and establishments. The question remains: in what form is the decision to be transferred or communicated to the threatened population? The form of communication can be critical. That form is a matter of shaping language (symbols, codes, etc.) in a manner (medium) that ensures that the decision for action to offset the threats of the storm are taken seriously and worked out.

One of the most frustrating things in life is to realize that you are not getting the point across. What does it take to ensure that the person who is supposed to get the message receives it and understands it? There are moments in our lives when we wish to ensure that there is a need for a message, awareness (information) of what is going out in the message, what is intended by the message, and that there is a corresponding sense of meaning (knowledge) in the message for the receiver. The task of shaping what we want done in a manner that insures that it is done or achieved can be a difficult task. All of this is included when we consider the transfer as a subcomponent of an ADIK system. It is a task of considerable importance to the information scientist. The word "transfer" is used to refer to a major part of the ADIK system. Transfer can be considered synonymous to communication as used in the present text. Often, the physical processes of transmission and communication have been used interchangeably with an absence of distinction. But the distinction is of importance to the information scientist. For the present treatment, transmission represents the physical movement of energy in space, time, and given expression (language) in a message (medium). Communication is the intention of the transmission.

Humans have a diverse but limited capacity to transfer their intentions to others, to meet the demands of the events they confront to which they may be required to respond. Organisms have the capacity to use tools to extend and add to their native capacities. In no area other than communications is the need to augment this native capacity more explicit. From early times, humans have used pebbles, rocks, smoke, dress, riots, voting, speaking, writing, and other means for conveying intentions. Communications is an innate subsystem of the human information and knowledge system. It represents an extension of our thinking, learning, and feelings, enabling the applications of our intentions, whatever they may be—whether to enhance personal and collective development or safeguard us against harmful contingencies that present themselves in the process of achieving desired goals and objectives.

Definitions

Communications

Varied applications of the term "communication" are acknowledged in the following definition: "giving or giving and receiving information signals or messages by talk, gesture, writing, etc." (*Webster's New World* 1966, 296). Transfer can be understood through the following definition: "the process whereby experience in one task has an effect (either positive or negative) on performance on a different task subsequently undertaken" (*Penguin Dictionary of Psychology* 1995, 810).

A crucial distinction between the terms "transmission" and "communication" rests simply on the following: transmission refers to the physical movements of signals (energy, matter), while communication refers to the reception, use, and transfer of ideas and intentions.

Information Science and Communications

In addition to the definitions cited, consider communications as a "means of access." All species communicate to survive. Communication as a human-to-human process is a person-to-person, organization-to-organization experience—doing, giving, and sharing awareness (information) and knowledge (understanding) with one another. It is also a human-machine process. When we communicate, we have at our disposal a variety of technologies that we invent, create, and produce. These include the primitive assembling of pebbles, rocks, and smoke and the creation and production of pens, pencils, chalk, and light to the present use of computers and displays that, we shall learn, are links to the Internet and the World Wide Web. It is a primary research interest of the information scientist to develop the laws and principles of how these can best be used solving problems and making decisions that impact on the welfare of the individual, group, or organization.

An understanding of communications, by its very nature, remains interdisciplinary. Information scientists use theories and laws from all of the physical, social, and engineering disciplines when structuring an ADIK system. The information scientist, in the attempt to integrate technology with human demands for greater awareness and knowledge, brings together the understanding of all these sciences in the analysis, design, and evaluation of ADIK systems.

Language

Language, in all its diversity, is a means for reaching out, extending the self, capturing and commanding resources in the endeavor to survive, and thrive in the world. It is a fundamental and unique instrument of augmentation as well as ADIK transfer/communication for our species. Language has generated several sciences dedicated to the applications, origins, and understanding of this complex phenomenon. It is also a critical area in information science. It spans the domain of doumentation, processing, decision making, and broad areas of media. Language provides an underlying unity for the efforts of information scientists in results of their discoveries and research efforts, both practical and theoretical (Chomsky 1968).

Mass Communications

Mass communication is a particular form of communication in which media are used to disseminate data, information, and knowledge to a large number of people and institutions locally, nationally, and internationally. It should be noted at the outset that it may be difficult at times to separate transmission of signals (data) from the reception of the signal (awareness, information) for which there is intention (some idea, some thought) that the signal encodes. Our study of mass communication attempts to make this idea clear. In mass communication, the objective is to use transmission devices for the movement of ideas from a sender to a receiver. In the case of mass communications, there are many different kinds of transmission applications. These are directed to many different populations of receivers with different cultures, social purposes, and practices (anthropology).

Mass communication can be considered a sociological and sociopsychological experience. Information scientist Patrick Penland has provided us an important view of mass communication:

> The desire to communicate is the pervasive fact of social life. In a very fundamental sense, communication is culture and culture is communication. The public buildings, the arts, the rhetoric and the sociodramas of civic life have all

served to communicate the cultural heritage and to engender a common under-standing among a group of people. In this sense, these public arts have always been mass communication. (*Ency LIS* 1971, 458–59)

The medium is what transforms experience into knowledge (Inglis 1951, 3). Media is the plural form and includes all sign systems. Media are defined as "a medium of communication that has an important influence on the dis-semination of knowledge over space and over time and it becomes necessary to study the characteristics in order to appraise its influence in its cultural settings" (Inglis 1951, 33). Marshall McLuhan, a communication scientist in the late 1960s, expressed this sentiment:

The medium, or process, of our time, electric technology, is shaping and restruc-turing patterns of social interdependence and every aspect of our personal life . . . electrical information devices for universal, tyrannical womb-to-tomb surveil-lance causing a very serious dilemma between our claim to privacy and the com-munity's need to know[1] . . . All media work us over completely. They are so per-vasive on their personal, political, economic, aesthetic, psychological, moral, ethical and social consequences that they leave no part of us untouched, unaf-fected, unaltered. The medium is the massage.[2] . . . Any understanding of social and cultural change is impossible without knowledge of the way media work as en-vironments. All media are extensions of some human facility = psychic or physi-cal. (McLuhan 1967, 12, 26)

Display: What is It?

Before we begin to learn about displays, just think of the following circum-stances: driving a car without a speedometer, gas gauge, and oil gauge or fly-ing an airplane without an altimeter to tell the pilot whether the aircraft is high enough to miss the mountain ahead. How about telling time without a clock? Perhaps the location of the sun would do the trick, depending on how accurate one must be.

What is a display, and what does it have to do with information science? A display can be many things—the television we watch, the books and newspa-pers we read, even the clothes we wear. To be clear, a display is actually a trans-mission device, very much like a letter that you mail and that someone reads. One might ask an information scientist, "Why not study displays in transmis-sion?" Indeed, it could. However, the point of emphasis in the study of dis-plays is not the engineering structure (the hardware) of a display (like paper, ink, paint, electronics, etc.). When we study displays in communication, we study how the content of the display influences and directs the viewer to thought and action. Actually, we can say that the first thing that a baby sees when born into this world is a display, although it may be only a blob of light. The display can be something that is part of our life and, as we will learn, a physical tool or a major technological component of an ADIK system. The display is a thing, something physical. It is something that tells us what is involved in a particular system. The display gives us the time of day (e.g., clock) and tells us what is happening. The display is an important way of communicating what we enter into the computer and what the computer did to what we put into it. It is an important way of telling the computer to do whatever we wish with what we command. In other words, the display is a way of telling ourselves and others of our presence and intentions. The display is an important way for us to extend and express our affections and desires and to learn. The display is one way we communicate.

Why is a display important to information science? Displays are a critical part of the ADIK system because they can be an important source for moving the viewer from awareness (what, where, when, who) to knowledge (how, why). The display helps us in our development, in solving problems and making decisions. Displays are a representation of our existence, our state of being. The information scientist is very much interested in understanding how displays, particularly electronic displays, help us integrate what we receive from our sensors and from our data-processing machinery (computers) to accomplish tasks and deal with the day-to-day demands the world imposes on us.

Displays are tools we invent, create, and engineer to move our ideas from one place to another—that is, communicate. They extend, complement, and augment our ability to write, draw, and give to ourselves and others what we have on our minds. Displays help humans move (transfer) ideas from one person and place to another. Displays bind the various parts of the ADIK system together.

The nature and design of the display are important to the information scientist. How the data or signals are organized and presented on a display can set the limits and quality of a person's awareness (information) and understanding (knowledge) and influence matters of personal and organizational development including function and survival. This aspect of displays is studied in chapter 10, where the human factors important in the design and use of displays are studied.

Kinds of Displays

Displays are material, physical things (tools). They can be static, mechanical, and/or dynamic. A road sign is a static display. It can only be changed manually when a change is warranted. Another example of a static display is a photograph of an event. Books are static displays. The symbols that are used and printed on the page you are now reading is a static display. It can only be changed by physically erasing what is written, printed, painted, and/or sketched. A mechanical display is one in which gears are used to move the data captured from one scene to another. A motion-picture camera and the output from the projector presented on a screen comprise mechanical displays. A dynamic display allows for the continuous inputting and outputting of data, information, and knowledge. Computer monitors and TV screens are dynamic displays because of the continuous data input/output. The radio and cell phone are dynamic electronic displays. Each kind of display extends or limits what we can do with the data it delivers about the events that surround and impact on us.

Displays and Communications

The display is a way of communicating. Flying the American flag outside your home communicates your patriotism. A book is a form of display (static) that records the ideas, thoughts, and other accounts of human living. Displays move (transmit) data from one place or person to another. Displays are a potential source for meaning and human understanding (knowledge). Communication refers to the meaning that is contained in that which is moved (transmitted) and presented (displayed). Communication is behavioral. What this means is that the way we act is defined in the way we communicate. The use of language, both spoken and unspoken, is central to communication (linguistics). Communication science refers to the study of how thoughts, ideas, and intentions are represented in the way we move these aspects of living among ourselves. Such processes (way of doing things) direct and influence all the things we do.

Information science and communication science are often discussed by information professionals as being the same. The difference, however, is in their objectives. Although these objectives are very much related, the laws and principles pertaining to each address different, specific things. While the information science function is to derive the laws and principles that relate directly to the analysis and design of ADIK systems (that include information-knowledge transfer), communication science directs its attention to understanding how transmission impacts on the content of the transmitted displays in media, print journalism (press), and museums and art. For example, museums and films have an impact on each other.

Display Factors

There are two major factors that help information scientists understand the nature and importance of displays and how they function in ADIK systems. One factor concerns the display itself and what makes it work. This is the technological-physical factor. The second factor is how what it presented on the display helps us perform as persons or organizations. This is the human-organizational factor.

You're watching a terrific show on TV and, all of a sudden, what is shown is obscured by "snow," a sort of clutter. Engineers call this "noise." You are distracted and annoyed. For example, you are talking to your friend on the phone and all of a suddenly there is static and you cannot hear what your friend is saying. You may hang up and try again. These are instances where the electric energy that makes up the display (what you are hearing, seeing) is changing; getting weaker or stronger. You can experience this at home at times when the lightbulbs seem to be dimming, or in some instances, the lights go out. There is no display. You wonder what is going on. Actually, the amount of electric energy is changing, producing a change in the display (light). These are all examples of the technological-physical factor.

In many, if not all banks and stores, there are sensors placed in different locations to spot thieves in action. These sensors present data on a monitor (display) that police and others investigating crimes can examine to establish what the culprits look like and what they did. The position and angle in which these sensors are placed determine the quantity and quality of the data that will be available for study. The point is that the value and function of a display depends very much on how and where the display is placed and used (programmed). Try to leave the library with a book that you have not checked out! The sensor will catch you. This is also an example of the technological-physical factor.

An example of the human-organizational factor is if you are sitting in the back of the classroom and the instructor places a slide on the screen, the letters are so small that you would need binoculars to see the print. There is nothing wrong with the physical aspect of the display. The screen is there. The projector is working correctly. There is a display of the material that is presented from the projector. You can see the screen (display), but you cannot see what is on it. The print is so small that it is impossible for you to read what is on the display. The human factor of the data has not been taken into account, and therefore the data are not presented in a way that you, seated in the back of the classroom, can read them.

In the previous chapters, we became aware of some computer fundamentals. In the process of using computers and particularly, the Internet, the occasion can arise where something done by the user leads to either an unexpected or wrong outcome. For example, when browsing the Internet, a user incorrectly navigates to a page. They scan the menu for a possible approach to correct the situation, or go back to the main page. The options displayed on the menu failed to match the situation the user was facing, or there was no "back" button. Here the function of the display was compromised because of the poor testing of the application software to match human requirements. This hypothetical menu does not succeed in meeting the human-organizational factor required although it is physically sound.

Application: The Third Dimension

Displays of all kinds, whether static, mechanical, or dynamic, are everywhere. Aspects that are important to the information professional are the light, sound, smell, paint, chalk, and print that make up a display. Each singularly or together can be used in a different form and manner. Years ago those who went to movies were given a special kind of eyeglasses that enabled them to see things in the third dimension (3-D). They were awkward to wear, yet it was a thrill to watch a Western movie showing the battle between the Indians and the Pioneers with arrows going directly at your eye! In the TV show *Murder, She Wrote*, Americans watched a sequence that showed how the main actress, who was serving as the detective solving a murder, could wear specific equipment that made her actually live the sequence of actions taken by the murderer, a technical representation of reality called virtual reality. Virtual reality is actually a technique where different images are processed by the computer and the human, equipped with special equipment such as those 3-D glasses, receives and responds to images of the presumed "real world."

Visualization

Visualization is the use of different kinds of displays with some tool to create images that make sense of reality. Think of the computer and the displays such as paint and canvas that enable you to produce a picture of an idea that you may have. Suppose that you want to send a greeting card to a relative via e-mail. This is a visual representation of an idea in your head (a seasonal greeting). Visualization is what happens when humans use computers to create their ideas visually. Visualization is a good example of how humans, with the aid of the computer, can be creative.

Visualization is a way of combining a number of displays in a manner such that your presence in the visually created space is similar to one that someone would experience in the real world (virtual reality). This is made possible by using the computer to process data in a manner that extends (augments) our visual capabilities, so that we can see objects in space that we can actually manipulate and structure as we do in real life. This capability can be very helpful in all kinds of research. It can teach future pilots to fly, help basketball champions to play a better game, and identify and help catch criminals.

Wireless Communications

In chapter 4, we learned about wireless transmission, the movement of signals from one source to another. In that chapter we discussed the Internet and the

World Wide Web as transmission networks. Now we apply this understanding to the intent of the transmission, namely communications, the sharing of ideas and intentions.

During the latter part of World War II, a physical scientist and electrical engineer by the name of Vannevar Bush served as a consultant to the president of the United States as part of his appointment as director of the Office of Scientific Research and Development. There, he was responsible for over six thousand scientists engaged in military projects. That office was responsible for bringing together many scientific efforts in conducting warfare. In 1945, Bush wrote the article "As We May Think" in *The Atlantic Monthly*. In this article, Bush tried to relate the technology developed in World War II to other applications. Bush proposed "Memex," a system that would allow users to look up any kind of periodical or book and even bookmark their favorite places. The application of this kind of system came in 1969 with the formation of the Advanced Research Project Agency (ARPA) by the Department of Defense to support military activity. This led to a system called the Advanced Research Project Agency Network (ARPANET), the objective of which was to increase the sharing of scientific information among several of the research communities conducting research for the military. Advances in technology provided a further expansion of ARPANET, to serve as a transmission-communication system serving both public and private global interests. This led to the development of the Internet.

In the early 1980s a computer scientist named Tim Berners-Lee was working at CERN, a research laboratory in Europe. He studied how data files could be linked together. He invented the World Wide Web communication system in 1989, and wrote the first Web client (browser-editor) and server in 1990. These and other efforts led to hypertext, a method in which a hyperlinked text in a file is highlighted by using a computer mouse, providing the user the related file on the display. A hyperlink is a symbol (icon), picture (graphic), or word in a file that, when selected or highlighted, automatically opens another file for viewing on the computer display. A set of standards known as the "Hypertext Transfer Protocol" (HTTP) were developed, which allowed information to be shared between researchers at the laboratory in which Berners-Lee worked. The idea led to the development of the World Wide Web (WWW), which uses the same basic technology that Berners-Lee developed. In 1992, the first Internet service provider offered access to the Internet, both commercial and private. Berners-Lee is now the head of the Computer Science Laboratory at MIT and is considered to be the father of the WWW.

The Web is simply a conglomeration of many networks all serving the purpose of communication. There are many ways to access the WWW today, but most often it is done via a computer and a browser. A browser is a software program that allows you to view and navigate Web pages. A present example would be Mozilla Firefox, which enables tabbed browsing, a spell checker, incremental find, live bookmarking, a download manager, and an integrated search system for a user's desired search engine. Other technologies that allow you to access the Web include cell phones, personal digital assistants (Palm handhelds), and Web-enabled televisions. The WWW will be discussed in further detail in the next chapter.

SUMMARY

Communication of data, information, and knowledge transfer is a vital part of human existence and a critical part of ADIK systems. All species communicate, varying in kind and degree. Communication is a function where thought and intention expressed in language, in its many forms, plays an important role, where thought and intention are shared and extended for the individual and for the common benefits and purposes (commonwealth). Communications is of considerable importance to the information scientist because it is the experience (function) that ties together (integrates) the various parts of an ADIK system in meeting its human and organizational objective(s). The medium is the source through which communication functions and through which thought and action are taken. The media, the plural of medium, are diverse forms of expression ranging from a scribbled note to newspapers, television, radio, photographs, etc. Each enables humans and organizations to relate, to communicate with each other. Each can be considered a display, a medium.

Displays are an essential part of our lives. They are the physical means for the movement (transmission) of ideas from one place, person, and organization to another. There are three kind of displays; static, mechanical, and dynamic. Static displays do not allow for continuous change to the content without erasing or replacing the text or content. Mechanical displays move static images from one place to another on a screen by gears in the machinery. Dynamic displays use electronics and computers to move images from one place to another. These displays allow for presenting data, information, and knowledge in various ways. These displays, with computers, enable the presentation of reality in different dimensions (virtual). This capability can serve a number of functions important to research (artificial intelligence, visualization, and robotology), education (computer-mediated presentations), and crime control and organizational management. Finally, the Internet and the WWW are the two most prominent forms of transmission technologies that, with computers, serve communications. The information scientist is directly involved in understanding how these various communicative capabilities, both human and technological, can be tied together (integrated) ensuring an efficient and effective data and knowledge environment (system) that extends human capabilities.

EXERCISES

1. Why is it possible to conclude that most wars, if not all, reported in history are the result of ADIK system failure?
2. Identify three areas in the structure of an ADIK system where breakdown could impact communications.
3. Is it possible to communicate without displays? If yes, how? If not, why?
4. Is a cartoon a display? Explain.
5. How can a display directly influence your learning? Explain.
6. In what way is transmission of an idea different from the communication of an idea?
7. In what way is the library the same or different from the media other than the fact that they both contain physical reports of human experience?
8. Describe a current case detailed either on television or in newspapers that clearly shows the difference between transmission and communication.
9. Is it possible to have a transmission failure yet not result in communication breakdown?
10. What did Marshall McLuhan mean when he stated that the "medium is the massage"? Give an example.
11. In what sense is the Internet/World Wide Web a concern of both the information scientist and the computer scientist?

Notes

1. McLuhan refers to the book as an extension of our eye; clothing, an extension of the skin; electric circuitry, an extension of the central nervous system (1967, 39–41). Among some information scientists, communication and information are considered related, if not synonymous, experiences.

2. Note spelling is as used by McLuhan: massage is defined as "rubbing and kneading the body to reduce pain or stiffness" (*Oxford Dictionary* 1996, 383).

10

Human Factors (Ergonomics) and Information Science

LEARNING OBJECTIVES

- Compare the terms "ergonomics" and "human factors."
- Cite examples of ergonomic aspects of ADIK systems.
- Draw and explain a model of human information processing.
- Synthesize principles of human information processing and information science to describe the philosophy of user-oriented design.

OVERVIEW

Information scientists attempt to understand in the analysis, design, and evaluation of ADIK systems those human factors (resources) that can influence, limit, and/or enhance data, information, and knowledge processing and use.

Definitions

The terms "human factors" and "ergonomics" are often used synonymously. Early in the history of human factors, the expression "human engineering" was used.

Human factors is the study of those elements that influence the efficiency with which people can use equipment to accomplish the functions of that equipment, the physical environment in which the equipment must be operated and maintained, the characteristics of the jobs that people must perform in order to accomplish goals, and the capabilities and limitations of equipment and personnel in accomplishing the tasks (abstracted from D. Meister 1971).

Ergonomics is "the study of workplace design and the physical and psychological impact it has on workers. Ergonomics is about the fit between people, their work activities, equipment, work systems, and environment to ensure that the workplace is safe, comfortable, efficient, and that productivity is not compromised" (www.powerhomebiz.com/Glossary/glossary-E.htm#E).

Alphonse Chapanis (1995, 4), noted human factors specialist (ergonomist), defines human factors and ergonomics in this way: "Ergonomics and Human Factors use knowledge of human abilities and limitations to the design of organizations, jobs, machines, tools and consumer products for safe, efficient and comfortable use."

Background

As humans, our sensors receive energy from an event and this energy is then transmitted to a processor, which can either be human or machine. Computers expand our means to process information at greater speed and with increased capacity. To get the most out of our human-computer systems, special consideration is given to how the input and output systems and the user interface are designed. This requires some understanding of human factors, or ergonomics.

Human factors specialists, or "ergonomists," are trained to ensure that systems are useful, efficient, effective, easy to learn, and safe. They strive to ensure that the optimal physical, technical, and environmental conditions required to complete a task are met through appropriate design. Table 10.1 lists some of the general interests of a human factors specialist. Ergonomics applies to the design of everything from input and output devices to the user interface of a software application in a computer system. From the location of every key on the keyboard to the brightness of the monitor to the number of menu options on the toolbar, human factors have an integral role in each design decision. For example, when searching for a database on a computer the user may need to shut down the system in order to get back to the initial menu. This is because the command is hidden behind a menu and not obvious or intuitive from the interface design and layout. Ergonomics, when applied to the design of a human-computer system, helps to ensure that people more fully benefit from the capabilities of the machine.

Origins of Ergonomics

The origins of ergonomics go back to Bernardino Ramazzini (1700), a physician and founder of occupational/industrial medicine. His research included studies of occupational diseases and the advocacy of protective measures for workers. Contemporary ergonomics has its roots in psychology and industrial design. The field of human factors can be traced to the Industrial Revolution. Workers labored long hours with machines that required mostly routine but also some complicated operations under conditions that would be considered inefficient, even inhumane, today. The owners of factories at that time were interested in getting the most out of their workers. At the beginning of the twentieth century, Frederick Taylor and Frank and Lillian Gilbreth were the first to note that if they changed some of the conditions with which labor workers had to contend, their productivity improved. Several of these same principles are applied today in the information age to the design of human-machine systems. In this text the study of ergonomics will be centered on both the physical characteristics of technology and the role that human (cognitive/perceptual) factors assume in ADIK system performance.

General Area of Interest of Ergonomists

Ergonomists are interested in almost all aspects of human behavior and system performance. Some of these are included in table 10.1.

Theory

The theoretical background of ergonomics and its application to information science in the analysis, design, and evaluation of ADIK systems is broad. It includes the application of most, if not all, of the knowledge of the physical, behavioral and social sciences, and engineering. Physical, technological systems have characteristics that can extend and/or limit system performance. How these system characteristics are joined with other human properties is the ap-

Table 10.1.
Some Areas of General Interest to a Human Factors Specialist.

- Design of streets and displays for highway control and safety
- Passenger comfort on aircraft to reduce fatigue
- In general, impact of media violence on children and adults
- Proper placement and lighting around computers to lessen fatigue and eye injury
- Proper level of sound used at airport terminals for announcements
- Placement and use of smoke detectors and other alarm systems

plication of ergonomics in the system analysis, design, and evaluation of ADIK systems.

System Components and Ergonomics

Each component (subsystem) of the ADIK system possesses physical characteristics, the design of which influences the extent of human capabilities. Sensors capture the characteristics of events and situations in time and space. Data from these events and situations are received by humans and/or machines. Response to these states is a function of the limits of human sensory, cognitive-perceptual ability, aided by technology. Two examples are used to clarify this idea.

Example: The Public Announcement Communication System

Throughout an airport, loudspeakers (public announcement system) are installed to alert travelers to the status of their aircraft. These loudspeakers are used in addition to the visual displays located throughout the airport to inform (alert) travelers about the status of various flights. The volume of the sound with which the message is sent could be sufficiently loud but the lack of sharpness (articulation) in the speaker's voice in transmitting the message could cause some passengers to miss the content of what is intended. The ADIK transmission subsystem failed (chapter 6).

Example: Audiovisual Presentation

The instructor of the course decides to use an overhead projector to display the essential points of the lesson. In so doing, the instructor guides the presentation of course content on the overhead by verbally reiterating much of the lesson material that is presented visually. If the timing of the verbal-visual presentation of the lesson material is not considered properly, there is a high probability that the main points of the lesson may be missed by the student.

Cognitive/Perceptual Functions

In addition to those things we do with our senses, day-to-day living (events, situations) requires the use of our heads, our minds, and our brains. While our sensors enable us to be aware of what is going around us, there is both the need and requirement (chapter 4) to understand and then take the appropriate action required of the event and situation. This is a matter of cognition and perception.

Table 10.2.
Properties of the Cognitive Conscious and the Cognitive Unconscious.

Property	Conscious	Unconscious
Engaged by	Novelty	Repetition
	Emergencies	Expected Events
	Danger	Safety
Used in	New circumstances	Routine situations
Can handle	Decisions	No branching tasks
Accepts	Logical propositions	Logic or inconsistency
Operates	Sequentially	Simultaneously
Controls	Volition	Habits
Capacity	Tiny	Huge
Persists for	Tenths of seconds	Decades (lifelong)

Source: Raskin (2000, 16). Used by permission of Addison-Wesley.

Cognition is "a broad (almost unspecifiable so) term which has been traditionally used to refer to such activities as thinking, conceiving, reasoning, etc." (Reber 1995, 132), and "how . . . human beings process information from their environment in order to form concepts of that environment" (Littlejohn 1978, 135). In this process, it has been suggested that more attention should be paid to the type of "conscious" activities and give the computers more of the automatic or unconscious type of work and calculations. Table 10.2 is a list comparing automatic and conscious activities.

Cognitive: Information System Processing Models

Several information system processing models have been discovered in humans. For instance, several cognitive psychologists have tested theories by constructing models that parallel human thought. When giving their computer software a list of words, it "remembers" some words better than others. If these words match the structure and timing of enough real humans taking the same test, it implies that their theory of human information processing (HIP) is right. After years and years of research, cognitive psychologists have developed models of how we think and learn. A simplified sketch of one of these is shown in figure 10.1.

Information Processing Model: Perceptual Representation

Perception is defined as "awareness of the elements of physical environment interpreted in light of personal experience" (*Webster's Seventh New Collegiate*

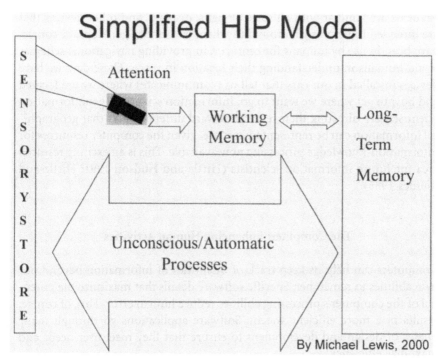

Figure 10.1. A Theory of Human Information Processing. Source: personal communication from Dr. Michael Lewis at the University of Pittsburgh.

Dictionary, 626). Table 10.3 represents the sensory processes used in obtaining information from an environment.

In this configuration, the sensory (eye, ear, etc., acquisition subsystem) picks up the energy (data) emitted from the event and situation (stimulus), enabling an awareness (information) of the event and situation. This state is then extended to include the segmentation of what is acquired by the central nervous system (brain). A process of sensory stimulations, results, and features leads to the identification of a pattern(s).

An area of major interest and importance to the information scientist with respect to cognition and perception concerns the use of present technologies to aid people in navigating the space in their environment (spatial knowledge).

Table 10.3.
A Model of the Sensory and Perceptual Processes in the
Flow of Information from the Environment.

Stimulus Energy . . .	Sensory Processes . . .	Segmented Feature . . .	Pattern Recognition . . .	Pattern Identification

Source: Anderson (1990, 84).

All of us are familiar with all sorts of signs, displays, and other devices that are intended to help us get around to where we want to go. Maps, of course, have been in use by humans for centuries in providing navigational schemes to aid humans in understanding their location in space. These days we have devices installed in our cars that tell us (communicate) where we are located and how to get where we want to go. Information scientists (geoinformation scientists) are directing their research toward different ways that geographical information can be represented in space, given the computer resources for information-knowledge processing now available. This is an exciting research area for future information scientists (Hirtle and Hudson 1991; Hirtle and Jonides 1985).

The Computer: Enhancing Human Activities

Computers can help us keep track of quantities of information beyond our own abilities to remember. Specific software details that maximize the potential of the computer's processing abilities reduce human error. This, of course, results in a more efficient system. Software applications go through many phases of design and development to ensure that they meet user needs and maximize efficiency.

Paradoxically, it may be essential to think of humans as augmenting computers (which augment humans). If there had been no human interaction, computers never would have come about. They are put together by people and machines, and are programmed to assist in daily tasks from simple to complex. Computer software and hardware have become essential to our society.

Humans engineer their own environment, whether it is a building, a room, an automobile, an airplane, a classroom, or even an airport terminal that creates a usable environment. More often than not, designers and engineers, as well as other professionals, do a good job ensuring that these structures and machines function in safe and efficient ways. But as much as there are examples of good design and engineering, poor examples still can be found. There are instances where insufficient attention is paid to the limits and substance of human performance (the human factors). Situations exist where the environment that is constructed does not match needs and requirements. Computers are tools that, when placed in the right environment, can powerfully extend our innate as well as learned capabilities. Yet, there are other occasions where insufficient attention is applied to what the individual can and cannot do given the tools at hand. The human factors specialist (ergonomist) and information professional must work together in the analysis, design, and evaluation of augmented data, information, and knowledge systems.

The computer allows us to collect and process more information, faster than we can unaided. However, these physical components do not make up the total processing system alone. People are the most important part of the processing system. Our ingenuity determines how the machinery can be applied to solve problems, aid the decision-making process, and accomplish simple or complex tasks on both the macro and micro levels. Computers can reduce time and distance. Computers can also reveal what is not visible to the human eye, near and far. Computers can create, or be the means for creating, physical suffering and harm. This is one of the tasks of the information scientist working with the computer scientist, ergonomist, and others. It all depends on how we employ this powerful technology (chapter 10).

Many of us are most familiar with the computer as practical tools. They enable us to do more than we ever thought possible, and in more ways. In this section, we highlight some of the very practical yet out-of-the-ordinary ways computers can extend our abilities.

Recognizable benefits that many of us take for granted include searching for goods, services, and information online, communicating with friends and family near and far, and having unlimited resources at our fingertips. Moreover, we have to remember that computers have the ability to enrich our lives in a number of ways. Only our ingenuity limits the way we apply them. Computers are being used in medical devices that save and restore lives. They are being used to deliver education everywhere. They are being used to reunite missing children with their families. We are aware of how the computer can boost our cognitive ability. It helps us store more information than our own brains can recall and retain. However, computers enhance other human abilities. For a person with visual impairment, a computer can provide access to information via screen-reading technologies. For a person with hearing impairment, a computer can provide text for an audio presentation. For a person with visual and mobility impairment, a computer can provide access to the community. Studying how people think and learn has helped guide the people who developed software, such as the aptly named artificial intelligence (AI) programs. In turn, the new programs become ways to extend human capabilities—for instance, the development of computer programs that could learn to plot possible chess moves of opponents, far into the future, beyond human capacity. This may seem inconsequential to some of us but has led to many significant consequences, such as the ability to predict approaching weather disasters (involving up to two thousand or more factors). The impact of computers in our daily lives is almost beyond description. The computer scientist, working with the information scientist, continues to probe how information systems can be analyzed, designed, and evaluated to ensure that computer abilities can effectively respond to the needs and requirements of all people of the globe.

User-Centered Design

While often overlooked in the design process, considering the human factors that go into any design is imperative for ensuring optimal usefulness. User input and feedback are critical components in designing and redesigning an application. A software developer has to understand the user's task to create an application that meets the user's needs. User-centered design principles need to be applied in the design of everything, from business forms to processes to packaging—in other words, anything you can think of that humans would interact with or use.

The Human-Computer User Interface (HCI)

The computer is what the user interacts with to enter, retrieve, and control data. Optimally, a designer wants the interface to be transparent to the task at hand. It should be obvious: the user shouldn't have to think about how to do something, because it takes effort away from performing the actual task. Considering how humans interact with the computer to accomplish the tasks allows designers to minimize problems for the user through design. However, this is not simple; it requires a thorough understanding of the user's abilities, the task to be performed, and human cognition (perception and memory), as well as aesthetic design, information architecture, and interaction design. Careful consideration needs to be given when designing input and output methods, especially to the software applications that run on the machines.

While we will discuss input and output methods in more detail later in this chapter, the mouse, keyboard, and screen display are the most commonly used input and output devices. Many people are familiar with using a mouse to point and click as they navigate through a graphical user interface. Observing the number of times users must point and click to find what they are looking for is one example of how human factors play a role in interface design. The user controls and manipulates the system via software applications. Each application has its own screen interface designed to perform tasks through controls—those elements on the display such as icons, menus, push buttons, radio buttons, sliders, and scroll bars.

Software Applications

Software development is a key part of designing efficient human/computer systems. The software is what makes it possible for people to use the machines. The goal of any computer software application is to provide ways for the user to have access to and manipulate information. Applications can sup-

Figure 10.2. Computer Science and Human Information Processing. Drawn by S. Masters.

port general tasks such as word processing. They can also be very specific to a task, as for example, architectural design. Software applications automate repetitive tasks for us.

Several information system models can be discovered in humans. For instance, in cognitive psychology and cognitive science, psychologists have tested their theories by constructing computer models that parallel human thought processes. When giving their computer software a list of words, it "remembers" some words better than others. If these words match the structure and timing of enough real humans taking the same test, it implies that their theory of human information processing (HIP) is right. After years and years of research, cognitive psychologists have developed models of how we think and learn, as seen in figure 10.2.

Information Science and Ergonomic Challenges

Technology is present in all quarters of our environment (libraries, schools, hospitals, media, entertainment, etc.). The challenge is to increase awareness among individuals and the general public of the role and importance of ergonomics (human factors) to their welfare.

Advances in ADIK technologies (ubiquitous and virtual) demand greater attention and care in the analysis, design, and evaluation of ADIK systems.

These advances support the requirement, specification, application, and compliance of standards (regulations) in the use of these advancing technologies by individuals, organizations, and institutions. Particular note should be made of the increasing attention and application of these technologies throughout the world (globalization). This directs attention to differences in culture with respect to attitudes toward the use of technology in general, and specifically to technology at the personal level.

Improper use of ADIK technologies can injure and harm individuals and organizations. With changing capabilities of advancing technologies, it is important to acknowledge and understand how these changes are included in the engineering, system development, and educational process.

There is the necessity of understanding the needs and requirements (cognitive/affective) of an aging population in the design and application of future information processing technology. This area offers increasing challenges in the education of future information scientists, particularly those interested in ergonomics.

SUMMARY

Humans adapt their own surroundings—whether it is a building, a room, automobile, airplane, classroom, or even a railroad station—in ways that create a suitable environment. More often than not, designers, engineers, and other professionals do a good job ensuring that these structures and machines function in safe and efficient ways. But although there are examples of good design and engineering, poor examples can be found. There are instances where insufficient attention is paid to the limits and substance of human performance (the human factors). Situations exist where the environment that is constructed does not match the needs and requirements of its users. Computers are tools that, when placed in the right environment, can be a powerful technology, extending our innate as well as learned (cognitive/perceptual) capabilities. Yet there are other occasions where insufficient attention is applied to what the individual can and cannot do given the tools and tasks at hand. The human factors specialist (ergonomist) and the information professional must work together in the analysis, design, and evaluation of ADIK systems.

EXERCISES

1. Students are now quite experienced in the use of their computers in completing their assignments, looking up references for their reports,

etc. Discuss an instance when the computer failed to provide the assistance you required and identify the "human factors" condition that led to that conclusion.

2. In what way(s) would a librarian be interested in applying the professional skills of an ergonomist?

3. In a previous chapter of this text, we studied the important role that electronic and other displays play in insuring that our ADIK systems are efficient and effective. Discuss how the information professional and the ergonomist can work together to ensure that the task objectives are accomplished efficiently.

4. Given your understanding of information system analysis and design, what aspects studied in the current chapter would you consider important in establishing their worth as human tools in responding to the problems of terror and other human conditions?

5. Relate the term "human computer interface" to ergonomics.

6. What are the consequences to human performance of motherboard failure?

7. Considerable research has been applied to space technology. What aspects of these advances are of importance to the information scientist?

8. Modern automobiles are being equipped with global positioning systems (GPS). Of what interest are these technological advances to the information scientist?

IV

SOCIAL ISSUES

Information scientists must always accept challenges and measure the success of their work in terms of the beneficial impact on human beings and their health and safety.

—Anthony Debons

"I've been waiting so long, I can't remember whether I'm uploading or downloading."
By permission of Bunny Hoest, *Parade Magazine*, October 6, 2002.

11

Value and Quality of Data, Information, and Knowledge

The important issue will always be for man to control development to mold it to his constant search for the quality of life. In this constant evolution, information will always be the major element of change.

—Myrtha B. Casanova (1990, 53)

LEARNING OBJECTIVES

- Analyze the value of data, information, and knowledge.
- Examine the major dimensions of quality of information.

OVERVIEW

More often than not, the value of information and knowledge is assumed, yet not counted in very practical ways. First, we present various views on the value of information by several noted information scientists. This is followed by the presentation of those factors that relate to value, particularly the measurement of cost and the benefits expected from information, and then knowledge. The quality of information and knowledge is then examined from different perspectives—first, the value of knowledge as a process and then as a product. The discussion of the quality of information centers on various dimensions such as accuracy, timeliness, age, and the availability of the source.

Views on the Value of Information and Knowledge

Information science attempts to understand how the tools (technology) we invent and create enable us to be aware and understand the world about us. Psychologists advise us that depriving individuals of sensory stimulation (awareness) has an important effect on an individual's behavior and well-being. A total blackout of a city can jeopardize the safety of individuals and also prevent the exercise of many services necessary to individuals and organizations. The failure of a traffic light can lead to serious road accidents. Day-to-day commerce could not exist without information. Our lives are totally dependent on information. Information is crucial to meaning and understanding/knowledge. A number of information professionals and information scientists have expressed their views on the value of information.

Robert M. Mason

Robert M. Mason, an information system and management expert, directs our attention to the functions of information analysis centers. These centers provide clients with specific information tailored to specific needs and requirements in the management of organizations. His studies of information analysis centers revealed that their value is centered on four basic factors:

1. Quality: accuracy and credibility;
2. Scope: recentness and completeness;
3. Difficulty: lag time, ease of use, and staff use;
4. Cost of the service.

Mason's conclusion is that "although the users assigned higher values to the service characteristics related to information analysis, evaluation, and synthesis, the users' discrimination between information analysis centers and other information sources were not particularly strong" (1979, 339).

Robert Taylor

Robert Taylor (1986), an information scientist, studied the value of information from a broad perspective. He suggested four ways that the value of information can be understood. Consider:

1. Economics;
2. Utility: that which is added to data to make them useful;

3. Exchange value: what the person would give in terms of energy, time lost, opportunity, and money for information;
4. Benefits: what organizations accrue as the result of the information use, or nonuse.

Taylor concluded that the value of information cannot be understood without acknowledging the context in which information occurs. His research led him to consider that information has potential value in the messages sent, received, and the decisions made as a result. Thus, information is "value-added" when it is used for a specific purpose. The value of information is established when we give information to others in exchange for something we need and require. An apparent value of information rests in the time and effort an individual is willing to consume to receive what is seen as benefits from the information.

Taylor (1986) also concluded that information has value through the resources that are available to us. Resources include friends and associates who are part of the give-and-take of daily living. Libraries, museums, art galleries, and music halls are important resources because they provide us with awareness and the meaning of the many things that we experience. Applied to what we have studied in earlier chapters, information systems represent a valuable and important resource. These systems aid our development and, in particular, enable us to solve problems, make decisions, and generally deal with the many circumstances that come our way.

P. K. McPherson

McPherson's point of view on the value of information, like Mason's, stresses the role of information in an organization. Both regard information as an activity of the mind (cognition). The activity includes processing, reasoning, and judgment. The value of information lies in its potential to bring the numerous vital parts of an organization together, including knowledge, money, information, and intelligence (1994).

McPherson judges the importance of carefully developing an accounting process for establishing the value and impact of information on the organization. He considers the necessity of exercising care in identifying advantages and disadvantages gained from the use of information and knowledge. This includes an acknowledgment of the differences between the intangible and monetary value of information. Both Taylor (1986) and McPherson (1994) allude to the idea of value-added methods they used to define the value of information. While Taylor defines value as that gained by the information it provides a client by a service or an information system (chapter 4),

McPherson regards "value-added" as that which is gained by an organization using information for a purpose versus what it costs to obtain the information.

Tefko Saracevic and Paul Kantor

Information scientists Tefko Saracevic and Paul Kantor (1997) stress the importance of viewing the value of information broadly with a focus on the property of the mind. Information value centers on how we think, what stirs us to do what we do, and how we go about meeting the demands of the problem at hand as individuals and collectively (socially). A number of studies highlight the distinction of estimating the value of information as that which our minds enable us to do and the services and information systems that help in the process. In this view, the value of information can include the "satisfaction that state of mind can provide, success, utility, relevance, completeness, specificity, accuracy, timeliness, impact, effort, difficulty, failure, frustration, and the like" (Saracevic and Kantor 1997).

Other Information Scientists

Fritz Machlup, an economist and information scientist, stated that the value of information and knowledge is tied together in its production and distribution. There are other views on how to estimate the value of information from an event. For example, a person can gain important information (value) by simply taking action or by estimating the possible outcome of the event relative to what one can gain by action taken without such knowledge (Sheridan 1988). Hartmann (1995) reports that the value of information differs based on the client's field of interest and expertise. Hartmann states that anthropologists' requirements (value) for information differ from other scientists. Mowshowitz (1992) suggests that the value of information rests on the ability of the information to help the user make decisions, choose one alternative from others, and take "control of actions." Svoboda (1995) claims the value of information increases with the degree of focus, interpretation, and accessibility. Lastly, Nicols and Isselman (1995–1996) provide an interesting perspective on the issue of defining the value of information by citing the competencies required to provide value in the services clients receive when they require information. These competencies include the ability to conceptualize information and knowledge of internal and external information resources, the understanding of information resource management, and the ability to synthesize and tailor information.

The Value of Information

Benefit

Benefit is defined as "something helpful or profitable" (*Oxford Dictionary* 1996, 52). An understanding of the benefits that accrue from the ADIK resource directly subsumes any source (agent, service, system, etc.) that augments or complements the human capacity for awareness, meaning, and understanding, and this creates a benefit.

Information professionals' perception of "benefit" comes from many different perspectives. In the information science literature, the term "benefit" is not generally operationally defined. One area in which "benefit" is directly examined is in the analysis, design, and evaluation of information systems. Although at times there is lack of understanding of information systems, other than the fact that they are computer-driven, the consensus is that they are essential and the organization can benefit from them. In this sense, benefits can grow from such systems when organizational change is needed to respond to new challenges and becomes a matter of necessity. Managers and other administrative people in the organization readily appreciate that such systems can provide the reasoning for the actions they plan to execute on behalf of the organization:

- Why is change needed?
- How certain are the benefits?
- How much will it cost to make the change?
- How sure are the costs?

The benefit from the information system is that it provides a rationale for action rather than action from political power (Dennis and Wixom 2000, 448).

Cost

Accessing, obtaining (retrieval), and using data, information, and knowledge for the things we need and require must involve costs. Information professionals are interested in these costs because they directly influence the level of services that are provided to individuals who depend on data and information as part of their work.

Bruce R. Kingma, a library and information scientist and professor at Syracuse University, New York, has extensively studied the costs that are part of functions and operations related to a library. These operations include the day-to-day operations, interlibrary loans, and journal subscriptions. Table 11.1 is the result of his extensive research in this area. Fixed and variable costs of production are those that remain the same regardless of the amount of energy and effort we apply to what we do. The costs of running a school, for example, can vary. More students require more teachers, meals, supplies, etc. The cost of running a library or a museum can vary based on how many people use the facility. Table 11.1 provides an example of such costs.

When ADIK costs refer directly to the management of an organization, the impact of the loss to problem solving and decision making when data and information are inadequately acquired, transmitted, and processed can be substantial. This could influence and compromise the integrity of the entire organizational structure and function.

Some of us may have had a problem with the inability to estimate or judge the value of information. For example, how much is the car worth that we are

Table 11.1.
Fixed and Variable Costs of Production.

Goods and Services	Time Period	Fixed Costs	Variable Costs
Copies of a novel	1 month	Editing, typesetting, author's time and effort, the building	Ink, paper, labor, postage for copies of the novel, marketing costs
Book publishing	1 year	The building	Cost per copy, author's time, set-up costs
Costs of a software program	3 months	Time and effort of programs	Packaging, CDs, and labor for copies
Books from the library	1 year	The library building	Librarians and books
Photocopies	1 day	Purchase of the photocopying	Paper, toner, or individual copy machine
Minutes of telephone service	1 day	Telephone circuits and network	An electric current, sometimes an operator
Viewing a television broadcast	1 hour	Labor, building, cameras, script, video, electricity	The electricity to power a television set (provided by the consumer)
Television broadcasting	1 year	Television building and broadcast	Labor, cameras, scripts, electricity

Source: Kingma (1996, 34).

intending to purchase? What is the value of spending time and money to obtain a degree in college when the salary from a job would lessen the burden of living on your own? Answers to these and many other questions could turn out to be quite significant in their consequences on our standard of living. We can obtain an idea of the complexity by examining table 11.2. For example, the value of the information for legal services to a client could rest on the background and experience of the lawyer, which is often difficult to estimate.

Jose Griffiths and Donald W. King (1986, 1993), both information scientists, have studied the value of services provided by libraries and other institutions (systems). Their area of interest is the role of time as a value of information. Time consumed in accessing and providing aid and service to clients is measured together with the time spent acquiring the information and knowledge commodities (books, journals, etc.). Resource use is the center of their attention. Their study of value is based on statistical measures applied to surveys, personal interviews, and other methods that determine application of resources. Time as value is translated into dollars paid for services rendered, the amount of usage of the resources, and the time spent in the use of these resources. Table 11.3 provides us with the results of one of their studies.

Information centers are extensions of the library environments. The time spent in serving these centers indicates their value in meeting their objectives. The sketches in figure 11.1 provide us with an idea of the value of these centers.

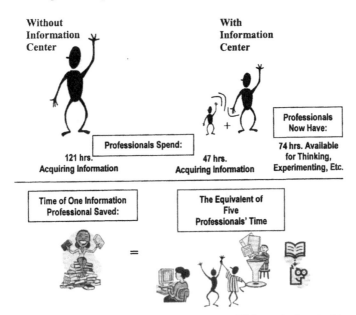

Figure 11.1. Information Centers. Source: Griffiths and King (1993, 89–126). Redrawn by S. Masters.

Table 11.2.
Markets with Imperfect Problems and Solutions.

Market	Problems	Solutions	
		Market	Government
Legal services	Client: quality of lawyer/legal service cannot be easily judged by client. Lawyer: guilt/innocence difficult to determine prior to employment	Lawyer's reputation and success, education, partnership in well-known firm, price	State bar exams, legal recourse of suing lawyer
Computer software	Customer: quality/usefulness of product difficult to judge prior to purchase. Seller: once purchased, customer has incentive to return product for refund after installation on hard drive	Limited guarantees, reputation of product/company, computer magazine reviews	Consumer product laws
Consumer credit	After receiving goods and services consumer has incentive to stop payments	Credit reports, requirements of collateral	Regulation of credit and credit reporting, criminal law
Insurance markets	Insuree incentive to misrepresent driving ability, health, quality of car, house, etc.	Physicals, home inspections, data on driving record, contractual obligations	Insurance laws and reporting agencies, criminal laws

	Incentive to take fewer precautions or less care when driving or maintaining home or health. Insurer incentive to underfund investments. Potential for declaring bankruptcy under large claims	for fire alarms, health care, etc., company reputations	
Labor markets	Employee incentive to misrepresent abilities, incentive to shirk while on the job. Employer incentive to misrepresent employee duties, dangers of workplace	Potential employee: education and work history, references. Potential employer's reputation, ability to terminate (fire/quit) employment	Regulation of employment contracts, regulation of workplace safety
Stock market	Incentive for corporate managers to initiate value/profitability of organization, uncertainty about corporate value	Corporate annual reports, investment experts, stock prices a signal of market information on corporate value, diversification of stock portfolio	Enforcement of general accounting principles, criminal law, monitoring by Securities and Exchange Commission
Journal subscription	Individual subscriber/library cannot determine quality of journal until after paying for and receiving subscription	Journal reputation and age, reputation of editors, citation of published articles, library use	None

Source: Kingma (1996, 105).

Table 11.3.
Time as Value.

Average Additional Time (of Professionals and Others on Their Behalf)
Required to Acquire Documents Provided by Libraries
If There Were No Libraries

	Journals	Books	Internal Reports	Other Documents
			Type of Document	
Time Spent by Professionals (minutes)				
Going to the library	20.9	26.7	0.6	14.1
Identifying needed documents	11.0	8.6	16.4	12.3
Locating a document	11.5	6.7	14.0	9.9
Obtaining a copy	2.2	2.8	4.6	4.6
Photocopying the document	3.6	4.2	4.1	4.1
Total	49.2	49.0	39.7	45.0
Time Spent by Someone Else on Behalf of Professionals (minutes)				
Going to the library	10.7	9.7	2.8	Unknown
Identifying needed documents	7.1	4.8	2.5	Unknown
Locating a document	2.4	3.0	1.3	Unknown
Obtaining a copy	3.5	1.6	0.9	Unknown
Photocopying the document	12.6	5.5	3.0	Unknown
Total	36.6	24.6	10.5	Unknown

Source: Griffiths and King (1993, 175). Reprinted with permission of SLA.

The Quality of Information

In chapter 4, we presented the factors that influence the quality of data (i.e., timeliness, reliability, accuracy, etc.). Now let's turn our attention to understanding that the quality of information is dependent on the quality of data. First, we should establish what is meant by the quality of ADIK systems as a resource in a world where technology is changing so rapidly and increasingly influencing each of our lives. What do we mean by quality? How do we know the quality of the data, information, and knowledge each of us uses every moment of our lives? When we shop for food—meat, fruits, and vegetables—the quality of these can easily be determined, often visually, or by taste, if necessary. It may not be as easy to determine the quality of the data, information, and knowledge (DIK) that come into our minds, that with which we do things, make decisions, and solve problems. Here we are not referring to data, information, and knowledge that society in general has allowed us to use and make available to others. Rather, we mean the quality of data, information, and knowledge that we use to solve problems and make decisions to run our lives.

Let's start with basics. We have learned that data are representations in some coded form of the energy that is received by our senses. If the energy that our sensors receive is not sufficient (weak), there is no response. Yet, curiously, this does not mean that if we do not have data that provide us with information, there is no awareness. The absence of energy that led to the lack of a light source can provide data about the state of the battery, the lamp, or other mechanisms that are used to shed the light. What we can say in this experience is that the quality of data is dependent on the state of the energy source and the ability of the receiver to receive the level of energy that is provided. Our ability to wake up at the sound of the alarm clock is dependent on how loud the alarm is that reaches our ears and our state at the time we receive that signal. That goes as well for the instance when someone shakes our shoulder to wake us up. One aspect of this quality of data is the capacity of the data to ensure responsiveness.

But it may not be that simple. Data appear on paper, in print, in lights, in paint, from people's mouths, and from film. Thus, when we consider the quality of DIK, we understand as well the medium through which these resources are provided to us and its impact on our awareness and our understanding. Media refers to the ways (light, paper, ink, radio waves, etc.) used to provide us and others with a sense of both what is and is not going on around us.

The quality—the excellence of data—depends on many factors. Two questions are considered particularly important. First, do the data tell us accurately the state of energy and matter (events) that are important to us, that is, do we have to do something or not? We can call this idea the isomorphic potential of the data, which means the ability of the data to tell us accurately the state of the world. The second question refers to the potential of the data to keep us aware. Let us look at these two aspects of the quality of data in our day-to-day experience.

For example, you received and proceeded to check your bank statement and found that a deposit you made was not included. You then become alarmed and immediately sought to ask why the missing item was not included. The fact that the data on your bank statement did not correctly relate to your action would indicate that the data provided in your statement was faulty. Someone or something made a mistake. There was a lack of correspondence (isomorphism) between what you did (happened) and what the data provided. The quality of the data you received was in question.

Data that do not match the capacity of the individual to receive and engage in the intended actions raise a question about the quality of the data. This means too much data, too little data, or data presented in a manner that does not instigate awareness and understanding affect the quality of the data. The potential of data to be manipulated either through exclusion or obfuscation (giving more than needed) reduces the quality of the data. Students often ignore their textbooks because the volume of data presented in the chapters challenges their capacity to be aware—and their memory as well.

At this point, we ask the question about the integrity of information and knowledge. Both of these depend on the quality of the data in responding to the questions of what, where, when, who, how, and why. Information deals with the questions of what, where, when, and who, and knowledge deals with how and why. We have learned that information and knowledge are considered as both human and physical resources. Information and knowledge as processes occur in our brains (minds). These processes are represented in physical products and actions that humans produce. A measure of the quality of information and knowledge is provided in the work of scientists and the many professions that are dependent on the quality of data, information, and knowledge and thus the integrity of information and knowledge. With this background, let us now examine some of the important factors that need to be considered when we attempt to understand the quality of DIK.

Accuracy as Quality

Perhaps one of the best ways anyone can understand the role of data, information, and knowledge accuracy is to apply it to a specific situation. Accuracy of DIK includes a number of things, ranging from the calibration (setting) of a timepiece, speedometer, weather/economic prediction, rail/air travel schedules, etc. In general, DIK accuracy can be viewed from the following four perspectives:

1. How sharp our senses (or technological sensors) are in capturing an event; how well instruments capture changes in temperature, climate, pollution, internal states of our bodies, space, etc. With poor glasses, you may not see what you should see for safety or other purposes.
2. The number of procedures, transformations (transactions) engaged in (taken) to move data, information, and knowledge from one place to another. Each time you move data from one place to another, you stand the chance of reducing its accuracy.
3. Coherence (sticking together) between human-machine operations and transactions demanded to engage an event. Moving data from one person to another or from one machine to another can change the accuracy of the data. Although the difference may be small for a particular incident, it can accumulate and lead to large errors in accuracy.

4. The degree of confusion that is generated by improper formatting of DIK. This leads to bewilderment, the result of the level of understanding, language, accurate translation. For example, how many times have we been confused by how airports present their departure and arrival schedules?

Timeliness as Quality

There are a number of ways that the information professional can consider timeliness as a quality of data, information, and knowledge. By timeliness, we mean that the information is available at the time we need and require it.

Obsolescence

Data on a particular subject can change quickly while some data never seem to change. Each day, new books are available to us on almost any subject. Before we realize it, new books on the subject appear that make the old book possibly obsolete. Data on a particular event that is continuously changing dramatically and continuously causes the DIK to bias the problem-solving and decision-making processes required in response to an event. This is an important problem for the field of information. Yet, information professionals are continuously studying the problem of obsolescence of material for a number of reasons, one of which would be storage. There is a limited amount of space for the collection of books on bookshelves. Another reason is that obsolescence can be a matter of value in addition to quality. Scholarly activities are very much dependent on DIK written in the distinct past, and although the DIK may be considered obsolete, their value to scholarship could be considered important.

Completeness and Format Check as Quality

Completeness is an idea that is subsumed in an understanding of data validation. A completeness check ensures that all data have been accounted for and entered. Format check ensures that data are of the right type (e.g., numeric) and are presented in the right format (e.g., month, day, and year) (Dennis and Wixom 2000, 321).

Age as Quality

Age as quality can mean the date of origin of DIK and its value to present thinking and work. The adage that those who hasten to ignore history will soon learn its value reflects the idea that the aging of data, information, and knowledge has a quality of its own—and, as a matter of fact, is the basis for scholarship. The other perspective on age as quality refers to the life cycle of information technology. All mechanical and electrical devices, ranging from the wheel and lightbulb to electronic devices (TVs, computers, etc.), age as a function of time and with this, change in the quality of the resource. Age, and thus, the efficiency (quality) of a particular technology are accounted for in the specifications accompanying that technology.

Source Availability as Quality

For any area where data, information, and knowledge are required to meet the demands of a task, it is of considerable importance that the source of such resources be identified and accessed. The transition between information (awareness) and meaning (knowledge) is of considerable interest to information professionals, particularly those whose interests focus on information retrieval. During the past decade and in the present, information scientists have been attempting to identify some of the basic principles and laws that could govern the search process for the information and knowledge needed and required to support a particular intellectual engagement, decision making, and problem solving. This aspect has been discussed in other chapters of this book. Our immediate attention is directed to the identification of a source of information and knowledge. Technology has aided considerably in the search for information and knowledge. Numerous databases can be brought to view via the computer. Services such as those provided by special and reference librarians, information/knowledge counselors, information brokers, and area specialists can be employed to identify specific sources required by individuals.

Level of Summarization

The quality and utility of DIK can be influenced by the completeness and clarity that is applied toward bringing together much of the source material to the client. This can be quite important when the time available and demanded of the task is limited. Care is taken in summarizing DIK so that what is given to the client or patron is not skewed in a specific direction or not supported by the locally available sources.

Format Check

This refers to insuring that the available data correspond directly to the source on which the data are based. Text and numeric data should carefully reflect the state (day, month, year) for that which the data represents. Graphs and other tables should be presented in a manner whereby the variables presented or described are accurate. As previously stated, a format check of the data can ensure that the data are of the right type (e.g., numeric).

Security and Quality

DIK can be compromised in different ways (discussed previously). It is sufficient at this point to briefly account for the following:

1. Copyright protects the authorship of the DIK source.
2. Documentation about the DIK system procedures enables a clear understanding of system operations and function, insuring the integrity of the system.
3. DIK systems have value. The value is commensurate with the quality of these resources. The efficiency and effectiveness of the DIK depend, to a considerable degree, on the steps taken to ensure that the resource is not tampered with, misdirected, or obliterated. The case of the Timothy McVeigh trial that followed the Oklahoma City bombing (wherein the FBI failed to account for literally thousands of reports considered relevant to the case) tells us how the security of DIK can serve both as a negative and a positive force in the actions that are taken.

A situation in which security and timeliness interfered with proper governmental responses happened during 9/11, shown in figure 11.2. Useful information that might have prevented the disaster existed, but a lack of communication between departments, caused by security walls and human possessiveness, blocked departments from realizing that the information was pertinent, in a timely fashion.

Other Dimensions of Quality

Data is continuously changing (transitory), so that the reason for the change from one moment to another is incapable of a fixed point of reference (i.e., backward-forward; forward-backward). Data are obscured for a particular time (temporal masking), then reappear without an acknowledgment of the time that they were obscured. Authorship of a particular source is unknown and the completeness of its ideas is taken into account when considering the validity of the source's data to support a claim or proposition.

The Integration of Information Resources

by S. Masters
with ESRI fonts
and MS Clip Art.

"**Lack of resources impeded work before 9/11, FBI says.**"
* All quotes—The Associated Press, Wire Service, Sept. 25, 2002.

What they mean is that the resources and leads they did have weren't integrated:

No 9/11?

"At a hearing…lawmakers asked what would have happened if someone had linked the two earlier. Could the attacks have been prevented?"*

The two leads arrived at FBI headquarters weeks apart in the summer of 2001. The first, from a Phoenix agent, warned that Osama bin Laden's terrorists may be learning to fly at U.S. schools. The second described a suspicious student pilot in Minnesota named Zacarias Moussaoui. But the leads weren't put together until after terrorists crashed four hijacked airliners at the World Trade Center, the Pentagon, and a rural Pennsylvania field.*

Yes, it happened because—

An FBI counterterrorism supervisor told them it was unlikely those leads ever could have been connected, given headquarters' limited staff and poor computer systems…I don't think one individual could keep this all in his head.*

What if all computers had the same information (for example, if they had been connected to the same database)?

Or what if someone had picked up the phone and called another government department?

He's the same man!

Figure 11.2. U.S. Government Information Systems. Information systems must be able to talk to each other—so that there can be an integration of data, information, and knowledge from multiple sources. If it had been augmented by even a low technology like a telephone and people's willingness to share, information might have saved the day!

The Value of Knowledge

In this text, we have differentiated knowledge from information by defining knowledge as the human state of understanding and the product of that state represented in some physical form. In this view, knowledge is dependent on information, and in turn, information is dependent on data. The values of these three human and physical resources are interdependent.

Society's recognition of and commitment to education and the importance applied to literacy and learning provide a starting point in considering the value of knowledge. One way to view the value of knowledge is to relate the resource to our capacity to question the how and why of experience.

From one perspective, we can readily appreciate the value of knowledge: the meaning, the understanding of the function, and significance of those things around us. We go to school to obtain knowledge, learn history, geography, arithmetic, the nature of energy and matter. We appreciate those who have knowledge and contribute to it. We appreciate and benefit from those in and out of government who run our country, provide and maintain law and order, protect us from threat and crime, as well as those who provide us with these resources that maintain our health.

Now we ask how information professionals and scientist relate to these benefits. The value of knowledge derives from the structure of environments (people, technology, and procedures) that information professionals create and serve. The value of knowledge is derived from information systems analysts and designers who structure and evaluate such environments, enabling us to extend our capabilities to understand what we need and want to do.

Knowledge is a property of our minds that at times is reproduced or transmitted in physical form—by smoke, odors, paper, film, music, art, even vague physical gestures. Let us examine first the value of knowledge as a process, then as the result of that process.

Value as Process

Knowledge as a resource and as a property of the mind provides us with one view of the value of knowledge. Nicholas Rescher, a philosopher from the University of Pittsburgh, refers to the value of knowledge as the cognitive economy (Rescher 1998). The value of knowledge is connected to the process of communication, giving ideas, thoughts to others. In this view, knowledge is a basic need of humans. Lack of knowledge can represent real discomfort and a source of puzzlement. Further, humans desire knowledge. It reduces the possibility of loss while providing the prospect of gain. Knowledge has value against the price of ignorance, lost opportunity, and even death. While knowledge represents power, people realize that not sharing it with others can be counterproductive. Rescher, a prominent philosopher, states that it should be understood that knowledge, as a process of the mind, has a price tag in the time, effort, and ingenuity that is applied to ensure its presence.

Value as Product

Fritz Machlup devoted a lifetime of scholarly attention and research to understanding and estimating the value of knowledge. Although directed toward the cost/benefit involved in the production and use of information and knowledge, Machlup (1983) bridges the value of information and the value of knowledge. To Machlup, the value of information is not necessarily the value of knowledge. He advises that something will not have value if there is no need for it (need versus requirement). Basically, values are based on our expectations, not on what we don't obtain (regrets). Knowledge is valued not because of what we have but by that which we do not have (ignorance). The value of knowledge centers around how much we are willing to pay to get it. Moreover, the fact that we may value knowledge does not necessarily mean that we will act based on it.

One of the more approximate measures of the value of knowledge is education. Schools are the repositories of knowledge. By using the base year of 1972, Rubin, Huber, and Taylor provide us with some measure of the value of knowledge through the costs that are applied to it in table 11.4.

Table 11.4.
The Cost of Education in Billions of Dollars. Although it was derived in 1972, the principles behind it are still relevant.

At-home mother's foregone earnings	9.3
Preschool	1.4
Elementary and secondary	
Monetary expenses	54.0
Implicit expenses	5.9
Students' foregone earnings	47.0
Higher education	
Monetary factors	20.8
Implicit expenses	6.7
Student's foregone earnings	27.8
Education in church	8.0
Education in military	4.3
Commercial education	1.7
Federal programs	0.7
Public libraries	1.0
Total	**188.6**

Adapted from Rubin, Huber, and Taylor (1986, 16).

Administration of ADIK

When should some data, information (what, where, when, who), or knowledge (how, why) be useful? That depends on the task. It also depends on the criteria established for the satisfaction (completion) of the task. This generally includes a validation check, discussed previously. The legal profession has established norms for the admissibility of the DIK in court that conform to certain standards (rules of evidence) on which the legal profession is based.

Information professionals' interest in the admissibility of DIK centers on the following:

1. Identification of the need and the extent to which this identification relates to an appropriate requirement of an individual or organization that satisfies the need.
2. Authentication of the source.
3. Correlation of the DIK source to the client's need and requirement.

SUMMARY

We have learned that data, information, and knowledge are both physical and human resources. As resources, they have value and quality. This value can be estimated based on costs that are part of their acquisition and usage. As well, the value of these resources can be judged based on their quality, namely accuracy, timeliness, availability, completeness, aging, admissibility, clarity, formatting, and security.

EXERCISES

1. What are some of the problems a student is likely to face in judging the value of a textbook in helping to obtain a good grade for an examination?
2. Based on your understanding of the differences between data, information, and knowledge, what would you claim to be the main factor or factors that discriminate between the value and quality of these resources?
3. Identify the problem or problems likely to be faced when a person presents a quotation (from any source) in an English composition assignment without citing the reference accurately.
4. Individuals refer to "shelf life" for items that are stored and accessible for a particular time. Relate this idea to the value or quality of a knowledge resource (books, periodicals, etc.).

5. Listed items on a credit report for an individual state whether bills have been paid on time. These items are kept on the report by the credit agency for seven years. These reports are used by financial institutions to support decisions made about the credit allowed to individuals. Discuss the value of this practice as a quality of information or knowledge measure.

6. A member of the family is diagnosed with a medical problem, and you want to find information about it on the Web. How will you evaluate the information you find and how will you decide which are high-quality sources?

12

Security, Privacy, and Ethics

Yours is mine and mine is yours.
Shared but not in impunity.

—*Anthony Debons*

LEARNING OBJECTIVES

- Assess the relationship among security, privacy, and ethics.
- Summarize the potential ethical issues involving the use of ADIK systems according to system components.

OVERVIEW

Political systems vary in their views on the ways that individual privacy and ways of behavior are defined and supported. These views are important because they correlate with the manner in which data, information, and knowledge systems are designed and evaluated. The prevalence of threat to national security increases the attention applied to data, information, and knowledge systems and their role in safeguarding individual and collective liberties. Thus, a number of issues are important to the information scientist. If information is valuable, then what are the factors that make it secure? Are the methods used to obtain, employ, manage, preserve, and distribute information from numerous individual and collective sources in the application of financial and medical status ethical? Do the methods conform to acceptable standards? This chapter directs its attention to these security issues.

Security

Information technology is varied. It includes tools such as sensors (radar, sonar, satellites, MRI, PET) and other devices that can acquire data as small as the smallest needle in a haystack! Information technology includes cell phones, computers, and techniques such as artificial intelligence, storage devices such as radio frequency identification (RFID) tags, and even robots that help us handle dangerous substances and vacuum our floors. These tools can do much good as well as harm. They enable us to obtain and process data, information, and knowledge in amounts that we could not begin to imagine just a decade ago.

One of the major impacts of information technology is that it makes large amounts of data accessible to others about almost every detail of our lives. Each time we buy an item at a store with a credit card, that transaction is recorded and assembled by someone, some agency who has an interest, private or general (commercial), to serve a purpose. The interest of the information scientist is to learn how such technologies can best be used to improve our lives.

While information technologies can help humans in many ways, this technology can also be used to harm people. While the computer can process large amounts of data to help our understanding of many aspects of our lives, the computer can be used to hurt people. The computer is an interesting tool because it could cause crime as well as be the object of a crime. By making data about a person's credit line on a credit card available, persons could use the credit card (or Social Security) number obtained from the computer to make purchases against another individual's credit line. The owner of the credit card usually discovers the fraudulent act long after the transaction has occurred. Computers can be used to harm the capacities of other computers to provide important data. Understanding how computers work inside and out, criminal hackers can disrupt what computers do by creating what is called a virus. A virus is a computer program that attaches itself to another program, thereby providing false data or no data at all. There are many kinds of viruses (application, system, etc.). Computer scientists continuously study how these viruses can be identified and dealt with. Computer and information scientists are working together to establish ways to deal with such computer crimes (e.g., the CERT Coordination Center at Carnegie Mellon University).

Privacy

Supreme Court Justice Louis Brandeis recognized in 1890 that "the right to be left alone is the most valued right of civilized man" (Warren and Brandeis 1890, 643). Information technology raises important social issues about privacy. Cameras and sensors located in stores, libraries, office buildings, schools, and even on individuals can continuously monitor the presence and behavior of all things (human/material) within their scope of view. These sensors can serve as tools to ensure our safety. They can be used as surveillance of all human and other activities. This surveillance can be used to follow the moment-to-moment activity of the individual for whatever purpose, legal and/or illegal. Information systems consisting of sensors, transmission links, and computers enable the government to collect data on all aspects of an individual's life, workplace, and community. Computers account for what individuals do at work—for example, how many breaks an employee takes during a given shift or how often the Internet/World Wide Web is accessed for personal communication rather than for work. As a matter of fact, the government authorizes these checks. This monitoring of privacy can be substantial and significant.

The government has come to realize the impact of information technology and has established laws to protect the right to privacy of the individual. The Privacy Act of 1974 gives the individual the right to control what records can be collected, held, used, or given to others. The records cannot be used without the individual's consent. The individual has the right to have a copy of the records and to make changes to them as warranted. When used, the records should be used for lawful purposes, kept up to date, and their use safeguarded. The records could be used if there is a public need for them and when the individual's rights are not violated. In another act (1992), the transmission of unsolicited information (advertisements) through fax (written material transmitted electronically) is prohibited. Yet how many of us experience unsolicited telephone calls asking for donations, subscriptions to magazines, or other endeavors? There is a requirement for laws restricting this abuse of an individual's privacy.

Ethics

Webster's New World Dictionary defines ethical as "conforming to the standards of conduct of a given profession" (1966, 499). Basically, "ethics" deals with matters of right or wrong behavior (moral issues) that a person engages in during the conduct of their profession. The medical profession, for example, guides its ethical behavior by the Hippocratic oath, in which doctors pledge to hold morality as the highest standard in their work. In information science, the behavior of information professionals (information scientists, computer scientists, and others) is guided by codes established by professional societies. There are numerous societies interested in safeguarding the rights of individuals in the use and misuse of information and knowledge. People in these societies include professionals in specific parts in their field (computer scientists, librarians, information managers, archivists, etc.).

Four issues have been identified as representing ethical conduct in the information age:

1. Accuracy: responsibility for the authenticity, fidelity, and accuracy of information. Accountability for errors.
2. Property: ownership of information. This includes the price paid for the exchange, identification and ownership of the transmission mediums, and how a scarce source of information is to be allocated.
3. Accessibility: What information does a person or organization have a right or a privilege to obtain? Is public information provided equitably to everyone?
4. Privacy: Divulging information about oneself to others. What information should one be able to keep strictly to oneself?

One of the chief functions of the information professional is the analysis, design, and evaluation of data, information, and knowledge systems that augment human capacities. The following are some of the ethical issues identified for the analyst, designer, and evaluator of augmented data, information, and knowledge systems:

1. ADIK systems can play an important role in society. How can we learn about the impact of these systems on society and the individual?
2. The influence of education and training on his/her perceptions regarding the work engaged in and issues pertaining to appropriate standards of behavior.
3. The need to acknowledge and define the human and institutional dimensions that are part of the events and to which these systems must respond.

Ethics and the Augmented Data, Information, and Knowledge System

ADIK systems in the hands of individuals, organizations, and institutions are important tools for governing people while also enabling these entities to meet the demands of the broader environment. These systems, in their entirety and in part, are complex and often embedded in many functions that are part of the data, information, and knowledge environment. For example, hardware sensors can be installed at different locations in the environment, thus avoiding the physical presence of human agents who would serve the same purpose. A wide variety of transmission devices (flags, sirens, telephones, radios, etc.) can transport data from one location to another. Individuals, likewise, have the capacity to distribute data, information, and knowledge to others at different places and at different times. Individuals have the ability to process data with or without technological assistance. In the course of each of these transactions that are often part of an ADIK system, there is the possibility of error (capricious and/or intended). This can influence directly the solution of problems, the making of decisions, and the distribution of knowledge that could significantly affect the well-being of both individuals and organizations. The following are some of the analysis and design factors of the essential components of an ADIK system that can materially impact individuals and institutions.

Event

The system captures only those aspects of an event based on the analyst's or designer's point of view and/or preference. This can include ignoring certain aspects of events by pretending they are transitory or unimportant without documenting the rationale, which can distort data and/or information. Failure to account for the details of an event because of the likely consequences that would ensue if reported also can create distortions. Adding aspects (variables) to an event beyond those that are captured by sensors can do the same. Not documenting an aspect of an event to insure that it doesn't interfere with the analyst's desired perceptions is another source for errors.

Acquisition Subsystem

By focusing a sensor on a specific aspect of an event, for a specific purpose not in line with system needs and requirements, a misperception is created. Obtaining more data than needed to achieve personal or institutional objectives or gathering personally identifiable information (not in public space) without permission of the individuals is ethically questionable.

Transmission Subsystem

Obtaining and forwarding data not relevant to the system and directed to personal ends, creating noise to disrupt data flow, and using someone's name or PIN to access computers are unethical uses of an ADIK system.

Processing Subsystem

Processing problems include providing more data than needed and required to support a decision, failure to check the assumptions that support the organization and presentation of data to the user (decision maker, problem solver) of the system, and failure to document changes in coding or database structure.

Utilization Subsystem

Problems in utilizing data include applying personal values that go beyond the available data for decision making and problem solving and avoiding data that would indicate errors in judgment in the decision-making/problem-solving process.

Transfer (Communication) Subsystem

Communication problems include creating unnecessary complexity in the data received on which the decision was based (obfuscating), informing others of matters in order of importance not consistent with the available data or their interests (ordering), and highlighting data that is not consistent with the importance of content, but consistent with individual, selfish purposes (centering). Purposefully delaying an action for a benefit (the "float") or preserving, removing, or excluding information from the system or services (such as a website) because it conflicts with an individual's personal views, religion, etc., also create problems in communicating data.

SUMMARY

It has been said that information and knowledge represent power. One of the responsibilities of an information scientist is to understand when and how data, information, and knowledge can be incorporated in the analysis and design of systems that are intended to help us live life efficiently. There are parts of our lives that we would like to keep to ourselves. Exactly how this requirement for privacy can be safeguarded in the structure of our systems for the public good is an aspect that is important to the work and study of today's information scientist. Lastly, it could be said that there is always a right or wrong way to do almost anything, but the distinction is usually not a simple either/or choice. Understanding difficult points of views, questioning assumptions, and understanding our own biases are all critical for ethical actions and reflect moral issues. Different people have different views as to what is right or wrong and the human behavior related to it. We search and yearn for standards by which we can guide our actions and keep things secure. More and more, we are finding that the technology around us directs what we can do and do better, often at a price, but almost always with a sense of power and purpose. The information scientist's role in the creation and assessment of data, information, and knowledge systems is critical in reminding us to ask the "why" questions. We must remember that although we can do something with technology, it doesn't always mean we should.

EXERCISES

1. Why is cheating on an exam or test considered to be an unethical behavior? Respond to this question from the information science point of view.
2. Jim Dobbs was a homeless person who found shelter in the local library during the cold winter months. Jim represented a problem to the librarian because of his dirty attire and lack of sanitary habits. The librarian asked Jim to leave the library because of his condition. Jim resisted and mentioned to the librarian that the library was a public place. Was the librarian acting appropriately in this case? If not, why not?
3. The cost of textbooks is increasing yearly. Meanwhile, advances in our understanding of technology are also increasing. What factors should be of concern to the information scientist related to these circumstances?
4. Students may be concerned that they do not know what harmful things are really going around in school. This could be dangerous. What steps other than "stepped up" security can be taken to insure that the students are always informed as to what is going on and yet maintain privacy of the students?
5. Is privacy of information the same as privacy of knowledge? Which is most important? Explain why you think so.

13

The Future of Information Science:
The Knowledge Sciences

Wonder, dream with the sickle
To reap the future.

—*Author Unknown*

Figure 13.1. "Daddy, Tell Us What the Twentieth Century Was Like."
By permission of Bunny Hoest. Source: *Parade Magazine*, April 7,
2002.

LEARNING OBJECTIVES

- Identify some of the world conditions that will direct the future of information science.
- State why it is accurate to consider information science as one of the knowledge sciences.
- List at least one aspect of each of the subsystems of the augmented data, information, and knowledge (ADIK) system that can be expected to change.

OVERVIEW

Although information science has its roots in antiquity, as we have learned, current information science is shaped by dramatic developments in technology and the responsiveness of ADIK systems to current events. An understanding of these factors and how they can influence career development is relevant to those who aspire to devote their working lives to such a purpose. The present chapter identifies relevant sources that sketch the present and future direction of the science. It identifies several areas that merit attention as to their influence in shaping a career in the science. Lastly, this concluding chapter proposes an overall view of what can be considered the knowledge sciences and the function of information science as part of that perspective.

Introduction

The information revolution emerged as the result of many technical and theoretical advances in response to military requirements. These advances provided us with a greater span of awareness from earth to space. We are now in the early stages of the knowledge revolution fueled by advances in data acquiring, transmitting, and processing technologies that promise to extend the rapid growth in knowledge that started early in the twentieth century. Information scientists—with library, computer, and communication scientists—are now shaping this knowledge revolution to serve the common good (from processing to insight).

It is difficult to predict the future. What we can say about the future is that it is unknown. But we can reflect on the state of things today and project them as the objectives for tomorrow. For this, we examine three sources, beginning with the World Future Society, whose mission is to examine and comment about the future. We will inventory the interests of information scientists and other information professionals as represented in the work reported at their annual convention as the second source. A third source is contemporary literary commentary (books, news, etc.).

The World Future Society

The purpose of the World Future Society is to forecast trends and develop ideas about the future. It publishes a magazine that includes the thoughts of scientists, technologists, and others about the future. The society forecasts the following (World Future Society 1998):

- Forecast 1: The "echo-boom" generation, comprising eighty million people born between 1977 and 1997, will soon wield even more economic power than their baby boomer parents.
- Forecast 2: "Tissue engineering," the growing of new human organs, skin, and cartilage, will become one of the hottest growth areas of biotechnology. A $400 billion market in health services alone, the technology can also be used to make food, clothes, and other products.
- Forecast 3: The "war on terrorism" may spur the creation of a new "Marshall Plan" for the Third World. Compared to global military expenditures, investments in eliminating poverty and improving living conditions, the root causes of terrorism, are modest: as little as $9 billion per year could offer near-universal access to clean water and sanitation in developing countries. According to development experts, $13 billion annually could provide basic health and nutrition for all.
- Forecast 4: The ten most important new technologies for the next ten years are: genetic mapping, super materials, high-density energy sources, digital high-definition television, miniaturization, smart manufacturing, antiaging products and services, medical treatments, and hybrid-fuel vehicles, to name a few.
- Forecast 5: Most of the major cities in the developing world will face severe water shortages in the next two decades. By 2009, at least 3.5 billion people will run short of water, almost ten times as many as in 1995.

Of course, all these forecasts are dependent on the data, information, and knowledge systems that enabled their gathering and construction. Indeed, these and other forecasts are based on the results of current data, information, and knowledge systems. Of great interest to the information scientist as well as the informed citizen are the following projections also derived from ADIK systems.

Computing Research Association

In June 2002, the Computing Research Association, supported by a grant from the National Science Foundation, held a conference at the Airlie House in Virginia to discuss and explore the grand research strategies in computer science and engineering, with particular attention to the role of information systems. They identified five major challenges (Computing Research Association 2003):

- Challenge 1: Determine the best use of information technology to help humans deal with events that may be difficult to predict and respond to.
- Challenge 2: Discover ways that information systems (software agents, robots, etc.) can help increase productivity and effectiveness.
- Challenge 3: Learn how to use information systems to help individuals learn and increase their potential.
- Challenge 4: Discover how to analyze and design systems so they can be assured to function efficiently and effectively when needed.
- Challenge 5: Find ways in which to use technical parts and functions to help humans do more and more important things with information technology.

Professionalism and the Future

One way that we can develop some estimate of the future of information science is to examine the works and interests of information professionals now in the field and in the laboratories who are currently advancing the science. The annual meeting of these professionals, in which they report on their work in progress, is a source that can provide an estimate as to where the science is now and where it is headed in the near future. The following are some of the areas of work and study that library, information, and communication scientists share.

- Digitalization of information and knowledge: retrieval and use;
- Global electronic access to data, information, and knowledge;
- Greater attention to the application of information systems in specialized areas (e.g., medicine, law, disaster control, etc.);
- Wireless communications and computing in library and information centers;
- Expansion of interests in cognitive processes in reference work;
- Use and management of the Internet/WWW.

Specific Areas of Implementation and Future Developments

Distance Learning

One can attend and complete an educational program at a school, college, or university far away from home via lectures and seminars that are presented electronically. There will be many advances in the way that courses are conducted, enabling instructors to use computers and other technological techniques in improving student learning.

Computer Sensory Recognition

Voices, handwriting, eyes, fingerprints, and optical devices are coupled with computers, enabling people to interact with machines and with each other. Privacy and sensitivity concerns are also pushing these developments.

Parallel Processing

Large mainframe computers are becoming important again after having been overshadowed by personal computers. These supercomputers have more powerful capacity due to massive parallel processing technology (figure 13.2).

Figure 13.2. Big Ben the Supercomputer. Big Ben is a Cray XT3 MPP system, named after a Pittsburgh Steeler, at the Pittsburgh Supercomputing Center. It can perform ten trillion calculations per second! Photo courtesy of the Pittsburgh Supercomputing Center.

Intelligent Agents

Knowledge robots, navigators, and other intelligent software agents will filter and retrieve information routinely for users as computer capacity increases and is more widely applied at all levels and for a greater variety of tasks.

Embedded ADIK

Presently, computers run many things without ever being seen. These computer chips are embedded in almost everything that is touched and used. More and more, they will become part of our daily lives without most of us realizing it.

Expert Systems

Expert systems will increase in their ability to aid problem solving and decision making. This will enable information scientists to apply this approach in the design of ADIK systems used for personal and organizational management, medical diagnosis, engineering, and other fields.

Computer Translation

Computers will help us translate languages found throughout the globe. The translations will become more accurate and rapid. Optical computers will use the smallest unit of light energy to code information, enabling the processing of data at almost unbelievable speed and in large quantities.

A Projection of Possibilities

The immediate future of information science will be influenced heavily by the data production and dissemination trends that emerged in the first decade of the twenty-first century. What are these trends? First, with the advent of digital-only data production devices (e.g., new generation of telephones, digital cameras, and recorders) the need to have a stand-alone analog to digital converters is likely to disappear by 2015. Masses of digital data that will be created will require a qualitatively new approach to their management. The second trend that will continue to transform our lives is the convergence between consumer electronics and personal computing technologies. Just as stand-alone printers, scanners, copiers, and faxes gave way to a single device in the early 2000s, so will other data management devices. The age of multifunctional devices is here already, making data generation and transmission devices easy and convenient for humankind. Today many consumers can subscribe to data transmission services which enable them to use personal computers to watch television and talk to friends in other countries from their local library. The convergence of hardware and software will continue as well. In fact, similar to operating systems in mobile phones or computer chips in automobiles, most devices people use in the near future will operate with software that is built into a piece of hardware. Conversely, the demand for operating systems that would accomplish a multitude of tasks and provide interface and management of multiple devices will increase (Sterostine 2008).

Michael Dertouzos (1998), a noted information scientist, was the director of MIT's research lab for twenty years before his death in 2001. He spent his life analyzing the information age's inception and growth—ever since he was an undergraduate student. Based on his expertise, he wrote a book titled *What Will Be*, which highlights his predictions for the future of information sciences. It should be stated that what Dertouzos projected for the future is now in the present reality in many instances.

Dertouzos claims that the word "cyberspace" will be replaced by what he calls the Information Marketplace. He defines it as a twenty-first-century village marketplace where people using computers buy, sell, and freely exchange information and information services—or will the computers be agents with "intention, i.e., intelligence and free will?" (Dertouzos 1998, 10). In the Information Marketplace, people will use new technologies to simply perform a variety of actions. For example, Dertouzos talks of a World Shop, a store where a person can shop for anything—from a car to clothing—by entering a cubicle equipped with the latest technologies. Holographic projections, goggles, video screens, a mouse, specialized gloves, and other new technologies would let the user try out products before buying them. A person shopping for a dress will be able to see herself in the dress before it is actually made. The shop may also be able to tailor the user's interests from their selections during past visits. The interactive technology would take shopping into the next century by adding attractive technology and letting manufacturers make products on demand rather than before they are sold. "Just-in-time manufacturing" already exists and is being applied more and more to consumer goods.

Human computer interfaces have changed since Dertouzos's projections in 1998. Gloves let computers register precise finger movements, and glasses and head-tracking helmets with mechanical electromagnetic and optical gadgets can track your eye and head movements so that the computer knows where you are looking. This technology could be useful for developing glasses that can depict images normally seen on a computer (such as e-mail and television) by simply moving your eye to the left and up, for example.

Perhaps the most notable human/computer tool he describes is speech recognition. This is leading to voice-activated lights, computers, cars, almost anything that could be reached by voice (cell phones) instead of by normal manual techniques. Computers can now translate voices into a variety of languages, making a phone call from Japan to the United States possible even though the two people on the phone do not speak the same language. This leads to literacy programs that can recognize the mistakes being made by the person trying to read. This is better accepted by those who are trying to learn to read because they will be less embarrassed. Machines are infinitely patient.

Bank transactions have changed as well. Digital credits are passed from a buyer to a seller like cash, using a number given to you by the bank. It is untraceable like cash. Another advancement, called micropayments, has been invented that will allow for electronic transactions that convey small amounts of money in units of 1/1,000 of a dollar. A recipe for apple pie might cost 256/1,000 of a dollar (25.6 cents), or a song to be downloaded might cost 60/1,000 of a dollar (6 cents).

People's daily lives will change as well. A program could be created that has music built into your bed as an alarm clock, with selections coming from an initial questionnaire and individual tastes read from modifications over the years. Again, this implies thinking machines that can tailor their performance (in this case, songs) to user interest. Programs could exist that would allow the user to see what they will look like in certain clothes while getting ready in the morning. The program would inventory available clean clothes, and voice commands ("formal"/"informal") would be used to tell what style of clothing the user is looking for on that day.

Video games, which are already being played online and on home systems, will become even faster and more realistic and will incorporate more complex actions such as speech, goggles, body suits, and window walls which will be used to display superb graphics and game play.

Health care will be improved by making lifelong medical records available to any distant physician rather than being broken up into many different doctors' offices in handwritten paper files. Dertouzos (1998) also talked about Guardian Angel, a product that will monitor a newborn baby's medical history step by step. This could determine potential conflicts between prescribed drugs and patterns that may forecast potential illness and would allow for more accuracy in both diagnosis and treatment.

The way that we learn will no doubt be affected in the future. Although they already exist, simulators will become faster and more realistic. A person could see exactly how it looks and feels to drive a car or fly a plane without ever moving an inch. There may also be simulations that are educational in other ways. For example, you could put a teenager through a simulation of a peer pressuring him or her to do drugs, or a simulation for a CEO that would allow him or her to talk to a union representative or avert a crisis.

That last thought brings us to businesses. E-commerce will undoubtedly grow even larger as we move into Dertouzos's Information Marketplace. Manufacturing by the order will also increase as people pick out exactly what they want, and then the company can make it for them. That would cut down on costs for the company because they would never produce products that would go unsold. All organizations will benefit from technologies such as visualization, simulation, rapid assembly, and lifelong product monitoring.

According to Dertouzos's (1998) views, people who go to work will not report to an office but to a "work center." A work center is a place with high bandwidth, a cafeteria, group work software, and other technologies that will be important in the Information Marketplace. People at work centers would work at different jobs but use the place for its technological advancements as well as for a chance to interact with people—which doesn't happen when you work from home unless you have housemates or preschool/homeschooled children.

Governments will use technologies like electronic polling and voting. It is valuable for emergencies as well as for a general poll. Yet, if governments can instantly poll everyone, they may think they have a license to do it very often, leading to leaders who do not think for themselves but only react to what the constituents want them to do. The military will also be affected. A soldier may find himself or herself behind enemy lines, and then he or she can put up an instant network that can go up within minutes. A commanding officer can then see exactly where the soldier is and provide him or her with directions for where to go, showing the soldier radar and satellite of places that he or she cannot see.

A major issue concerning any new economic trend such as the Information Marketplace is whether it will affect the gap between rich and poor. The Information Marketplace might increase the gap between rich and poor slightly because poor people may not use the Information Marketplace as much, while those who can afford it will rely on it more and more. Another issue is employment. Will the new technologies of the Information Marketplace create more jobs? Dertouzos (1998) asserts that it will increase productivity slightly but will have no upward pressure on the employment rate. History suggests he may be too pessimistic about this.

Finally, Dertouzos (1998) talks about a "work-free society" deep into the future, a couple of centuries away. In this futuristic society there will be fully automated factories and fully automated service centers. People of the world will do no manual/mental work because they will derive all the revenue that they need from the machines they own. Their machines will make other machines, and the owners would just sit back and do whatever they want. Some people would use this time effectively to pursue hobbies, art, or spend time with people, while others would simply vegetate in front of a media-producing device—more immobile than even today's "couch potatoes." These projections exist in selected ways now (e.g., ATMs). But these machines require maintenance, etc., so jobs are created by automated services.

The Knowledge Sciences

The world of the future, although impossible to predict, can be guessed at. Throughout the millennium, humans have continuously sharpened their sensory capabilities through the tools they have developed and the new insights that were possible. The emergence of symbol-processing capabilities has opened new vistas for experimentation far beyond those of past millennia. Information—the product of awareness—is more than plentiful; it is often rather overwhelming. The next stage is extending this capability to meaning and understanding the needs and requirements of a complex (and at times threatening) world. There lies the challenge. The what, where, when, and who questions can be answered almost instantly today, thanks to technology developed in the past century. And the pace continues to accelerate. The vital how and why questions that Plato and Aristotle first raised now offer a future challenge for the information scientist.

Understanding the nature and exercise of knowledge has been a perennial human quest. We continuously question the how and why of our experiences to some degree. The central point for the information scientist is to determine how our technological resources can be used to extend or augment our capacities in dealing with knowledge.

It should be clear in the study of information science that the objectives of this science can merge with the work and interests of every other science and profession. As we have studied, the augmented data, information, and knowledge system brings together theories and laws from the many sciences in the analysis and design of such systems. Figure 13.3 illustrates major divisions within the knowledge sciences.

We are now moving toward the knowledge revolution. Translated to our present study, this means an integration of documentation, computers, and communications as a science that finds expression in the analysis, design, and evaluation of knowledge systems. Information science brings together the idea of interdisciplinarity. From another perspective, information science is a "uniscience." A uniscience is a science that integrates the various research activities and field experiences of the respective related sciences into a unified set of theories, laws, and principles.

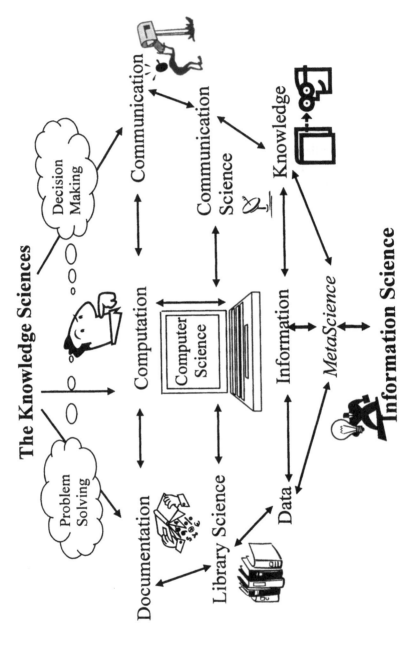

Figure 13.3. Major Divisions within the Knowledge Sciences. By A. Debons, drawn by S. Masters.

No less attention to questions of what, where, when, and who will continue to be required in the business of dealing with the complexity of life and the circumstances that it presents, but life will demand a greater focus on the integration of the questions of how and why. Such circumstances as hurricanes, tornadoes, climate change, poverty in the global environment, and control of terror will demand knowledge systems that can efficiently and effectively respond to such states. Greater availability of data—and thus awareness (information)—will increase the demand for understanding (knowledge). This includes the ability to analyze, evaluate, and synthesize current and projected states of events. Advances in technology will augment human capacities beyond those now present in current data, information, and knowledge systems. In the hands and minds of future information scientists lies a future of challenge and adventure.

Within the framework of the knowledge sciences, advances in sensor, transmitting, and processing technologies will continue to challenge information scientists for a long time to come. There are some aspects of the future of the knowledge sciences that merit our attention.

Library Science

The local library will continue to be around—a place where we can get our favorite books, where children can exercise their imaginations, and where others can explore their own interests. Changes are now occurring in the library that will continue to be part of the library landscape. There will be more computers around the library where individuals can explore many aspects of knowledge in ways that could not have been experienced a decade ago. Patrons can obtain articles from books and journals that are not physically available at the library where they are visiting. This is possible through the Internet and also interlibrary exchange where knowledge needed and required but located elsewhere can be obtained. There will be changes in the reference desk where the skilled reference librarian will serve almost like the local doctor, analyzing one's needs, identifying the requirements to meet such needs, and then prescribing a course of action (requirements) to meet these individual needs. Bookmobiles will continue to serve specific groups and communities where access to the library is not easy but perhaps with electronic technologies as well. Libraries will continue to be located in large commercial companies to serve specific needs of groups and individual workers in such companies. From the scientific perspective, data, information, and knowledge retrieval will continue to engage the interest and work of library scientists. Questions of access to documents (books, articles, etc.) that may infringe on local codes of ethics will continue to occupy the center of library science interest as the electronic age changes the nature and importance of the information and knowledge necessary to serve the common good.

Computer Science

With increasing advances in teletransmission and telecommunication, computers will increase the capability of the Internet, World Wide Web, and related systems to meet individual needs and requirements. This technological capacity to deal with the rapid growth of available knowledge will influence and extend the training of information professionals. These information professionals will utilize the resources of the virtual and digital library system, dissect the basic tasks faced by clients, diagnose the respective needs of clients, and match the available hard and electronic information and knowledge resources required of the tasks at hand.

Computer scientists will continue to explore and expand the power of computers to animate robots that augment human motor and cognitive capabilities in normal as well as hazardous environments on earth and in space. Sophisticated sensors (radar, sonar, even eyeglasses and hearing devices) that capture multidimensional aspects of events will be linked directly with computers in design to achieve medical, diagnostic, and investigative objectives. Vehicles will travel along major interstate superhighways guided by sensors allowing the driver the luxury of more composed, safe, and stress-free driving. Computer scientists will continue to establish new models of teaching—both in and outside the prevailing classroom—made possible by advances in computer technology.

Communication Science

Advances in communication science will continue to be directly influenced by understanding and advances in teletransmission technologies. These include the application of fiber optics and expanded network and bandwidth technologies. The mobile transmitting and receiving technologies (cellular phone, etc.) will establish, promote, and allow for greater freedom of communicative contact and expression. The electronic display (TV, etc.) will continue to dominate the communicative resource while radio and film will maintain their private and public interest as accessible entertainment, informative, and educational mediums. The communications scientist will be consumed by a greater interest in public policy regarding ethics, privacy, and censorship.

Information Science

The critical role of the augmented data, information, and knowledge system in public function and welfare will predominate. At present, information scientists are consumed by a wide spectrum of issues that overlap the attention of library, computer, and communication scientists. The professional organization ASIS&T, representing the interests of information scientists, is broad in perspective. In general, many sciences (disciplines) begin with a wide expression of interest in a subject. Subsequently, there is a greater refinement of focus, motivated by developments and discoveries that influence member interest in the science. Thus, there are many interrelated fields such as

- arts and humanities;
- automated language processing;
- classification research;
- computerized retrieval services;
- digital libraries;
- history and foundations of information science;
- human-computer interaction information, analysis, and evaluation;
- information architecture;
- information generation and publishing;
- information needs (seeking and use);
- information policy;
- knowledge management;
- library automation and networks;
- management of medical information systems;
- scientific and technical information systems;
- information and society;
- visualization, images, and sound.

The future of information science may be unclear, but the challenges to those who seek its understanding are defined. Events and situations, broad in scope and consequence, will continue to challenge the human will and capacities. This state of being will demand continued attention in maintaining and increasing the power of present ADIK systems to meet the challenge. The technologies that relate to these systems will increase rapidly with wider applications, all requiring skilled minds and hands. Present and future students and professionals of the science will assume an important identity and role in their ability to apply and synthesize the knowledge of all the sciences. The information age will merge with the knowledge age, fueled by advances in technology, and information scientists will face greater complexities, the result of prevailing and emerging cultural/political issues coupled with the increased use/misuse of energy resources that demand greater application of prevailing and future ADIK systems.

SUMMARY

The future portends significant changes. Longevity will continue to increase with growing knowledge of human physiology and health maintenance. Computers will continue to be increasingly invisible as they are incorporated throughout our homes, in the automobile, and throughout other places in our environment. These changes will have impacts on entertainment, the way individuals study and learn, the way that young are cared for, individual and collective health, local and international commerce, and political influence and processes. The Internet will continue to increase in importance as a medium for communication. Meanwhile, issues of privacy, ethics, and security related to the use of data- and information-processing technology will command increasing attention. These factors and others will create an increasing requirement for the services of information professionals—both practitioners and scientists—who, with engineers and physical, behavioral, and social scientists, can provide data, information, and knowledge systems to meet these demands.

EXERCISES

1. Apply what you have learned about information science to the kind of high school environment that students will be likely to attend ten years from now. Describe that environment. What kind of problems do you see ahead for that kind of school?
2. Based on the predictions that were provided for the knowledge sciences, what area do you estimate will be most important for the development of a career in information science? Explain.
3. Some claim that the computer will be invisible in years ahead, if not now. What can this mean for specialists in the knowledge sciences?
4. Describe what you consider to be the characteristics of the information professional of the future.
5. What do you consider to be the major similarities and differences in what computer scientists and information scientists study and do?
6. What common idea do the knowledge sciences share?
7. Discuss the relationship between information science and the knowledge sciences.
8. List the questions that come to mind with respect to the role of the information scientist in the library and then in the business environment.
9. Some claim that the library will not exist in the future due to the influence of the Internet and the resources it offers. Discuss.
10. Discuss the role of the information scientist in counteracting international terrorism.

Appendix

THE NATURE OF INFORMATION
By Edward M. Housman

Information is the substance that passes between us when I tell you something.
Information persists for a time, then fades back into chaos.
Information cannot move without making noise.
Laughter is information dancing.
Information occupies space.
And time.
It takes energy to move information.
Information is necessary for life, for any organized activity.
Information is form without substance, substance without form. Both.
Information, like light, has weight; a gigabyte weighs less than a fingerprint.

Information involves the displacement of form through space and time.
An insight is information crashing into information.
Information implies structure.
Information can be in motion or frozen in time.
Information is crystalline order in a cloud of chaos.
Information is the satisfying, perhaps disturbing, answer to a question.

The weight of a stone, and the information needed to describe it, are equal.
Information is a substance, a form; like light, both wave and particle.
Information has a solid state; it freezes into rigidity (storage).
Information has a liquid state; it flows (communications).

Like matter, it slowly crumbles (entropy).
Information is sculpture, an idea encrypted into nature, a fact.
Somewhere information moves; the cosmos rumbles, roars out the fact.
In their egocentricity, humans think that information is for us alone. Not so.

There are two kinds of information: the physical and the biological.
The cosmos would be immobile darkness without them.
One is a sortie of bits; aircraft in-formation.
One is a star screaming, "I am here!"
One requires no observer.
Two is essential to life, its very fiber.
Two is a cat doping out its prey, a flower opening to the sun.
Information makes all objects in the universe, and teenagers, jitter.
It is the great mystical life force that drives us through wisdom, to death.

The same information can be expressed in different ways: a voice, a letter.
Unlike matter, information can be in many places at once.
A handshake is information. A nod. A look. A sigh.
Information is formed by rubbing two bit-streams together.
Information dwells in bit-streams, on paper, on stone, in a gesture.
Information craves a medium, a shard of tumbling time-space to dwell upon.

Information is easily confused with knowledge, certainty, wisdom, and data.
The meaning of a picture, a scene, a sensation, is information.
Information glows in a sea of randomness.
An organization is not physical; it's people bound by information.
An organization, any organized activity, is impossible without information.

Noise and randomness are information's constant companions
Poetry is a tangle of bits on a pedestal, in the mind.
Poetry is information fireworks.
A poem is a hard, sparkling diamond of information.
Poetry is compressed insight, unstable and likely to explode.

The author's affiliation with The MITRE Corporation is provided for identification purposes only, and is not intended to convey or imply MITRE's concurrence with, or support for, the positions, opinions, or viewpoints expressed by the author.

Glossary

Abstract. A summary of what is included in a technical research paper; usually a paragraph included prior to the formal presentation of a written paper or technical presentation.

Accessibility. Rendering written, verbal (audio), graphic material available to others. This includes the access policy, which manages the delivery of materials based on certain laws, principles, and regulations.

Affect. In the broadest sense as used in psychology, refers to the feeling of experience (Gould and Kolb 1964, 13).

Application. A computer program that allows one to do what is needed and/or required outside of maintaining the computer itself.

Architecture. The design of a structure that conforms to certain functions or work.

Augmented data system. Methods, procedures, and related technologies that extend the human organizational capacity to account for states (events) that occur in space and time.

Augmented data and information system. An environment of people, technology, and procedures, the purpose of which is to extend the human capacity to be aware, this enabling the formation and execution of action.

Augmented data, information, and knowledge (ADIK) system. An environment of people, technology, and procedures, the purpose of which is to extend the human capacity to derive meaning and understanding of actions to be taken or not taken.

Awareness. Cognition; a source of both consciousness and unconscious states of being; a state of receptivity to energy and matter in time and space.

Bandwidth. The frequency that a range of energy (sound, light) uses when moving from one source to another.

Bits. Abbreviation of binary digit. The most basic unit of digital computing, a bit can be in only one of two states, zero or one (Cohen 1991, 93).

Bus. An electronic connection that allows a signal to move from one point in space and time to another.

Byte. A grouping of eight bits (see above). Bytes are commonly used to represent alphanumeric characters or the integers from 0 to 255 (Cohen 1991, 94).

Central processing unit (CPU). The brains of the computer. It performs all of the functions that are required of an electronic data processing technology.

Chief information officer. The top organization level position, the function of which is the management of all information resources (i.e., library, mailroom, computers, program scheduling, etc.).

Cognitive needs. Cognitive, an adjective, is a broad term applied to the work of the mind (brain). Need, a noun, is a state of absence, a want, often assumed as a requirement. In the present text, a cognitive need refers to the classification of the mental processes engaged when responding to the tasks and the interest (motivation) to do so.

Content. A noun; included in something. On a Web page, this is the meaning in the text, not the formatting.

Content of awareness. That which is experienced (consciously and unconsciously) both in cognition and affection (emotions).

Communication. A broad term that includes the role of language, the practice of journalism, the position of the media, and other sources that result in the transmission of data and information.

Data. Symbols organized according to a set of rules (algorithms) that allow processing for numerous purposes.

Data acquisition device. Usually considered as a sensor that scans the environment based on a program that serves a purpose. Humans, however, can serve as sensors for a similar purpose. Also, a human and/or technology that accounts for the presence of energy in space and time.

Data link layer. The connection through which data are transmitted from one component to another (*Computing Dictionary*, 129).

Data system. Interrelated, organized set of symbols that enables the execution of functions for a variety of purposes (e.g., census, weather, employment, etc.).

Database. A collection of related information in an easily accessible format such as in a table form or report (*Computing Dictionary* 1999, 131).

Design. The arrangement of people, technology, and procedures to achieve a specific function or objective.

EATPUTr. The structure (event, acquisition, transmission, processing, utilization, and transfer) used as a metaphor for an augmented data, information, and knowledge system.

Encapsulation. Placing a set of rules, usually related to telecommunications, that is presented in one way into another. Encapsulation is a process of finding all the details of an object that do not contribute to its essential characteristics

Feasibility study. An assessment to determine whether the user's needs and requirements can be met through the ADIK system that is requested.

Floppy disk. A storage device that is composed of a plate of thin, flexible ("floppy") magnetic storage medium encased in a square or rectangular plastic shell.

GANTT. An orderly process engaged in the system analysis, design, and evaluation of ADIK system.

Hub. A device that physically connects two or more cables together. 1. The hub is the central point in the star physical topology (Cohen 1991). 2. Hardware or software device that contains multiple independent but connected modules of network and Internet work equipment. Hubs can be active (where they repeat signals sent through them) or passive (where they do not repeat, but merely split, signals sent through them) (*Cisco Internetworking Terms and Acronyms* 2005).

Information. That which is in our heads (from our senses, mind), and that which is produced physically from such (i.e., speeches, writings, documents, etc.). Defined differently by information scientists (see Tokens in Fox 1983).

Information analysis center. An environment of people, technology, and procedures, the objective of which is to determine the data, information, and knowledge needs and requirements of clients (individuals, groups, organizations).

Information management. Identifying, using, and directing the processes and products of information (i.e., documents, people, libraries, computers, etc.) toward specific objectives—individual and collective, organizational, institutional, public/private.

Information management system. An environment of people, technology, and procedures, the purpose of which is to plan, operate, and control the actions of organizations (public or private).

Information officer. Defined differently in different countries; librarian who directs patrons to specific library resources upon request.

Information retrieval system. An environment of people, technology, and procedures, the objective of which is to aid in the identification and obtaining of data, information, and knowledge important to the user's task.

Information scientist. A professional trained to study and establish theories and the laws that define and determine the relationship between the limits of human and organizational functions and the tools that serve to extend these functions.

Information system. The physical organism entailing consciousness and awareness; also, an environment of people, technologies, and procedures, the object of which is to extend (complement/augment) human awareness in dealing with decision making and problem solving.

Knowledge. A subject long considered and studied by philosophers. Knowledge is a state of extended consciousness or awareness; processes of the brain as part of properties of matter and energy; human thought, leading to meaning and understanding; also, the product of the state, in physical form, storable, retrievable, transferable, possessing utility and value.

Knowledge (explicit). That which is understood through experiences and learning.

Knowledge (implicit). The understanding and meaning that we infer as the product of experience and that is not readily verifiable.

Knowledge (tacit). Silent, unspoken, hidden, and implied. How we understand the world around us and yet we cannot explain why.

Knowledge system (KS). A formal way of looking at the world (Popper 1965; Churchman 1971); an environment of people, technology, and procedures directed at enhancing the objective of organizations.

Mainframe. A large, powerful computer that often fills a huge room and is shared by many users via terminals. These terminals may be far away from the mainframe.

Management information system (MIS). Environment of people, technology, and procedures, the objective of which is to aid the process of operating, directing, and controlling the resources of an organization.

Media access control. A protocol by which two or more stations could share a common media in a switchless environment when the protocol does not require central arbitration, access tokens, or assigned time slots to indicate when a station will be allowed access to transmit (*Cisco Internetworking Technology Handbook* n.d., 100).

Medium. An intervening thing through which a force acts or an effect is produced (*Webster's New World* 1966, 914).

Message. A communication sent from a person or program. An assembly of characters and sometimes control codes that is transferred as an entity from an originator to one or more particpants (*IBM Dictionary of Computing,* McGraw Hill, 10th edition, 1993, 428). A set of information electronically transferred between devices (*Computing Dictionary,* 4th edition, summer 1999, vol. 3, issue 3, 200).

Metaphor. A way of thinking, acting, and understanding (Lackoff and Johnson 1980).

Microcomputer. Small, one-person computers, often called PCs.

Modem. A device that lets the computer send and receive signals (data) over telephone lines.

Need. A broad term (noun) more often than not associated with requirements for data, information, and knowledge. In the present text, the idea of need is associated with what happens in the brains of individuals (cognition) when confronted with situations in the "real" world.

Network. A computer system that links two or more computers (Beekman and Rathswohl 2001, 540).

Network protocol. A set of rules, or ways of doing things, that tell computers how to talk to each other over a network medium.

Networking. The bringing together of a number of technologies that are chained together by cable or by telephone lines or satellites (*Computing Dictionary*, 4th edition, summer 1999, vol. 3, issue 3, 207).

Object. In the object-oriented approach, an object is a computer representation of some real-world thing or event. Objects can have both attributes and behaviors (Kendall and Kendall 2002, 898).

Operating system (OS). Software (programs) that controls a computer and its peripherals (*Computing Dictionary*, 4th edition, summer 1999, vol. 3, issue 3, 213).

PERT. A scheme for the management of those processes involved in system analysis and design.

Physical layer. The first layer in the seven-layer open systems interconnection (OSI) standardized model of computer network communications (*Computer Dictionary*, 4th edition, summer 1999, issue 3, 224).

Process. A series of steps or a progression toward some aim or goal (*Penguin Dictionary of Psychology* 1985, 600).

Product. A thing brought into existence (*Oxford Dictionary* 1996, 94).

Receiver. Responsible for requesting resource reservations (*Collins Essential English Dictionary*, 2nd edition, 2006).

Remote terminal. Computer screen that is connected to a distant computer, which may be a long distance away. Terminals don't work unless they are connected to a computer; however, a remote *computer* may also work independently.

Request for proposal (RFP). An invitation for suppliers, through the bidding process, to submit a program of work (research and study) on a specific product, service, or general operational objective.

Requirement. That which satisfies an individual organizational objective; purpose and state of being. Often used interchangeably with the term "need."

Router. A hardware device or software program that routes messages as they travel between networks; typically on the Internet (Beekman and Rathswohl 2001, 544).

Schemas. Organized ways of thinking for storing and retrieving information efficiently (*Encyclopedia of Creativity* 1999, 17).

Scripts. Special schemas that relate to expected sequences of events in various social or physical settings, for example, restaurants, barbershops, etc. (*Encyclopedia of Creativity* 1999, 17).

Search engine. A program that allows users to locate specified information from a database or mass of data (*Computing Dictionary* 1999, 247).

Security. A broad term that includes the maintenance of safety, confidence, and obligation.

Strategic command control center. An environment of people, technology, and procedures used by the military to aid leaders to plan and direct action prior to, during, and following military action.

Subsystem. A system within a system that contributes to the overall function of an environment, consisting of people and technology. From the field of physiology and/or biology with which we are familiar, the cardiac system is a subsystem of the human organism. From the computer field, a modem (see above) is a subsystem of the computer as a technological system.

System. An environment of parts (human or physical) working together to achieve an objective or purpose.

System development cycle. A series of actions that are taken to create an environment to meet individual and organizational needs and requirements. The process follows the analysis and design of the system responding to user needs and requirements.

Telecommunications. The movement of messages in space and time with specific emphasis on the role of language (symbolic) information and knowledge.

Teletransmission. The movement of electronic signals in space and time.

Token. A sign; indication; symbol (*Webster's* 1966, 1532). One application is information science (Fox 1983), as something over and above sentence types, that uses it (i.e., for communication).

Training program. A step-by-step preparation of individuals to meet the demands of the present and technology (ADIK systems) used in the work environment.

Transmitter. A human and/or technological resource that moves and passes signals from an event in a specific place in time and space to another.

User. Any person, organization, institution that captures data, information, and knowledge in any form for a task.

User need. An individual's state of mind, which directs a person's action. Often the expression is used to indicate a state that is synonymous to the physical requirement that satisfies it. Often used interchangeably with the term "requirement."

Web. A network of separate things or functions as is found in a spider's strands.

Wireless transmission. Movement of signals from one place and time without the familiar usage of wire. Often associated with the Internet and other applications. The terms wireless transmission and wireless communication are used interchangeably.

References

Note that terms in brackets, such as [*ALA Glossary*], are abbreviations that are cross-referenced in this section.

ALA Glossary of Library and Information Science [*ALA Glossary*]. See Young, Heartsill.

Allen, Bryce L. 1996. *Information Tasks: Toward a User-Centered Approach to Information Systems.* Library and Information Science Series (New York). San Diego, Calif.: Academic Press.

Anderson, John R. 1990. *Cognitive Psychology and Its Implications.* 3rd ed. New York: W.H. Freeman and Company.

Aristotle. n.d. http://en.wikipedia.org/wiki/Aristotle (accessed Jan. 16, 2006).

Ballard, Patricia T., ed. 2001. *Encyclopedia of Associations.* Vol. 1. 37th ed. Detroit, Mich.: Gale Research Inc.

Ballesteros, Elissa Rosemary. 1995. Unconscious Cognition in the Conduct of Inquiry: An Information Counseling Approach. PhD diss., University of Texas at Austin.

Baretto, A. A. 1996. Technical and Economic Efficiency and the Viability of Information Products and Services. *Ciencia-Da-Informacao* 26, no. 3 (Sept./Dec.): 405–14.

Barnes-Svarney, Patricia L., ed. 1995, 1998. *The New York Public Library Science Desk Reference* [*Science Desk Reference*]. The New York Public Library Series. New York: Macmillan.

Beekman, George, and Eugene J. Rathswohl. 2001. *Computer Confluence.* Upper Saddle River, N.J.: Prentice Hall.

Belkin, N. J. 1978. Information Concepts for Information Science. *Journal of Documentation* 34, no. 1: 55–85.

———. 2005. Anomalous State of Knowledge. In *Theories of Information Behavior,* ed. Karen Fisher, Sanda Erdelez, and Lynne McKechnie, 44–48. ASIST monograph series. Medford, N.J.: Published for the American Society for Information Science and Technology by Information Today.

Belkin, Nicholas J., and B. H. Kwasnik. 1986. Using Structural Representation of Anomalous States of Knowledge for Choosing Document Retrieval Strategies. In *1986 ACM Conference on Research and Development in Information Retrieval: Palazzo dei congressi, Pisa, Italy, September 8-10, 1986*, ed. F. Rabitti. [Pisa, Italy]: Organization of the Conference.

Beniger, James R. 1986. *The Control Revolution: Technological and Economic Origins of the Information Society*. Cambridge, Mass.: Harvard University Press.

Bernstein, P. 1997. Moving Multimedia: The Information Value in Images. *Searcher* 5, no. 2 (Sept.): 40–49.

Betz, Joseph A. 1996–1997. Constructing Cooperative Learning Systems in Engineering Technology. *Journal of Educational Technology Systems* 25, no. 2: 97–108.

Blackwell Encyclopedia of Social Psychology, The. See Manstead and Hewstone.

Bliss, Henry E. 1929. *The Organization of Knowledge and the System of the Sciences*. New York: Henry Holt and Company.

Bloom, Benjamin S. 1956a. *Taxonomy of Educational Objectives: The Classification of Educational Goals, Handbook 1*. New York: David McKay Company, Inc.

———. 1956b. *Taxonomy of Educational Objectives: The Classification of Educational Goals, Handbook 2*. New York: David McKay Company, Inc.

Boehm, B. 1993. *Software Engineering Economics*. Englewood Cliffs, N.J.: Prentice Hall.

Booch, Grady, James Rumbaugh, and Ivar Jacobson. 1999. *The Unified Modeling Language User Guide*. The Addison-Wesley Object Technology Series. Reading, Mass.: Addison-Wesley.

Borko, Harold. 1965. *The Conceptual Foundations of Information Science*. Report No. SP 2507, AD-615 718. Santa Monica, Calif.: System Development Corporation.

———. 1998. Information Science. In *Historical Studies of Information Science*, ed. Trudi Bellardo Hahn and Michael Buckland. ASIS Monograph Series. Medford, N.J.: Information Today.

Borko, Harold, ed. 1962. *Computer Applications in the Behavioral Sciences*. Englewood Cliffs, N.J.: Prentice Hall.

Boulding, Kenneth E. 1968. General Systems Theory—A Skeleton of Science. In *Modern Systems Research for the Behavioral Scientist*, ed. W. Buckley. Chicago: Aldine.

Brittain, John Michael. 1970. *Information and Its Users*. New York: Wiley-Interscience.

Buckland, Michael. 1991. *Information and Information Systems*. New York: Greenwood Press.

———. 2004. Information as Thing. *JASIST*, 42.5: 351–360.

Bush, Vannevar. 1945. As We May Think. *The Atlantic Monthly* 176, no. 1 (July): 101–8. www.theatlantic.com/doc/194507/bush/4 (accessed Aug. 21, 2005).

Carbo, Toni, and Stephen Almagno. 2001. Information Ethics: The Duty, Privilege and Challenge of Educating Information Professionals. *Library Trends* 49, no. 3 (Winter): 510–18.

Carey, Jane M. 1988. *Human Factors in Management Information Systems*. Norwood, N.J.: Ablex Publishing Corp.

Casanova, Myrtha B. 1990. Information: The Major Element of Change. In *Information Quality: Definitions and Dimensions* 53, ed. Irene Wormell. Cambridge/Los Angeles: Taylor Graham Publishing.

Case, Donald O. 2002. *Looking for Information: A Survey of Research on Information Seeking, Needs and Behavior.* San Diego: Academic Press.

Chapanis, Alphonse. 1995. Ergonomics in Product Development: A Personal View. *Ergonomics* 38, no. 8 (August): 1625–38.

Chaplin, J. P. 1985. *Dictionary of Psychology.* 2nd rev. ed. New York: Bantam Doubleday Dell Publishing Group, Inc.

Children's Dictionary. See Neufelt.

Chomsky, Norman. 1968. *Linguistic Contributions to the Study of the Mind.* New York: Harcourt Brace Jovanovich.

Churchman, C. West. 1971. *The Design of Inquiring Systems: Basic Concepts of Systems in Organizations.* New York: Basic Books.

———. 1979. *The Systems Approach and Its Enemies.* New York: Basic Books.

Cisco Internetworking Technology Handbook. n.d. San Jose, Calif.: Cisco Press. www.cisco .com/univercd/cc/td/doc/cisintwk/ito_doc/index.htm (accessed Mar. 30, 2006).

Cisco Internetworking Terms and Acronyms. 2005. San Jose, Calif.: Cisco Press. www.cisco .com/univercd/cc/td/doc/cisintwk/ita/index.htm (accessed Mar. 30, 2006).

Clark, Ruth C. 1999. *Developing Technical Training: A Structured Approach for Developing Computer-based Instructional Materials, Second Edition.* Boston: Addison-Wesley.

Clemen, Robert T., and Terence Reilly. 2001. *Making Hard Decisions with Decision Tools.* Pacific Grove, Calif.: Duxbury Press/Thomas Learning.

Cleveland, Donald B., and Ana D. Cleveland. 2000. *Introduction to Indexing and Abstracting.* 3rd ed. Westport, Conn.: Libraries Unlimited.

Coad, Peter, and Edward Yourdon. 1991. *Object-Oriented Analysis.* Yourdon Press computing series. Englewood Cliffs, N.J.: Yourdon Press.

Cohen, Alan M. 1991. *A Guide to Networking.* Boston: Boyd & Fraser/Southwestern Publishing Co.

Collier's Encyclopedia. See Halsey.

Computing Dictionary: The Illustrated Book of Terms and Technologies [*Computing Dictionary*]. See Kobler.

Computing Research Association. 2003. *Grand Research Challenges in Information Systems Final Report.* Washington, D.C.: Computing Research Association. www.cra.org/ reports/gc.systems.pdf (accessed Sept. 2, 2005).

Coombs, Clyde H. 1964. *A Theory of Data.* New York: John Wiley & Sons.

Daily, Jay Elwood. 1971. Classification and Categorization. In *Encyclopedia of Library and Information Science*, vol. 5, ed. Allen Kent, 44. New York: Marcel Dekker.

Davies, Paul. 2000. *The Fifth Miracle: The Search for the Origin and Meaning of Life.* New York: Simon & Schuster, Inc.

De Solla Price, Derek J. 1986. *Little Science, Big Science . . . and Beyond.* New York: Columbia University Press.

Debons, Anthony, Consuelo Figueras, and Annie Thompson. 2000. Knowledge Counseling: The Concept, the Process and Its Application. In *Knowledge Management for the Information Professional*, ASIS Monograph Series, ed. T. Kanti Srikantaiah and Michael E. D. Koenig, 459–80. Medford, N.J.: Information Today, Inc.

Debons, Anthony, Donald W. King, Una Mansfield, and Donald L. Shirey. 1981. *The Information Professional: Survey of an Emerging Field.* New York: Marcel Dekker, Inc. [ASIS Best Information Science Book Award, 1981.]

Debons, Anthony, Esther Horne, and Scott Cronenweth. 1988. *Information Science: An Integrated View,* Professional Librarian Series. Boston: G. K. Hall. [ASIS Best Information Science Book Award, 1989.]

Debons, Anthony, ed. 1972. *Information Science: Search for Identity.* New York: Marcel Dekker, Inc.

Dennis, Alan, and Barbara Haley Wixom. 2000. *Systems Analysis and Design.* Hoboken, N.J.: John Wiley & Sons, Inc.

Dertouzos, Michael. 1998. *What Will Be: How the New World of Information Will Change Our Lives.* New York: HarperSanFrancisco.

Dervin, Brenda. 1989. An Overview of Sense Making Research: Concepts, Methods and Results. Paper presented at the annual meeting of the International Communication Association, Dallas, Texas.

Dervin, Brenda, and Michael Nilan. 1986. Information Needs and Users. *ARIST* 21.

Desiano, Salvator. 2002. Robotology. In *Computer Science, Volume 4,* ed. Rodger R. Flynn, 169–73. New York: Macmillan.

Devlin, Keith. 2001. *Infosense: Turning Information into Knowledge.* New York: W.H. Freeman and Company.

Dictionary of Psychology. See Chaplin.

Do Amaral, Sueli-Angelica. 1999. Library and Socio-Economic Development: A Challenge for Information Professionals. *Investigacion-Bibliotecologica* 13, no. 26 (Jan.): 50–63.

Due, R. T. 1996. The Value of Information. *Information Systems Management* 13, no. 1 (Winter): 68–72.

Duhon, Bryant. 1998. It's All in Our Heads. *Inform* 12, no. 8 (Sept.): 10.

Eliot, T. S. 1963. Choruses from the "The Rock." In *Collected Poems, 1909–1962,* 147. New York: Harcourt.

Encyclopedia of Creativity. 1999. Vols. 1 and 2. Burlington, Mass.: Academic Press, Elsevier.

Encyclopedia of Library and Information Science [Ency LIS]. 1968–2003. New York: Marcel Dekker, Inc. Also see these authors: Daily 1971, Lancour 1972, Penland 1971, and Thompson 1978.

Engelbart, Douglas C. 1962. Augmenting Human Intellect: A Conceptual Framework. AFOSR-3223 Summary Report, 134. SRI Program No. 3578. Menlo Park, Calif.: Stanford Research Institute. www.liquidinformation.org/engelbart/62_paper_top.html.

Evans, Gerald E., and J. R. Riha. 1990. Assessing DSS Effectiveness Using Evaluations Research Methods. *Information Management* 16, no. 4: 197–206.

FDA Consumer Magazine. January–February 2005. U.S. Food and Drug Administration. www.fda.gov/fdac/departs/2005/105_upd.html (accessed Jan. 14, 2006).

Fine, Sara. 1996. How the Mind of the Censor Works: The Psychology of Censorship. *School Library Journal* 42 (Jan.): 23–27.

Fitts, Paul. 1954. The Information Capacity of the Human Motor System in Controlling the Amplitude of Movement. *Journal of Experimental Psychology* 47: 381–91.

Fleetwood, C., and Shelley, K. 2000. The Outlook for College Graduates, 1998–2008: A Balancing Act. *Occupational Outlook Quarterly* 44, no. 3: 2–9.

Flynn, Roger R. 1997. Introduction to Information Retrieval. In *Information Science: Still an Emerging Discipline*, ed. J. G. Williams and Toni Carbo. Pittsburgh, Pa.: Cathedral Publishing.

Flynn, Roger R., ed. 2002. *Computer Sciences.* Vol. 1–4. The Macmillan Science Library. New York: Macmillan.

Fox, Christopher John. 1983. *Information and Misinformation: An Investigation of the Notions of Information, Misinformation, Informing and Misinforming.* Westport, Conn.: Greenwood Press.

Friedman, Thomas L. 2005. *The World Is Flat: A Brief History of the Twenty-First Century.* New York: Farrar, Straus, and Giroux.

Ganzorig, M. 2002. Remote Sensing and Geographic Information Systems: Their Use in Mongolia. *Focus on Geography* 47, no. 1 (Fall): 30–32. www.amergeog.org/focus/fall02.htm (accessed Jan. 14, 2006).

Garfield, Eugene. 1979. *Citation Indexing: Its Theory and Application in Science, Technology and Humanities.* Hoboken, N.J.: John Wiley & Sons.

———. 1977, 1978, 1980. *Essays of an Information Scientist.* Vol. 1–3. Philadelphia, Pa.: ISI Press.

Gaur, Albertine. 1992. *A History of Writing.* London: British Library.

Gerdy, G. P. 1995. *The Value of Information for Executives.* Medford, N.J.: Learned Information.

Gerhardus, D. 2003. Robot-Assisted Surgery: The Future Is Here. *Journal of Healthcare Management* 48, no. 4: 242–51.

Global Trends 2015: A Dialogue about the Future with Nongovernment Experts. 2000. NIC 2000–2002 (Dec). Washington, D.C.: National Intelligence Council. www.cia.gov/cia/reports/globaltrends2015 (accessed Sept. 2, 2005).

Goleniewski, Lillian. 2002. *Telecommunications Essentials: The Complete Global Source for Communications Fundamentals, Data Networking and the Internet, and Next-Generation Networks.* Boston: Addison-Wesley Professional.

Golub, Andrew Lang. 1997. *Decision Analysis: An Integrated Approach.* Hoboken, N.J.: John Wiley & Sons.

Gould, Julius, and William L. Kolb, eds. 1964. *A Dictionary of the Social Sciences, First Edition.* Alameda, CA: Tavistock Publishers.

Gray, R. D., and Q. D. Atkinson. 2003. Language-Tree Divergence Times Support the Anatolian Theory of Indo Origin. *Nature* 426: 435–39.

Grice, Paul. 1989. *Studies in the Way of Words.* Cambridge, Mass.: Harvard University Press.

Griffiths, Jose-Marie, and Donald W. King. 1986. *New Directions in Library and Information Science Education.* Westport, Conn.: Knowledge Industry Publications (Greenwood Press).

———. 1993. *Increasing the Information Edge.* Washington, D.C.: Special Libraries Association.

Grochow, Jerrold M. 1996. *Information Overload: Creating Value with the New Information Systems Technology.* Upper Saddle River, N.J.: Prentice Hall.

Guralnik, David Bernard. 1971, 1973, 1974. *Webster's New World Dictionary of the American Language.* Nashville: Southwestern Co.

Hahn, Trudi Bellardo, and Michael Buckland, eds. 1998. *Historical Studies in Information Science.* ASIS Monograph Series. Medford, N.J.: Information Today.

Halsey, William D., and Emanuel Friendman, eds. 1983. History of Libraries. In *Collier's Encyclopedia,* vol. 14, 558–60. New York: Macmillan Educational Company.

Harmon, Glynn. 1971. On the Evolution of Information Science. *Journal of the American Society of Information Science* 22, no. 4: 235–41.

————. 1975a. Information and Metaenergy. In *Perspectives in Information Science,* ed. Anthony Debons and William J. Cameron, 93–99. Amsterdam: Noordhoff- Leyden. Also 1973. Information and Metaenergy, *Proceedings of the N.A.T.O. Advanced Institute on Information Science.* Brussels: North Atlantic Treaty Organization, 183–86. Reprinted in 1974. *Information News and Sources* 6 (December): 301–3.

————. 1975b. The Invisible Manpower Market for Information Scientists. *Proceedings of the American Society of Information Science (ASIS) 1975 Annual Meeting: Information Revolution,* volume 12, part 1, ed. Charles W. Husbands, 59–60. Medford, N.J.: Information Today.

Hartmann, J. 1995. The Information Needs of Anthropologists. *Behavioral and Social Sciences Librarian* 13: 34.

Havelock, Ronald G. 1971. *Planning for Innovation through Dissemination and Utilization of Knowledge.* Ann Arbor, Mich.: Center for Research on the Utilization of Scientific Knowledge, Institute for Social Research, University of Michigan.

Hawker, Sara, ed. 1996. *Oxford MiniReference Dictionary and Thesaurus.* New York: Oxford University Press, Inc.

Heise, David R. *Understanding Events: Affect and the Construction of Social Action.* Cambridge: Cambridge University Press, 1979.

Heilprin, Lawrence B. 1989. Foundations of Information Science Reexamined. *ARIST* 24: 343–72.

————. 1995. Science and Technology: From Prescientific Times to the Present. *JASIS* 46, no. 8: 574–78.

Hirtle, S. C., and J. Hudson. 1991. Acquisition of Spatial Knowledge for Routes. *Journal of Environmental Psychology* 11: 335–45.

Hirtle, S. C., and J. Jonides. 1985. Evidence of Hierarchies in Cognitive Maps. *Memory and Cognition* 13: 208–17.

Hirtle, S. C., and M. Sorrows. 2007. Navigation in Electronic Environments. In *Applied Spatial Cognition from Research in Cognitive Technology,* ed. G. Allen, 103–26. Mahwah, N.J.: Lawrence Erlbaum Associates.

Hjerppe, Roland. 1992. Libraries of the Future: Real and Virtual. In *Essen Symposium 1992,* 83–97. www.informatik.uni-trier.de/~ley/db/indices/a-tree/h/Hjerppe:Roland .html (accessed Jan. 14, 2006).

Howard, Nicole. 2005. *The Book: The Life Story of a Technology.* Greenwood Technographies Series. Westport, Conn.: Greenwood Press.

Huizinga, Gerald. 1970. *Maslow's Need Hierarchy in the Work Situation.* Groningen: Wolters-Noordhoff Publishing.

Hyman, R. A. 1982. *Charles Babbage: The Pioneer of the Computer.* Oxford, U.K.: Oxford University Press.

Inglis, Fred. 1990. *Media Theory: An Introduction.* Oxford, U.K., and Cambridge, Mass.: Basil Blackwell, Ltd.

Inglis, Harold A. 1951. *The Bias of Communication.* Toronto: University of Toronto Press.

Ingwersen, Peter. 1996. Cognitive Perspectives of Information Retrieval Interaction: Elements of a Cognitive IR Theory. *Journal of Documentation* 52, no. 1 (Mar.): 3–50.

Ito, Masahiro, and Daniel Sigg. 2002. Event Analysis Tool Quick Start Guide. http://www.ligo-wa.caltech.edu/~sigg/quickstart/EventAnalysis/quickstart.html.

Kalseth, K. 1991. Business Information Strategy: The Strategic Use of Information and Knowledge. *Information Services and Use* 11, no. 3: 155–64.

Kamel, N., and K. Toraskar. 1997. An Approach to Value-Based Modeling of Information Flows. *Information Society* 13 (Jan.–Mar.): 93–105.

Kaplan, Michael. 2004. *Cultural Ergonomics.* Advances in Human Performance and Cognitive Engineering Research, v. 4. Amsterdam: Elsevier JAI.

Kendall, Kenneth E., and Julie E. Kendall. 2002. *Systems Analysis and Design.* Upper Saddle River, N.J.: Prentice Hall.

Kent, Allen. 1972. *Unsolvable Problems in Information Science: Search for Identity.* New York: Marcel Dekker.

King, Donald W., ed. 1978. *Key Papers in the Design and Evaluation of Information Systems.* White Plains, N.Y.: Published for ASIS by Knowledge Industry Publications (Greenwood Press).

King, Donald W., and Jose-Marie Griffiths. 2002. U.S. Information Retrieval System: Evolution and Evaluation (1945–1975). In *IEEE Annals of the History of Computing* 24, no. 3 (July–Sept.): 35–55. Ed. Boyd Rayward and Rebecca Graham. Los Alamitos, Calif.: IEEE Computer Society.

King, Donald W., Nancy K. Roderer, and Harold K. Olsen, eds. 1983. *Key Papers in the Economics of Information.* Hoboken, N.J.: John Wiley & Sons.

Kingma, Bruce R. 1996. *The Economics of Information: A Guide to Economic and Cost-Benefit Analysis for Information Professionals.* Englewood, Colo.: Libraries Unlimited, Inc.

Kobler, Ron, et al., eds. 1999, 1998. *Computing Dictionary: The Illustrated Book of Terms and Technologies* 3, no. 3 (August), 4th and 3rd eds. PC Novice/Smart Computing Reference Series.

Korfhage, Robert R. 1997. *Information Storage and Retrieval.* Hoboken, N.J.: John Wiley and Sons.

Krathhwohl, David R., Benjamin S. Bloom, and Bertram B. Masia. 1956. *Taxonomy of Educational Objectives: The Classification of Educational Goals. Handbook II: Affective Domain.* New York: David McKay Company, Inc.

Kreie, Jennifer, and Timothy Paul Cronan. 2000. Making Ethical Decisions. *Communications of the ACM* 43, no. 12 (December).

Kuhlthau, Carol Collier. 1993. *Seeking Meaning: A Process Approach to Library and Information Services.* Norwood, N.J.: Ablex Publishing Co.

Kuhn, Thomas S. 1970. *The Structure of Scientific Revolutions.* 2nd ed. Chicago: University of Chicago Press.

Lackoff, George, and Mark Johnson. 1980. *The Metaphors We Live By.* Chicago: University of Chicago Press.

Lancour, Harold. 1972. Documentation. In *Encyclopedia of Library and Information Science*, ed. Allen Kent, 247. New York: Marcel Dekker, Inc.

Langridge, D. W. 1992. *Classification: Its Kinds, Elements, Systems and Applications.* New York: Bowker.

Licklider, J. C. R. 1960. Man-Computer Symbiosis: Human Factors. *Electron* 1: 4–11.

Littlejohn, Stephen W. 1978. *Theories of Human Communications.* Columbus, Ohio: Charles E. Merrill Publisher.

Longfellow, Henry W. 1860. "Paul Revere's Ride." www.legallanguage.com/poems/MidnightRide.html (accessed Sept. 27, 2005).

Losee, Robert M., Jr. 1990. *The Science of Information.* New York: Academic Press, Inc.

Lubetzky, Seymour. 1969. Phase I: Descriptive Cataloging. *Principles of Cataloging: Final Report* (July). Los Angeles: Institute of Library Research, University of California.

Lubetzky, Seymour, and R. M. Hayes. 1992. Bibliographic Dimensions in Information Control. In *Introduction to Information Science*, ed. T. Saracevic, 436. New York: R.R. Bowker.

Machlup, Fritz, and Una Mansfield, eds. 1983. *The Study of Information: Interdisciplinary Messages.* New York: John Wiley & Sons.

Mansfield, A. J., and J. L. Wayman. 2002. *Best Practices in Testing and Reporting Performance of Biometric Devices, Version 2.01.* Middlesex, Great Britain: Centre for Mathematics and Scientific Computing National Physical Laboratory.

Manstead, Antony S. R., and Miles Hewstone, eds. 1995. *The Blackwell Encyclopedia of Social Psychology* [*Blackwell Encyclopedia of Social Psychology*]. Oxford, U.K., and Cambridge, Mass.: Basil Blackwell, Ltd.

Marakas, George M. 2003. *Decision Support Systems in the 21st Century.* Upper Saddle River, N.J.: Prentice Hall.

Mark, D. M., C. Freksa, S. C. Hirtle, R. Lloyd, and B. Tversky. 1999. Cognitive Models of Geographic Space. *International Journal of Geographical Information Systems* 13: 747–74.

Martell, C. 1996. Must It Be? *Journal of Academic Librarianship* 22, no. 2 (Mar.): 85–86.

Mason, Robert M. 1979. Perceived Benefits of Information Analysis. In *Information Choices and Policies: Proceedings of the ASIS 42nd Annual Meeting*, ed. Roy D. Tally and Ronald R. Deultgen, 339. White Plains, N.Y.: American Society for Information Science.

Mayer, Richard E. 2002. *The Promise of Educational Psychology.* Boston: Pearson Education, Inc.

Mayhew, Jean. 1999. Knowledge Management: A U.S. Corporate Perspective. *Bulletin-of-the-Japan Special Libraries Association* 19 (Mar.): 15.

McCrank, Laurence J. 2002. *Historical Information Science: An Emerging Unidiscipline.* Medford, N.J.: Information Today, Inc.

McLuhan, Marshall. 1967. *The Medium Is the Massage.* New York: Bantam Books, Inc.

McPherson, P. K. 1994. Accounting for the Value of Information. *ASLIB Proceedings* 46, no. 9 (Sept.): 203–15.

Meister, David. 1971. *Human Factors: Theory and Practice.* New York: Wiley Interscience.

Menou, Michael J., ed. 1993. *Measuring the Impact of Information on Development.* Ottawa, Ontario, Canada: International Development Center.

Miller, F. G. 2002. I=0 (Information Has No Intrinsic Meaning). *Information Research* 8, no. 1 (Oct.). http://information.net/IR/8-1/pap.140.html.

Miller, George A. 1991. *The Science of Words*. New York: Scientific American Library.

Miller, James Grier. 1978. *The Living System*. New York: McGraw-Hill.

Morgan, E. L. 1997. Unique Collections and "Fahrenheit 451." *Computers in Libraries* 17, no. 9 (Oct.): 18–20.

Mowshowitz, Abbe. 1992. On the Market Value of Information Commodities. I. The Nature of Information and Information Commodities. *Journal of the American Society of Information Science* 43, no. 3 (Apr.): 225–32.

Murray, James Augustus Henry, William Little, and C. T. Onions. 1964. *The Shorter Oxford English Dictionary on Historical Principles*. Oxford: Clarendon Press.

Nahl, Diane, and Dania Bilal, eds. 2007. *Information and Emotion: The Emerging Affective Paradigm in Information Behavior Research and Theory*. Medford, N.J.: Asist.

National Commission on Terrorist Attacks upon the United States. 2004. *The 9–11 Commission Report: Final Report of the National Commission on Terrorist Attacks upon the United States, Official Government Edition*. Washington, D.C.: U.S. Government Printing Office.

Negroponte, Nicholas. 1995. *Being Digital*. New York: 1st Vintage Books.

Neill, S. D. 1992. *The Dilemmas in the Study of Information*. New York: Greenwood Press.

Neufelt, Victoria, and Fernando De Mello Vianna, eds. 1997. *Webster's New World Children's Dictionary* [*New World Children's Dictionary*]. New York: Macmillan.

[*New World Children's Dictionary*]. *Webster's New World Children's Dictionary*. See Neufelt and De Mello Vianna.

New York Public Library Science Desk Reference, The [*Science Desk Reference*]. See Barnes-Svarney.

Newell, Allen, and Herbert A. Simon. 1972. *Human Problem Solving*. Englewood Cliffs, N.J.: Prentice Hall, Inc.

Nevitt, Barrington. 1982. *The Communication Ecology*. Toronto, Canada: Butterworths.

Nicols, M. T., and M. M. Isselman. 1995–1996. Survival in Transition or Implementing Information Science Competencies. *Bulletin of the American Society of Information Science* 22, no. 2 (Dec.–Jan.): 11–15.

Nitecki, Joseph Z. 1993. *Meta-Librarianship: A Model for Intellectual Foundations of Library Information Science*. Vol. 1 of the Nitecki trilogy, ERIC ED363–346.

Noe, Thomas H., and Buddhavarapu Sailesh Ramamurtie. 1995. Information Quality, Performance Measurement, and Security Demand in Rational Expectations Economies. Federal Reserve Bank of Atlanta, Working Paper 95–4 (June). *Journal of Finance* (Mar). www.frbatlanta.org/filelegacydocs/wp954.pdf (accessed Sept. 1, 2005).

Norman, Donald. 1988. *The Psychology of Everyday Things (The Design of Everyday Things)*. New York: Basic Books.

Norton, Melanie J. 2000. *Introductory Concepts in Information Science*. ASIS Monograph Series, 51. Medford, N.J.: Information Today.

Oberhofer, C. M. A. 1993. Information Use Value: A Test on the Perceptions of Utility and Validity. *Information Processing and Management* 29, no. 5: 587–600.

Osborne, Rep. Tom (NE03). 2001. Washington Round-up: Weekly Column—Week of May 7, 2001. www.house.gov/apps/list/speech/ne03_osborne/wc_010507_medprivacy.html (accessed Jan. 14, 2006).

Osif, Bonnie A., and Richard L. Harwood. 2000. The Value of Information and the Value of Librarianship (Manager's Bookshelf). *Library Administration and Management Magazine* 14, no. 3 (Summer).

Otlet, Paul. 1990. The International Organization of Bibliography and Documentation. Institut International de Bibliographie Publication no. 128 (unsigned, 1920). In *The International Organization and Dissemination of Knowledge: Selected Essays of Paul Otlet*, ed. and trans. W. Boyd Rayward. Amsterdam: Elsevier.

Otten, Klaus, and Anthony Debons. 1968. Opinion Paper: Towards a Meta-Science of Information: Informatology. *Journal of the American Society of Information Science* 21: 89–94.

Oxford MiniReference Dictionary and Thesaurus [*Oxford Dictionary*]. See Hawker, Sara.

Palfreman, J., and D. Swade. 1991. *The Dream Machine*. London: BBC Books.

Parker, J., and J. Houghton. 1994. *The Value of Information: Paradigms and Perspectives*. Medford, N.J.: Information Today.

Penguin Dictionary of Psychology, The. See Reber, Arthur S.

Penland, Patrick. R. 1971. Communication Science. In *Encyclopedia of Library and Information Science*, vol. 5, ed. Allen Kent, 558–59. New York: Marcel Dekker, Inc.

———. 1974. *Communication Science and Technology: An Introduction*. New York: Marcel Dekker, Inc.

Penland, Patrick R., with Aleyamma Mathai. 1974. *Interpersonal Communication: Counseling, Guidance and Retrieval for Media, Library and Information Specialists*. Vol. 1. New York: Marcel Dekker, Inc.

Plato. n.d. http://en.wikipedia.org/wiki/Plato (accessed Jan. 16, 2006).

Popper, Karl R. 1965. *Conjectures and Refutations: The Growth of Scientific Knowledge*. New York: Harper & Row Publishers.

Quint, B. 1993. *The Information Consumer in Transition*. Philadelphia, Pa.: National Federation of Abstract and Indexing Services.

Ranganathan, S. R. 1957. *The Five Laws of Library Science*. London: Blunt.

Raskin, Jeff. 2000. *The Human Interface: New Directions for Designing Interactive Systems*. Boston: Addison-Wesley.

Rasmussen, Edie, chair, and Elaine G. Toms, ed. 2002. ASIS&T: Preliminary Program, Annual Meeting. In *2002 Proceedings of the 65th Annual Meeting (Vol. 39) for ASIS&T 2002: Information, Connections, and Community, November 18–21, 2002*. Philadelphia, Pa.: American Society for Information Science and Technology.

Rayward, Boyd W. 1998. The Origins of Information Science and the International Institute of Bibliography/International Federation for Information and Documentation (FID). In *Historical Studies of Information Science*, ed. Trudi Bellardo Hahn and Michael Buckland, 22–33. ASIS Monograph Series. Medford, N.J.: Information Today.

Reber, Arthur S. 1995. *The Penguin Dictionary of Psychology*. New York: Penguin Books.

Repo, Aatto J. 1989. An Approach to the Value of Information: Effectiveness and Productivity of Information Use in Research Work. *Public Report Number*

PB89–191506/HCW, 191. PhD diss., University of Sheffield, 1988. Espoo, Finland: Technical Research Center of Finland, Public. 0358–5069: 51.

Rescher, Nicholas. 1982. *Empirical Inquiry*. Totowa, N.J.: Rowman & Littlefield.

——. 1998. *Predicting the Future: An Introduction to the Theory of Forecasting*. Albany: State University of New York Press.

Roach, Ronald. 2003. University of Pittsburgh Opens Digital Operating Room—Tech Briefs. *Black Issues in Higher Education* (2 Jan. 2003). http://findarticles.com/p/articles/mi_m0DXK/is_23_19/ai_96811015 (accessed Jan. 16, 2006).

Roiger, Richard J., and Michael W. Geatz. 2003. *Data Mining: A Tutorial-Based Primer*. Boston: Pearson Education, Inc., Addison-Wesley.

Rubin, Howard, ed. 1995. Building an IT Management Flight Deck. *Computerworld*. Leadership Series. Oct. 16.

Rubin, Michael Rogers, Mary Taylor Huber, and Elizabeth Lloyd Taylor. 1986. *The Knowledge Industry in the United States, 1960–1980*. Princeton, N.J.: Princeton University Press.

Sage, Andrew P., and William P. Rouse, eds. 1999. *Handbook of Systems Engineering and Management*. Hoboken, N.J.: John Wiley & Sons Inc.

Salton, Gerard, and Hans-Jochen Schneider, eds. 1983. *Research and Development in Information Retrieval: Proceedings, Berlin, May 18–20, 1982*. Berlin and New York: Springer-Verlag.

Salton, Gerard, and Michael J. McGill. 1983. *Introduction to Modern Information Retrieval*. New York: McGraw Hill.

Salvendy, Gavriel. 1997. *Handbook of Human Factors and Ergonomics*. New York: Wiley-Interstate Publication.

Saracevic, Tefko, ed. 1970. *Introduction to Information Science*. New York: R.R. Bowker.

Saracevic, Tefko, and J. P. Kantor. 1997. Value of Information Services. *Journal of the American Society of Information Science* (June): 543–63.

School of Information Sciences, University of Pittsburgh Catalogue, 1991–1993. c. 1991. Pittsburgh, Pa.: University of Pittsburgh.

[*Science Desk Reference*]. *The New York Public Library Science Desk Reference*. See Barnes-Svarney.

Schuurman, E. 1980. *Technology and the Future: A Philosophical Challenge*. Toronto: Wedge Publishing Foundation.

Shannon, Claude E. 1948. A Mathematical Theory of Communication. *Bell System Technical Journal* 27 (July, October): 379–423 and 623–56. Reprinted with corrections: http://cm.bell-labs.com/cm/ms/what/shannonday/shannon1948.pdf (accessed Aug. 19, 2006).

——. 1949. Communication Theory of Secrecy Systems. *Bell System Technical Journal* 28 (Oct.): 656–715. www.prism.net/user/dcowley/docs.html (accessed Sept. 27, 2005).

Shannon, Claude E., and Warren Weaver. 1949. *The Mathematical Theory of Communication*. Urbana, Ill.: University of Illinois Press, republished in paperback in 1963. Very similar to Shannon 1948, with preface by Weaver added. See Weaver for a link to the preface.

Sheridan, Thomas B. 1988. The System Perspective. In *Human Factors in Aviation*, ed. Earl L. Wiener and David C. Nagel, 27–52. San Diego: Academic Press, Inc.

Sillince, John A. A. 1995. A Stochastic Model of Information Value. *Information Processing and Management* 31, no. 4 (July): 543–54.

Smith, Linda C. 1987. Artificial Intelligence and Information Retrieval. *ARIST* 22: 51.

Solomon, M. 1997. Knowledge Management Tools for Knowledge Managers: Filling the Gap between Finding Information and Applying It. *Searcher* 5, no. 3 (Mar.): 10–14.

Spring, Michael. 1997. The Making of a Profession. In *Information Science: Still an Emerging Discipline*, ed. J. G. Williams and Toni Carbo. Pittsburgh, Pa.: Cathedral Publishing.

Srikantaiah, Taverekere Kanti, and Michael E. D. Koenig, eds. 2000. *Knowledge Management for the Information Professional.* ASIS Monograph Series. Medford, N.J.: Published for ASIS by Information Today, Inc.

Stair, Ralph M. 1996, *Principles of Information Systems: A Managerial Approach.* 2nd ed. New York: Boyd & Fraser Publishing Company.

Sterostine, Iouri. 2008. Personal Communication. Senior Conference officer, International Monetary Fund and World Bank.

Stone, Robert. 1967. *A Hall of Mirrors.* Portland, OR: Powell's Books.

Sveiby, Karl Erik. 1997. *The New Organizational Wealth: Managing & Measuring Knowledge-Based Assets.* San Fransisco: Berrett-Koehler.

Svoboda, Olga. 1995. Mining and Minerals-Processing Information: Where and How to Get It. *Electronic Library* 13, no. 4 (Aug.): 329–36.

Taylor, Arlene G. 1999. *Organization of Information.* Englewood, Colo.: Libraries Unlimited, Inc.

Taylor, Arlene G., David P. Miller, and Bohdan S. Wynar. 2000. *Wynar's Introduction to Cataloging and Classification.* Englewood, Colo.: Libraries Unlimited.

Taylor, Robert S. 1986. *Value-Added Processes in Information Systems*, ed. Melvin J. Voigt, 62–69. Communication and Information Science Series. Norwood, N.J.: Ablex Publishing Co.

Thompson, Lawrence S. 1978. Printers and Printing: 17th Century. In *Encyclopedia of Library and Information Science*, vol. 23, ed. Allen Kent, 294–512. New York: Marcel Dekker, Inc.

Thompson, Richard A. 2000. *Telephone Switching Systems.* Boston: Artech House.

Thompson, Richard A., David Tipper, Prashant Krishnamurthy, and Joseph Kabar. 2006. *The Physical Layer of Communication Systems.* Boston: Artech House.

Toffler, Alvin. 1972. *Future Shock.* New York: Bantam Books.

———. 1984. *The Third Wave.* New York: Bantam Books.

Tomer, Christinger. 1998. *Information Technology Guide.* Pittsburgh: Department of Library and Information Science, School of Information Sciences, University of Pittsburgh.

Trauth, Eileen M. 1978. A Study of Some of the Terms Relevant to the Field of Information Science. Unpublished collection of papers, Interdisciplinary Department of Information Science, University of Pittsburgh.

Trenholm, Sara. 2001. *Thinking through Communication: An Introduction to the Study of Human Communication.* Boston: Allyn and Bacon.

Tufte, Edward R. 1983. *The Visual Display of Quantitative Information.* Cheshire, Conn.: Graphics Press.

———. 1990. *Envisioning Information.* Cheshire, Conn.: Graphics Press.

Vickery, Brian C., and Alina Vickery. 2004. *Information Science in Theory and Practice.* 3rd rev. ed. Munich, Germany: K.G. Saur Verlag GmbH.

Von Bertalanfy, Ludwig. 1968. General Systems Theory—A Critical Review. *In Modern Systems Research for the Behavioral Scientist,* ed. W. A. Buckley, 11–30. Chicago: Adline.

Wang, William S. Y. 1991. *The Emergence of Language, Development and Evolution.* New York: Scientific American/W. H. Freeman and Company.

Warren, Rita. 2001. Information Architects and Their Central Role in Content Management. *ASIS&T Bulletin* 28, no. 1 (Oct./Nov.).

Warren, Samuel D., and Louis D. Brandeis. 1890. The Right to Privacy. *Harvard Law Review* IV, no. 5 (Dec. 15 1890). www.lawrence.edu/fast/boardmaw/Privacy_brand_warr2.html (accessed Jan. 14, 2006).

Weaver, Warren. 1949. Recent Contributions to the Mathematical Theory of Communication. Preface to *The Mathematical Theory of Communication* by Claude E. Shannon and Warren Weaver. Urbana, Ill.: University of Illinois Press, republished in paperback in 1963. http://academic.evergreen.edu/a/arunc/compmusic/weaver/weaver.pdf (accessed Sept. 27, 2005; page numbers are from PDF).

Webster's New Explorer Dictionary and Thesaurus. 1999. Springfield, Mass.: Merriam-Webster, Inc.

Webster's New International Dictionary, 3rd Edition. 1961. Cambridge, Mass.: Riverside.

Webster's New World Dictionary of the American Language, College Edition [*Webster's New World*]. 1966. Cleveland and New York: The World Publishing Company. See also Guralnik.

Wedgeworth, Robert, ed. 1993. *World Encyclopedia of Library and Information Services.* 3rd ed. Chicago: ALA.

Weiser, Mark. 1991. The Computer for the Twenty-First Century. *Scientific American* 265, no. 3 (Sept.): 94–10.

Wengert, Robert G. 2001. Some Ethical Aspects of Being an Information Professional. *Ethical Issue of Information Technology. Library Trends* 49, no. 3 (Winter). University of Illinois, Graduate School of Library and Information Science.

Wiegand, Wayne A., and Donald G. Davis, eds. 1994. *Encyclopedia of Library History.* New York: Garland Publishing, Taylor & Francis Group.

Wiener, Norbert. 1948. *Cybernetics: Or Control and Communication in the Animal and the Machine.* Cambridge, Mass.: MIT Press.

Williams, James G., and Toni Carbo, eds. 1997. *Information Science: Still an Emerging Discipline.* Pittsburgh, Pa.: Cathedral Publishing.

Williams, N., and A. S. A. du Toit. 1996. Determining the Value of Information: A Pragmatic Approach. *South African Journal of Library and Information Science* 64, no. 1 (Mar.): 8–14.

Wise, John A., and Anthony Debons, eds. 1987. *Information Systems: Failure Analysis.* NATO ASI series. Berlin and New York: Springer-Verlag.

Worboys, M., and K. Hornsby. 2004. From Objects to Events: GEM, the Geospatial Event Model. *Lecture Notes in Computer Science* 3234: 327–43.

World Future Society. 1998. Trends and Forecasts for the New Millennium. August-September. *The Futurist,* R-2175. Bethesda, Md.: World Future Society. www.wfs.org.

Wormell, Irene, ed. 1990. *Information Quality: Definitions and Dimensions: Proceedings of a NORDINFO Seminar, Royal School of Librarianship, Copenhagen, 1989.* London: Taylor Graham.

Wynar, Bohdan S., and John Phillip Immroth. 1976. *Introduction to Cataloging and Classification.* 5th ed. Englewood, Colo.: Libraries Unlimited.

Young, Heartsill, Terry Belanger, et al., eds. 1983. *The American Library Association Glossary of Library and Information Science [ALA Glossary].* Chicago: American Library Association.

Zahedi, Fatemeh. 1995. *Quality Information Systems.* Danvers, Mass.: Boyd & Fraser Publishing Co.

Zins, Chaim, 2005. Classification Schemes of Information Science: 28 Scholars Map the Field (One of four Critical Delphi Study papers). In *Proceedings of the ASIS 2005 Annual Meeting.* Medford, N.J.: Information Today.

———. 2007. Conceptions of Information Science. *Journal of the American Society for Information Science and Technology* 58, no. 3: 335–50.

"You're lucky the cable company doesn't bill us for roaming charges."
By permission of Bunny Hoest, *Parade Magazine*, December 6, 2002, 19.

Index

abstracts, 28, 95
acquisition. *See* libraries, technical services
acquisition subsystems. *See* subsystems, sensing
ADIK systems (augmented data, information and knowledge), xvii, 35, 45, 64; administration, 188–89; analysis, 75–76, 81, 195–96; communications and, 144–46; composition of, 69–70, 72–73, 75; computers and, 104, 121; cost, 176; data discrimination and, 87; design, 76, 195–96; development, 73–76, 81; displays, 149–50; documentation, 79; ergonomics and, 158–59, 165–66; ethics and, 194–96; future, 203, 210–11; maintenance, 78–79; management, 76–78; networks and, 104, 110; problem solving and, 134, 140–42; quality, 177–82; subsystems (*see* subsystems); testing, 78–79; transmission and, 102–3, 110; types, 70; user needs, 67–71. *See also* databases
agricultural revolution, 14–17

alphabet, 48–51
archivists, 31
Aristotle, 12–13, 25, 54, 91, 207
ARPANET, 153
artificial intelligence (AI), 56, 69–70, 96–97, 120, 129, 140–42, 154, 163, 192
augmentation, definition, 69–70
augmented data, information and knowledge systems. *See* ADIK systems

Berners-Lee, Tim, 153–54
bibliographers, 30
bibliometrics, 127
binary digits (bits), 21–23, 102–3, 108, 121
biometrics, 127
bits. *See* binary digits (bits)
Bloom, Benjamin, 68, 73–75
Bloom's taxonomy of cognitive and affective processes, 68, 69. *See also* user needs and requirements
books, history, 48–52
Borko, Harold, 57
Brittain, Michael, 67

bridge (computer hardware), 105
bus topology (networks), 109
Bush, Vannevar, 17, 118, 153

catalogers, 30
cataloging. *See* libraries, technical
 services
catalogs, 93
categorization, 93
central processing unit (CPU), 119,
 121–23
chief information officers (CIO), 36–37
chief knowledge officers (CKO). *See*
 chief information officers (CIO)
circulation. *See* libraries, access services
citation index, 93, 95
classification schemes, 92–93
coaxial cables (computer hardware),
 107, 108, 115
codex, 49–51
cognitive functions, 159–60
collection management. *See* libraries,
 access services
colon classification, 92–93
communication(s): accuracy, 18–21;
 definition, 33, 100, 146; displays and,
 150–51; history of, 33; information
 and, 9–10; mass, 147–48;
 technological perspective, 17–23;
 versus transmission, 101–2, 145, 146;
 wireless, 153–54. *See also*
 communication science
communication science, 17–23; as field
 of study, 33; definition, 56, 150;
 future of, 201, 210–11
communications models (Shannon),
 17–23
computation, 47, 55–56
computer hardware, 102, 105–7, 109,
 121–24
computer science: challenges to, 129,
 201; definition, 56; future, 210;
 history, 118–19; innovations,
 124–28
computer scientists, 32, 47–48, 128

computer software, 32, 121–22, 153–54;
 and transmission, 102; careers,
 37–38; decision analysis and, 138–42;
 ergonomics, 162–63, 164–65; future,
 203, 209–11; information processing
 and, 104–7, 110–12
computers: ADIK systems and, 56; and
 problem solving, 119, 140–42;
 composition of, 121–24; data mining,
 82, 120; displays, 148–50, 152–54;
 ergonomics, 162–65; future, 202–7;
 hardware (*see* computer hardware);
 history, 17, 118, 152–54; knowledge
 management and, 96–97; networks
 and, 105–13; practical uses, 119–21;
 privacy, 192; professions and, 32–42,
 44; security, 126–27, 192; software
 (*see* computer software);
 transmission and, 102–3
Computing Research Association, 201
counting, origins of, 55–56
cybernetics, 23–24, 57

data, 103; accuracy, 179–80; age, 180–81;
 acquisition, 82–86; communication
 of, 145; definition, 4–5, 81–82;
 discrimination, 86–87; format checks,
 180, 181; integration of, 187–89;
 nature, 82–88; obsolescence,180;
 quality, 177–82; reliability, 86;
 reproducibility, 87; security, 182;
 source availability, 181; technology
 and, 71, 82, 84–85; timeliness, 180;
 transmission, 99–103, 110–12, 146,
 147; validation, 86, 185; vulnerability,
 87–88
data mining, 82, 120
data systems, 72
database administrators, 35
databases: biometrics and, 126;
 definition, 85; professions and,
 35–39; types, 85. *See also* ADIK
 systems
decision analysis: models, 136, 138, 139;
 software, 138–42

decision making, 134–40. *See also* problem solving
Dertouzos, Michael, 204–7
Dewey, Melvil, 29, 92–93
Dewey decimal system, 92–93
displays: applications, 151–54; as forms of communication, 150; definition, 148–49; factors, 151–52; types, 150–51; visualization, 152–53
distance learning, 202
documents and documentation, definition, 29–31, 47–48, 53

e-commerce, 206
Engelbart, Douglas C., 69–70, 96–97, 118
ergonomics: applications, 157; challenges, 165–66; computers and, 162–63; definition, 56–57; history, 158; system components, 159; theory, 158–59; ergonomists, 157, 158, 162
ethics, 193–96
event, 64, 195
event analysis, 66–67
event world, 64
expert systems. *See* artificial intelligence

feasibility studies, 75
feedback, 24, 164
fiber-optic cables,107, 108, 115, 127, 210
file transfer protocol (ftp), 111
five laws of library science, 55
Flynn, Roger R., 58

GANTT charts, 76–78
geographics information systems (GIS), 125
global positioning systems (GPS), 125–26

hardware. *See* computer hardware
Harmon, Glynn, 57–58
holistic thinking. *See* systems thinking
human factors, 64, 69–70, 134–35. *See also* ergonomics

human computer user interface (HCI), 164, 204–5, 211
human information processing (HIP), 160–62, 165
Hypertext Transfer Protocol (HTTP), 111–12, 153–54

indexers, 30
indexes, 93
indexing. *See* indexes
Industrial Revolution, 14–17, 120–21
information: accuracy, 179–80, 194; acquisition, 88–93; age, 180–81; benefit, 175; characteristics, 9; communication and, 9–10, 17–23, 119–20; cost, 175–77; format checks, 180–81; meaning, 12; nature, 3–5, 9–12, 25, 88; needs, 67–68; obsolescence, 180; organization, 91–93, 120; ownership, 194; philosophy, xvii, 12–13; privacy, 193–94; processing, 120–21; quality, 177–82; retrieval, 90–91; security, 182; senses as source of, 3–4, 5; social perspective, 14–17; source availability, 181; task analysis and, 89–90; technological perspective, 17–24; timeliness, 180; transmission, 17–23; value, 172–75; visible and invisible, 10–12
information architects, 38
information brokers, 36
information consultants, 36
information counselors, 36
Information Marketplace, 204
information professionals, 86–88, 201; definition, 28; education, 43; employment, 43; types, 28–39. *See also* information scientists
information revolution, 14–17, 199–200
information science: communications and, 146–47; definition, xvi, 56–59; domains of, 29–33, 47; future, 35, 199–212; history, 47–57; professions in, 28–40; properties, 14, 57–59

information scientists: competencies, 39,
40; definition, xvi, 34–35; functions,
35, 39; future, 35, 201, 207–11;
interests, 39, 41–42; professional
organizations, 43; professions, 34–38.
See also information professionals
information specialists, 36
information system(s), 23–24, 72;
benefit of, 175; cognitive models, 160,
165; design, 75–76; future challenges,
201
information system analysts, 37
information system designers, 37
information system processing models,
160–62, 165
information system programmers,
37–38
information theory (Shannon &
Weaver), development, 17–23, 24
input devices (computer). *See* peripheral
devices
interface designers, 38
Internet protocol (IP) addressing,
110–12

Kantor, Paul, 174
knowledge: accuracy, 179–80;
acquisition, 94; age, 180–81;
communication, 33, 48–49, 72, 135,
147, 154; composition, 5, 13–14;
format checks, 180–81; nature, 5, 94;
obsolescence, 180; quality, 179–82;
retrieval, 95; security, 182; source
availability, 181; timeliness, 180;
transmission, 104; types, 94; value,
182, 187–88
knowledge management, 72, 95–97
knowledge revolution, 199, 207, 209
knowledge sciences, 135, 207–8
knowledge systems, 72
Korfhage, Robert, 90, 91, 93

LAN. *See* local area network (LAN)
language, 33, 48–51, 93, 103, 105, 147,
148

librarians: competencies, 39–40;
definition, 29; education, 29–30, 31,
43; future, 201; history, 29–30;
interests, 41–42; professional
organizations, 43; profession types,
30–31
libraries: access services, 54–55; costs,
175–76; data acquisition and, 85–86;
future of, 209–10; history, 53–54;
resource management, 55; technical
services, 54
library science: definition, 55; future,
201, 209–10
local area network (LAN), 105, 107,
108–10

Machlup, Fritz, 174, 181–82
Maslow's Theory of Human Motivation,
68–69
Mason, Robert, 172
mass communication, 147–48
McPherson, P. K., 173–74
medical informatics, 85, 127–28, 205
media, 87; communications and, 100,
105, 147; definition, 83, 147–48; of
networks, 107–8, 112–13; quality, 183
Memex, 17, 153
memory (computer), 122–23
motherboard (computer hardware),
121–22

needs. *See* user needs and requirements
network administrators, 38
network interface card (NIC), 102–3,
112
networks, 102–3; and transmission,
102–3; architecture, 109, 112–13;
definition, 104–5; hardware, 105–8;
protocol, 103, 105, 110–12; topology,
105, 108–10
Norton, Melanie, 91–92, 93

object-oriented analysis (OOA), 66
operating systems interconnection (OSI)
model, 110–12

organization of information, 92–93, 120
output devices (computer hardware).
  See peripheral devices (computer)

pattern-making, and data, 5, 124
peripheral devices (computer), 121,
  123–24, 157, 164
PERT Charts, 76–78
philosophy: and information, 12–13
Popper, Karl, xvii, 13–14
Privacy Acts, 193
problem, definition, 135
problem space, 136
problem solving, 119, 134–42. *See also*
  decision making
processing subsystems. *See* subsystems,
  processing
protocols, 103, 105, 110–12

quality of information, 177–82

radio frequency identification (RFID),
  128, 192
Ramazzini, Bernardino, 158
random access memory (RAM), 122
read-only memory (ROM), 122–23
receivers, 100, 102, 105–7
reference librarians, 30–31, 68, 90–91,
  209
reference and information systems. *See*
  libraries, access services
remote sensing. *See* sensing technologies
request for proposal (RFP), 73, 75
ring topology (networks), 109–10
robotics, 114, 120–21, 125, 128, 192, 201,
  203, 210
router (computer hardware), 105–6

Saracevic, Tefko, 57, 174
search processes, 91
security: and information quality, 187;
  and information technology, 125–26,
  151, 192
sensing subsystems. *See* subsystems,
  sensing

sensing technologies, 24, 32, 84–85, 87,
  103, 113–14, 125–26, 151, 192–93,
  202
servers (computer hardware), 106–7
Shannon, Claude, 17–23, 57, 118
signs and signals, 137, 161–62; as data,
  4, 83; and information, 5, 7, 88; and
  transmission, 103; definition, 5–7.
  See also information, visible and
  invisible
situation, 64, 65
software engineers. *See* information
  system programmers
special librarians, 31
star topology (networks), 109
subsystems: ethics and, 195–96;
  processing, 117–30, 196; sensing,
  81–98, 195; transfer, 144–55, 196;
  transmission, 99–116, 195;
  utilization, 133–43, 196
symbols. *See* signs and signals
system analysis, 75–76
system design, 76
system models, 75, 165
systems. *See* ADIK systems
systems maintenance, 78
systems management, 75–77
Systems Theory, 23–24
systems thinking, 64

task analysis, 89–90
Taylor, Arlene G., 92
Taylor, Robert, 172–73
technology, 32; and communications,
  33; and data, 84–85; and space,
  125–26; and transmission, 103, 105
telecommunications, 32; advances, 113,
  119–20, 210; as a field of study, 33,
  34; definition, 101
teletransmission, 32, 100–101, 113, 210
Three Waves theory (Toffler), xvii, 14–17
Three Worlds theory (Popper), 13–14
threshold (measurement), 84
Toffler, Heidi and Alvin, 14–17
topologies, 105, 108–10

transfer. *See* communication(s)

transfer subsystems. *See* subsystems, transfer

transmission: accuracy and, 19–21, 103–4, 110–12, 159; definition, 100, 146; devices, 148; of information, 17–23; of knowledge, 104; process, 102–3; subsystems (*see* subsystems, transmission); versus communication, 100–102, 145, 146; wireless, 100–101, 113, 115, 118

transmission control protocol/internet protocol (TCP/IP), 110–112

transmission subsystems. *See* subsystems, transmission

transmitters, 70, 72, 102, 105–7

tree topology (networks), 109–110

twisted pair wiring, 107, 108, 115

user needs and requirements: ADIK systems and, 67–69; definitions, 67–69; difference between, 67; ergonomics, 164–65; information retrieval and, 90–91

utilization subsystems. *See* subsystems, utilization

Vickery, Brian and Alina, 29, 55, 58, 144

virtual reality, 120, 129, 152–53

visualization. *See* displays

visible information, 10–12. *See also* signs and signals

Weaver, Warren, 17–23

webmasters, 38

Weiner, Norbert, 24

wireless transmission. *See* transmission, wireless

World Future Society, 199

World Wide Web, 153–54

writing and print, 48–49. *See also* books; language

Zins, Chaim, 58

About the Author

Anthony Debons is professor emeritus at the School of Information Sciences, University of Pittsburgh. He received his doctorate in experimental psychology at Columbia University. He retired as colonel from the U.S. Air Force after serving numerous duties, the last of which was as director of computers for the U.S. Air Force Research and Development Center at Hanscom Field in Lexington, Massachusetts. Following his Air Force retirement in 1964, he was appointed professor and chairperson of the department of psychology at the University of Dayton in Dayton, Ohio. In 1967, he established the first autonomous graduate program in information science in the United States while at that university. In 1968, he was asked by Professor Allen Kent to join him in establishing a doctoral program in information science at the University of Pittsburgh. He was then professor and vice chair of the interdisciplinary doctoral program in information science. He retired in 1986, following close to fifty years of teaching, which ranged from inspirational student seminars for a few students to international programs in Great Britain, Alaska, China, and Puerto Rico. During his tenure, he initiated a master's degree track in information counseling as part of the master's degree program in information science at the Graduate School of Library and Information Sciences, University of Pittsburgh.

CPSIA information can be obtained at www.ICGtesting.com
Printed in the USA
LVOW01s0338070815

449020LV00006B/12/P